Study Guide

Nancy P. Lynch, CPA, CMA
West Virginia University
Nancy C. Ruhe
West Virginia University

Financial Accounting: A Business Process Approach

Third Edition

Jane L. Reimers

*Rollins College, Crummer Graduate
School of Business*

Prentice Hall

Boston   Columbus   Indianapolis   New York   San Francisco   Upper Saddle River

Amsterdam   Cape Town   Dubai   London   Madrid   Milan   Munich   Paris   Montreal   Toronto

Delhi   Mexico City   Sao Paulo   Sydney   Hong Kong   Seoul   Singapore   Taipei   Tokyo

Editor in Chief: Donna Battista
Acquisitions Editor: Julie Broich
Editorial Assistant: Brian Reilly
Production Project Manager: Lynne Breitfeller
Operations Specialist: Diane Peirano

Prentice Hall
is an imprint of

www.pearsonhighered.com

10 9 8 7 6 5 4 3 2 1

ISBN-13: 9780136115304
ISBN-10: 0136115306

CHAPTER 1
BUSINESS: WHAT'S IT ALL ABOUT?

Chapter Overview

This chapter will help you to understand what a business does, how it is organized, and how the financial statements reflect information about the business. Business events are classified as operating, investing, or financing activities. These business transactions are recorded in the business' information system and are summarized and presented in four basic financial statements. You should gain an understanding of who uses the information reflected in these financial statements. You will also be introduced to the concept of risk and the importance of ethics in business.

Chapter Highlights

1. A business provides goods or services either to make a profit (**for-profit** firm) or just to help people (**not-for-profit** organization). A business acquires inputs (capital, equipment, inventory, supplies, and labor) and pays for these goods and services. The business then adds value to these inputs and creates and sells outputs (goods or services) to its customers and collects cash. The information about these activities is recorded in the company's information system.

2. There are four types of businesses:
(a) a **service** company does something of value for its customers, such as consulting;
(b) a **merchandising** company buys goods, adds value to them, and then sells them. A wholesale company sells to other companies and a retail company sells to customers who are the final consumers of the goods;
(c) a **manufacturing** company makes the goods it sells; and
(d) a **financial services** company adds value for its customers by providing monetary services such as lending, investing, insuring, or advising.

3. All businesses have owners, either individuals, groups of individuals, or governments. There are four general forms of ownership:

- A **sole proprietorship** has only one owner. For tax and legal purposes, the owner and the business are considered one and the same. Profits from a sole proprietorship are taxed on the owner's individual income tax return. The owner is responsible for all debts and may have to use personal assets to pay business debts. Even though the law considers the owner and the business to be one, the financial records of the business must be kept separate from the owner's personal financial records. Financial information from a sole proprietorship is not available to the public.

- A **partnership** has two or more owners with the details of their rights and responsibilities specified in the partnership agreement. The law considers the partners and the business to be one, just as it does with the sole proprietorship. The partners are responsible for the business' legal liabilities and debt.

- A **corporation** has one or more owners, called **stockholders** or **shareholders**, who own **shares of capital stock** in the corporation. It is considered a separate legal entity that is responsible for its own debts and pays its own taxes. The **Securities and Exchange Commission (SEC)** oversees the activities and financial reporting of corporations whose stock is publicly traded on a **stock exchange** (also called the **stock market**). Advantages of the corporate structure are (a) shareholders can own a small portion of the business, allowing them to diversify risk by investing in various other businesses, and (b) owners have limited liability. Disadvantages are (a) separation of management and ownership means that managers may make decisions that are not in an owner's best interest; and (b) corporate income is taxed twice, once on the corporation's own tax return and a second time on the individual owner's personal income tax return when he or she receives a distribution of corporate earnings (called **dividends**).

- Limited Liability Partnerships (LLP) and Corporations (LLC) are newer forms of organization that have the tax advantages of partnerships and the legal liability advantages of corporations.

4. Each business transaction consists of an exchange whereby the company gets something by giving up something. These exchanges are recorded from the company's (not the owner's) point of view in the company's information system. These exchanges can be classified as operating, investing, or financing activities. Operating activities are transactions related to adding value to inputs (such as inventory) to create and sell outputs (goods or services) and then collecting cash from customers. Investing activities are related to buying and selling items the firm will use in its business for longer than a year, such as land, buildings, and equipment. Financing activities deal with how a business gets capital to fund its business. Financing activities include receiving money from owners in exchange for ownership (called **contributed capital**) and from borrowing in exchange for an IOU. The repayment of the borrowing or loan (**principal**) is also a financing activity. However, the cost of the borrowing, **interest**, is an operating activity.

5. The information system provides managers with both financial and non-financial data to help make decisions and to plan, control and evaluate the operations of the business. The information system also provides the accounting records (commonly called the **books**) needed to prepare financial statements that are useful to investors, creditors, regulators, vendors, and employees. The guidelines followed in preparing the financial statements are called **generally accepted accounting principles (GAAP)** which are set by the **Financial Accounting Standards Board (FASB)**. Another similar set of accounting standards called the **International Financial Reporting Standards (IFRS)** set by the **International Accounting Standards Board (IASB)** are used worldwide. By 2014, the aim is to converge the two sets into one global set of accounting standards followed by all major economies. To help ensure the financial statements are accurate and reliable, the SEC requires companies whose stock is publicly traded to be audited by **Certified Public Accountants (CPA)**. In 2002, a new rule-setting group, the **Public Company Accounting Oversight Board (PCAOB)**, was mandated by the **Sarbanes-Oxley Act** to oversee the auditing profession and public company audits. The information system is also used for preparing reports required by other regulatory agencies such as the **Internal Revenue Service (IRS)**, the federal agency responsible for federal tax collection.

6. There are four financial statements: (a) balance sheet; (b) income statement; (c) statement of changes in shareholders' equity; and (d) statement of cash flows. A company's financial statements also include the **notes to the financial statements** (or footnotes) which describe the company's major accounting policies and provide other disclosures to help external users better understand the financial statements.

- The **balance sheet** shows the financial position at a particular point in time: Assets = Liabilities + Shareholders' equity. **Assets** (economic resources) are things of value owned by the business. **Liabilities** are amounts owed to others outside of the business (creditors). **Shareholders' equity** represents the owners' claim to the assets after the liabilities have been paid. Shareholders' equity is made up of **contributed capital** and **retained earnings** (earnings kept by the business). **Comparative balance sheets** show the balances at the beginning of the period and the end of the period.

- The **income statement** (also known as the statement of earnings, statement of operations, or profit and loss (P&L) statement) shows how well the company performed over a period of time. The period of time covered may be a month, quarter, or **fiscal year** (a year in the life of a business that may or may not coincide with a calendar year). The income statement summarizes **revenues** (amounts the company has earned by providing goods or services) minus **expenses** (costs incurred in earning revenues) which equals **net income** (or net earnings). A net loss results if revenues are less than expenses. A **single-step income statement** lists revenues first and then groups all expenses together. A **multi-step income statement** starts with sales revenue first, then subtracts cost of goods sold to get a subtotal called gross profit on sales (or gross margin). Other operating revenues are added and expenses are deducted to arrive at the next subtotal, operating income. Lastly, non-operating items and taxes are listed to arrive at net income.

- The **statement of changes in shareholders' equity** shows the changes over a period of time in shareholders' equity. A corporation's **statement of changes in shareholders' equity** has two separate sections, one for contributed capital and one for retained earnings. Contributed capital increases if additional shares of common stock are sold. Retained earnings increases by the amount of income the company has earned (from the income statement) and decreases by any dividends paid to owners. Ending retained earnings (which will also show up on the balance sheet) equals beginning retained earnings plus net income (from the income statement) minus dividends. Retained earnings is **not** the same as cash.

- The **statement of cash flows** summarizes the cash receipts and the cash disbursements during a period of time. The cash activities are classified into one of three sections, either operating activities, investing activities or financing activities. **Cash from operating activities** involves changes in cash from everyday, routine activities such as collecting cash from customers and paying suppliers, employees, and interest. **Cash from investing activities** involves changes in cash from buying or selling long-term assets used in the business. **Cash from financing activities** involves changes in cash from contributions by owners and long-term loans.

The SEC requires all publicly traded corporations to file their financial statements and other information regularly using a standardized, interactive format called **XBRL (Extensible Business Reporting Language)**.

7. All businesses face **risks** (potential injuries or losses) in order to earn rewards. **Controls** are designed to minimize or eliminate these risks. Management must always put good ethical behavior above appearing to be very successful.

Featured Exercise

Part A: Show the effect of each of the following events on the accounting equation.

The following events took place in the month of May, 2011.	Total Assets =		Total Liabilities +	Shareholders' equity	
	Cash	All other assets		Contributed capital	Retained earnings
1	Henney Penney started a farm by taking $15,000 from her savings account and depositing it in a business checking account. The business, which is a corporation, HP Farms, Inc., gives her shares of stock.				
2	On May 1, the business borrowed $5,000 on a two-year, 12% note. One month's interest will be paid in cash on the last day of each month.				
3	The company paid Old McDonald $1,000 for one month's rent on a farm.				
4	The company paid $6,000 cash for chickens to be held in inventory.				
5	Sold 2/3 of the chickens to Pop Weasel for $9,000. a. Record the sale. b. Record the cost of goods sold.				
6	Paid Tom Piper $100 for cleaning the chicken coop.				
7	The company declared and paid a $1,000 dividend to Henney Penney, its owner.				
8	On May 31, paid $50 interest on the loan.				
	Totals				

Part B: Using the information from Part A, prepare the four financial statements for HP Farms, Inc.

Part C: Answer the following questions using Parts A and B. For each question below, fill in the correct dollar amount and circle the correct financial statement on which it appears using the following codes:

IS for the income statement for the month ended May 31, 2011
BS for the balance sheet at May 31, 2011
SOCF for the statement of cash flows for the month ended May 31, 2011

a. Cash paid to suppliers for inventory of $_____ appears on the: **IS   BS   SOCF**

b. Inventory of $_____ appears on the: **IS   BS   SOCF**

c. Cost of goods sold of $_____ appears on the: **IS   BS   SOCF**

d. Total liabilities of $_____ appears on the: **IS   BS   SOCF**

e. Common stock of $_____ appears on the: **IS   BS   SOCF**

f. Net income of $_____ appears on the: **IS   BS   SOCF**

g. Retained earnings of $_____ appears on the: **IS   BS   SOCF**

h. Cash collected from customers of $_____ appears on the: **IS   BS   SOCF**

i. Sales of $_____ appears on the: **IS   BS   SOCF**

Solution

	Assets	=	Liabilities +		Shareholders' equity	
	Cash	All other assets			Contributed capital	Retained earnings
1	15,000				15,000	
2	5,000		5,000 Notes payable			
3	(1,000)					(1,000) Rent expense
4	(6,000)	6,000 Inventory				
5	9,000	(4,000) Inventory				9,000 Sales (4,000) Cost of goods sold
6	(100)					(100) Cleaning expense
7	(1,000)					(1,000) Dividends
8	(50)					(50) Interest expense
	20,850	2,000	5,000		15,000	2,850

Part B:

HP Farms, Inc
Income Statement
For the Month Ended May 31, 2011

Revenue
 Sales $9,000
Expenses
 Cost of goods sold $4,000
 Rent   1,000
 Cleaning   100
 Interest   50
Total expenses   5,150
Net income $3,850

HP Farms, Inc.
Statement of Changes in Shareholders' Equity
For the Month Ended May 31, 2011

Beginning contributed capital $ 0
 Stock issued during the month   15,000
Ending contributed capital $15,000
Beginning retained earnings   0
 Net income for the month   3,850
 Dividends   (1,000)
Ending retained earnings   2,850
Total shareholders' equity $17,850

```
                        HP Farms, Inc.
                     Statement of Cash Flows
                  For the Month Ended May 31, 2011
Cash from operating activities
Cash collected from customers          $ 9,000
Cash paid to vendors for chickens       (6,000)
Cash paid for rent                      (1,000)
Cash paid for cleaning                    (100)
Cash paid for interest                     (50)
Total cash from operating activities              $ 1,850
Cash from investing activities                          0
Cash from financing activities
Contributions from owners               15,000
Proceeds from loan                       5,000
Dividends paid                          (1,000)
Total cash from financing activities               19,000
Net increase in cash                              $20,850
```

```
                        HP Farms, Inc.
                        Balance Sheet
                        At May 31, 2011

      Assets                    Liabilities and shareholders' equity
Cash          $20,850    Note payable                      $ 5,000
Inventory       2,000
                         Common stock                       15,000
                         Retained earnings                   2,850
Total assets  $22,850    Total liabilities & shareholders'  $22,850
                         equity
```

Part C:

a. Cash paid to suppliers for inventory of **$6,000** appears on the **SOCF**.

b. Inventory of **$2,000** appears on the **BS**.

c. Cost of goods sold of **$4,00**0 appears on the **IS**.

d. Total liabilities of **$5,000** appears on the **BS**.

e. Common stock of **$15,000** appears on the **BS**.

f. Net income of **$3,850** appears on the **IS**.

g. Retained earnings of **$2,850** appears on the **BS**.

h. Cash collected from customers of **$9,000** appears on the **SOCF**.

i. Sales of **$9,000** appears on the **IS**.

Review Questions and Exercises

Completion Statements

Fill in the blank(s) to complete each statement.

1. A _____ company buys products and resells them to its customers.

2. A _____ is legally and financially separate from its owners.

3. The _____ oversees the activities and financial reporting of corporations whose stock is publicly traded.

4. In 2002 a new rule-setting group, the _____, was created by the Sarbanes-Oxley Act to oversee the auditing profession and public company audits.

5. U.S. GAAP is expected to converge with _____ by 2014 to form one set of global accounting standards.

6. Financial statements must be _____ (i.e., examined) by _____ who give an opinion on the fairness of the financial statements to ensure that they are accurate and reliable.

7. The _____shows the financial position of a company at a particular point in time.

8. The _____shows revenues minus expenses.

9. The _____ shows changes in contributed capital and retained earnings over a period of time.

10. All businesses face risks in order to earn rewards. _____ are designed to minimize or eliminate these risks.

True/False

Indicate whether each statement is true (T) or false (F).

_____1. The income statement shows the results of operations for a specific period of time.

_____2. Retained earnings is always equal to the cash balance of a company.

_____3. An asset is something of value that the company owns.

_____4. Retained earnings represents the amount owners have contributed to the business.

_____5. Dividends are a type of expense shown on the income statement.

_____6. Gross profit and operating income are sections in the statement of cash flows.

_____7. Net income appears on both the income statement and the statement of changes in shareholders' equity.

_____8. There are four financial statements a company uses to report its financial condition and results of operations.

Multiple Choice

Select the best answer for each question.

_____1. Which of the following groups uses accounting information about a business organization?
   A. Investors
   B. Managers
   C. Internal Revenue Service
   D. Securities and Exchange Commission
   E. All of these

_____2. Which of these businesses pays taxes on its income?
   A. Corporation
   B. Sole proprietorship
   C. Partnership
   D. Two of these
   E. All of these

_____3. How many of a company's four financial statements report information about the company over a specific period of time?
   A. One
   B. Two
   C. Three
   D. Four
   E. None

_____4. Dividends are _____.
   A. the same as revenues
   B. distributions to owners of a corporation
   C. owners' contributions to the firm
   D. another term for each partner's share of partnership income
   E. shown on the income statement

_____5. Which of the following is legally a separate entity from its owner?
   A. Sole proprietorship
   B. Partnership
   C. Corporation
   D. Two of these
   E. All three of these

_____6. What piece of information flows from the income statement to the statement of changes in shareholders' equity?
   A. Revenues
   B. Total expenses
   C. Cash
   D. Net income
   E. Gross margin

_____7. What is XBRL?
   A. It is the set of accounting standards that will be used by U.S. publicly traded corporations beginning in 2014.
   B. Extensive Business Reporting Language required to be used when filing reports with the SEC.
   C. The 2002 act that mandated the existence of PCAOB.
   D. Sales minus cost of goods sold.
   E. The distribution of excess business revenue over losses.

_____8. Which financial statement shows cash collected from customers?
   A. Balance sheet
   B. Income statement
   C. Statement of changes in shareholders' equity
   D. Statement of cash flows
   E. Two or more of the above.

_____9. Which of the following events increases retained earnings?
   A. Owners' contributions
   B. Purchase of inventory
   C. Sale of inventory
   D. Payment of rent
   E. Payment of interest on a loan

_____10. Which of the following events decreases retained earnings?
   A. Owners' contributions
   B. Purchase of inventory
   C. Purchase of land
   D. Payment of dividends
   E. Payment of the principal of a loan

Exercises

1. Identify each of the following as an asset, liability, or equity account by putting an "X" in the appropriate box. Only one box should be checked for each account.

Account Title	Asset	Liability	Shareholders' Equity
a. Notes payable			
b. Interest expense			
c. Sales revenue			
d. Cash			
e. Dividends			
f. Cost of goods sold			
g. Inventory			
h. Common stock			
i. Rent expense			

2. Put an "X" in the appropriate box to indicate the financial statement that is being described. Only one box should be checked for each item.

	Balance Sheet	Income Statement	Statement of Changes in Shareholders' Equity	Statement of Cash Flows
a. Reports the results of operations				
b. Reports the inflows and outflows of cash				
c. Reports assets, liabilities, and shareholders' equity				
d. Reports amounts as of a specific point in time				
e. Reports the company's financial position				
f. Reports the economic resources owned and the claims to those resources				
g. Summarizes revenues and expenses				
h. Reports the activity in contributed capital and retained earnings for the period				

3. Use the following information to fill in the missing amounts A, B, C, and D in the balance sheet below.

Tim's Wares, Inc. began its first year of operations by selling common stock for $6,000. During this first year, Tim's Wares earned revenues of $10,000. Expenses were $8,000. A cash dividend of $1,000 was paid to shareholders. At the end of the year, Tim's Wares' balance sheet looked like this:

Assets			Liabilities	
Cash	$ 1,000		Notes payable	$20,000
Accounts receivable	3,000		**Shareholders' Equity**	
Inventory	2,000		Common stock	B
Land	A		Retained earnings	C
Total assets	$ 27,000		Total liabilities & shareholders' equity	D

4. For each of the transactions below, show the effect on the accounting equation by circling one item in each column.

a. Paid $50 for a newspaper advertisement announcing an upcoming sale.

Total assets	Total liabilities	Total shareholders' equity	
		Contributed capital	Retained earnings
Increase	Increase	Increase	Increase
Decrease	Decrease	Decrease	Decrease
No effect	No effect	No effect	No effect

b. Paid $10,000 for merchandise (inventory).

Total assets	Total liabilities	Total shareholders' equity	
		Contributed capital	Retained earnings
Increase	Increase	Increase	Increase
Decrease	Decrease	Decrease	Decrease
No effect	No effect	No effect	No effect

c. Sold merchandise for $5,000 cash to a customer. Record the sale.

Total assets	Total liabilities	Total shareholders' equity	
		Contributed capital	Retained earnings
Increase	Increase	Increase	Increase
Decrease	Decrease	Decrease	Decrease
No effect	No effect	No effect	No effect

d. The merchandise sold in c. above originally cost the company $3,000. Record the cost of goods sold.

Total assets	Total liabilities	Total shareholders' equity	
		Contributed capital	Retained earnings
Increase	Increase	Increase	Increase
Decrease	Decrease	Decrease	Decrease
No effect	No effect	No effect	No effect

5. Tim's Wares, Inc. had the following assets and liabilities at the beginning and end of 2011:

	Assets	Liabilities	Shareholders' Equity
January 1, 2011	$300,000	$100,000	?
December 31, 2011	500,000	200,000	?

Compute net income for 2011 assuming no additional stock was issued and no dividends were paid.

Solutions

Completion Statements

1. merchandising
2. corporation
3. Securities and Exchange Commission (SEC)
4. Public Company Accounting Oversight Board (PCAOB)
5. International Financial Reporting Standards (IFRS)
6. audited, certified public accountants (CPAs)
7. balance sheet
8. income statement
9. statement of changes in shareholders' (or stockholders' or owners') equity
10. Controls

True/False

1. True
2. False   Cash increases or decreases from activities other than the collection of revenues and the payments of expenses and dividends. Changes in cash arise from many activities such as borrowing cash from creditors or paying cash for the purchase of land.
3. True
4. False   Contributed capital (or common stock) represents the amount owners have contributed to the business. Retained earnings represents the amounts earned and kept by the business.
5. False   Dividends are distributions of companies' profits to owners and are not expenses. Expenses are incurred to generate revenues; dividends do not generate revenues.
6. False   Gross profit (= sales – cost of goods sold) and operating income are subtotals found on a multi-step income statement.
7. True
8. True

Multiple Choice

1. E   All of these groups and many others use accounting information.
2. A   A corporation is considered a separate legal entity and thus must pay corporate income taxes on its profits. The shareholders must then pay individual income taxes on the dividends (or distributions of these profits). The law does not recognize sole proprietors or partners as separate from the business, so the owners pay taxes only on the profits of the business and not on the distributions of these profits.
3. C   The income statement, statement of changes in shareholders' equity, and the statement of cash flows report business activities during the accounting period covered by these statements. The balance sheet shows the financial position of the company at a specific point in time; it does not show the activity during the period.
4. B   Dividends are distributions (not contributions) of a corporation's (not partnership's) profit that are shown on the statement of changes in shareholders' equity and the statement of cash flows.
5. C   A corporation is considered a separate legal entity. The law does not recognize sole proprietors or partners as separate from the business.
6. D   The income statement shows net income (revenues minus expenses) for the period. Net income from the income statement is needed to determine the ending retained earnings balance (beginning retained earnings plus net income minus dividends) on the statement of changes in shareholders' equity.
7. B   XBRL (Extensible Business Reporting Language) is a technology that enables firms to report information in a standardized way that makes the data immediately reusable and interactive.
8. D   Cash collected from customers is in the operating activities section of the statement of cash flows.
9. C   Retained earnings is increased by net income. A sale increases net income and thus increases retained earnings. Although owners' contributions increase shareholders' equity, they increase contributed capital, not retained earnings.
10. D Dividends decrease retained earnings. Owners' contributions increase contributed capital; they do not decrease retained earnings. Purchases of inventory and land increase assets; they do not decrease retained earnings. Payment of the principal of a loan decreases liabilities, not retained earnings.

Exercises

1. Account Title	Asset	Liability	Shareholders' equity
a. Notes payable		X	
b. Interest expense			X
c. Sales revenue			X
d. Cash	X		
e. Dividends			X
f. Cost of goods sold			X
g. Inventory	X		
h. Common stock			X
i. Rent expense			X

2.	Balance Sheet	Income Statement	Statement of Changes in Shareholders' Equity	Statement of Cash Flows
a. Reports the results of operations.		X		
b. Reports the inflows and outflows of cash.				X
c. Reports assets, liabilities, and owners' equity.	X			
d. Reports amounts as of a specific point in time.	X			
e. Reports the company's financial position.	X			
f. Reports the economic resources owned and the claims to those resources.	X			
g. Summarizes revenues and expenses.		X		
h. Reports the activity in contributed capital and retained earnings for the period.			X	

3. First find the missing value for Land (A) which is $21,000 (= $27,000 - 1,000 - 3,000 - 2,000). Next find the missing value for total liabilities and shareholders' equity (D) which is $27,000 (= total assets of $27,000). Common stock (B) is equal to the $6,000 for which common stock was sold. Finally, retained earnings (C) is equal to $1,000 [= beginning retained earnings ($0 since it is the first year of business) + net income ($2,000 = $10,000 - 8,000) minus dividends ($1,000)].

4. Total assets	Total liabilities	Total shareholders' equity	
		Contributed capital	Retained earnings
a. Decrease (50) Cash	No effect	No effect	Decrease (50) Advertising expense
b. No effect 10,000 Inventory (10,000) Cash	No effect	No effect	No effect
c. Increase 5,000 Cash	No effect	No effect	Increase 5,000 Sales revenue
d. Decrease (3,000) Inventory	No effect	No effect	Decrease (3,000) Cost of goods sold

5.	Assets	Liabilities	Shareholders' equity
January 1, 2011	$300,000	$100,000	**$200,000**
December 31, 2011	500,000	200,000	**300,000**

Shareholders' equity has increased by $100,000. Since there has been no change in contributed capital (no additional stock was issued) and there were no dividends during the year, the increase in retained earnings is due to net income equaling $100,000.

CHAPTER 2
QUALITIES OF ACCOUNTING INFORMATION

Chapter Overview

In Chapter 1, you were introduced to the four basic financial statements: the income statement; the balance sheet; the statement of changes in shareholders' equity; and the statement of cash flows. For these financial statements to be useful, the information in the statements must be relevant, reliable, and prepared in a consistent way so that a user can compare the financial statements of one accounting period to other accounting periods, as well as compare one company's financial statements with other companies'. In Chapter 2, you will learn the qualities of financial statement information and the importance of accrual accounting in preparing the financial statements to ensure that they are useful to decision makers.

Chapter Highlights

1. GAAP are the guidelines and rules currently set in the U. S. by the SEC and FASB, and are generally considered to be rule-based and detailed. The International Accounting Standards Board (IASB) sets international financial reporting standards (IFRS), which are more concept based and require more judgment to apply. Most people who prepare and use financial statements believe that the world has become a global market and a single set of standards should be used worldwide.

The general and qualitative characteristics of accounting information are the same under both U.S. GAAP and IFRS: financial reporting should provide information that is useful. To be useful the information must be relevant, reliable, comparable, and consistent. **Relevant** information is reported in a timely manner and should be significant enough to influence business decisions. **Reliable** information is accurate, can be verified, and must faithfully represent what it intends to convey. The information should possess **comparability**. Companies must disclose the accounting methods they select to allow meaningful comparisons with similar companies' financial statements. The rules should be consistently applied because **consistency** is needed so that decision makers can compare the

financial statements of one accounting period with other accounting periods. For instance, **profit** (revenues minus expenses) for a period should be determined in a consistent manner with a prior period's profit so meaningful comparisons can be made.

GAAP provide guidance for measuring and reporting the elements of the financial statements. GAAP include four basic assumptions. The **separate-entity assumption** requires companies to keep the owners' personal financial records separate from the businesses'. The **monetary-unit assumption** requires the elements to be measured in dollars. The **time-period assumption** suggests that the life of a company and its performance can be divided into time periods. The **going-concern assumption** assumes that a company will continue in business for the foreseeable future.

GAAP also includes four principles. The **historical-cost principle** states that assets are initially recorded at cost, because cost is reliable (*i.e.*, unbiased and verifiable). However, both GAAP and IFRS have been increasing the use of **fair value** rather than cost in the financial statements. Some assets, although they are initially recorded at cost, are later adjusted to their **fair market value**, which is more relevant for investors, but less reliable. The **revenue recognition principle** says that revenue is **recognized** (*i.e.* recorded) when it is earned and collection is reasonably assured. Cash does not have to be collected before revenue is recognized. The **matching principle** requires that expenses be recognized in the same accounting period as the revenues that they helped earn. And the **full-disclosure principle** says that companies must disclose any circumstances and events that would make a difference to financial statement users.

Two constraints apply to the preparation of financial statements. GAAP must be followed when an amount is considered **material**, that is, large enough to affect someone's interpretation or decision. The **materiality** principle allows companies to report immaterial (insignificant) items in the most cost-effective manner, even if it means a departure from GAAP. The other constraint is **conservatism**. Accountants should select the accounting treatment that will be least likely to overstate income or overstate assets.

2. A complete set of financial statements includes (a) the income statement (also called the statement of earnings), (b) the balance sheet (also called the statement of financial position), (c) the statement of changes in shareholders' (or stockholders') equity, (d) the statement of cash flows, and (e) notes to the financial statements (sometimes called footnotes). Before financial statements are prepared, the company must be sure to adjust all account balances to reflect accurate amounts. This process is called **adjusting the books**.

3. The income statement is prepared first. It lists the revenues earned minus all the expenses incurred in generating revenue during the accounting period covered by the statement. Revenues increase and expenses decrease retained earnings which is part of shareholders' equity. Net income (sometimes called the bottom line) is the difference between the revenues (or sales) and the expenses (such as cost of goods sold, advertising expense, etc.). Dividends paid to shareholders are not expenses, even though they decrease retained earnings, too.

- Revenue equals the dollar amounts of goods or services delivered during the period; it does not reflect the amount of cash received during the period. Some sales may have been made **on account** (or on credit). The statement of cash flows will show the amount of cash collected from customers during the period. **Accounts receivable**, an asset on the balance sheet, will show the amount that has not yet been collected from customers. Thus, the three statements tell three important pieces of information about the sales and collections: 1) the income statement shows the dollar amount of goods or services delivered (revenue), 2) the statement of cash flows shows the amount of cash received, and 3) the balance sheet links the two and shows the amount of revenue not yet collected (accounts receivable).
- Expenses are matched with the revenues they helped to generate. Expenses equal the dollar

amount of goods or services consumed (used) during the period; they do not reflect the amount of cash paid during the period. Some expenses may have been paid for in advance (i.e., in a previous accounting period). **Prepaid insurance**, an asset on the balance sheet, will show the amount that has been paid for in advance but not yet used. Some expenses may not be paid for until a later accounting period. **Payables**, which are liabilities on the balance sheet, show the amounts still owed on items that may have been consumed (used) during the period. The statement of cash flows will show the amount paid during the period. The income statement shows the dollar amount of goods or services consumed (expenses), the statement of cash flows shows the amount of cash paid, and the balance sheet links the two and shows the amount of expenses not yet paid (payables) or the amount paid for in advance (prepaids).

4. The statement of changes in shareholders' equity shows the changes in contributed capital and retained earnings during the accounting period. Changes in contributed capital are shown by adding new shares issued during the period to the beginning contributed capital balance. Changes in retained earnings is shown by starting with beginning retained earnings adding net income (from the income statement) and subtracting dividends declared to arrive at the ending retained earnings balance. The ending balances of contributed capital and retained earnings balances from the statement of shareholders' equity are also shown on the balance sheet.

5. The balance sheet is prepared by calculating and summarizing the balance of each asset, liability, and shareholders' equity account as of the balance sheet date. The balance sheet balances because Assets = Liabilities + Shareholders' equity. The ending balance for each account is calculated by taking its beginning balance (*i.e.*, its balance at the end of the previous accounting period) and adding the changes in the account during the period.

6. The statement of cash flows shows every cash collection and every cash payment. Each cash

transaction is classified as one of three types: operating, investing, or financing.

7. The notes to the financial statements are a crucial part of the financial statements. The **full-disclosure principle** requires companies to disclose any circumstances and events that would make a difference to the users of the financial statements.

8. The assets, items of value that will provide future benefit, are listed in order of **liquidity** (the relative quickness with which each asset is to be turned into cash or used). A **classified balance sheet** categorizes assets (and liabilities) as either current or noncurrent. In the U.S., **current assets**, which will be turned into cash or used up within the year, are listed first, typically in this order:

- Cash, which is the most liquid asset.

- Short-term investments are investments made with the company's excess cash. An example is when a company pays cash to buy stock in another company.

- **Accounts receivable**, often listed next, represents the amounts owed by customers from credit sales.

- **Inventory** is merchandise the company has available to sell.

- **Prepaids** represent payments made in advance for items that will provide future benefit - for example, prepaid insurance.

In the U.S., **noncurrent** (or **long-term**) **assets**, which will last for more than one year, are listed below current assets. Often balance sheets prepared under IFRS list long-term assets (and liabilities) before current assets (and liabilities).

9. Liabilities are amounts a company owes and, like assets, are separated into current and noncurrent sections on a formal classified balance sheet. **Current liabilities** will be settled (or paid off) within the year.
- An example of a current liability is **accounts payable**, which is the amount owed to vendors for the purchase of inventory on account.

- Other payables are amounts owed to others for services or goods other than inventory.

Noncurrent (or **long-term**) **liabilities** are the obligations that will not be satisfied within the year and are listed below current liabilities.

10. **Equity** is the last section of the balance sheet and represents the shareholders' claims to the assets. Shareholders' equity for a corporation is separated into **contributed capital** (also known as **paid-in capital** or investments by owners) and **retained earnings** (capital earned and kept by the company). Contributed capital and retained earnings are the same ending balances from the statement of changes in shareholders' equity. The balance sheet of a sole proprietorship or partnership shows the two sections, investments by owners and earned capital, combined as one, called **capital**.

11. For financial statements to be relevant to users, GAAP requires them to reflect the economic substance of the company's transactions. **Accrual accounting** requires revenue and expense be recorded when in substance the revenue is earned and the expense is incurred, regardless of whether cash has changed hands. Often revenues and expenses are reported in a different accounting period than when the cash is received or paid. **Accruals** exist when the action (revenue or expense) comes before the cash (receipt or payment). **Deferrals** exist when the cash comes before the action.

- The rule for recording revenue is the **revenue-recognition principle**. Revenue is **recognized** (*i.e.*, reported) on the income statement in the period it is **earned**, even if cash has not been received or was received in advance. For example, when a company delivers a product to a customer on account, the revenue should be recorded when the product is delivered. In substance the company has completed its side of the bargain and should be able to reflect this revenue on its income statement. The company should not have to wait until later when the cash is finally received.

- The rule for recording expenses is the **matching principle**. Expenses are to be recorded (matched) on the income statement in the same period as the revenue they helped to generate, even if cash has not been paid or was paid in advance. For example, when a product is delivered to a customer, the expense of the product (cost of goods sold) should be matched with the related revenue (sales), regardless of whether the company has paid for the inventory in advance or still owes for the inventory.

12. In contrast to accrual-basis accounting, **cash-basis accounting** records revenue only when cash is received and expenses only when cash is paid. It often ignores the substance of the transaction and can result in manipulation and inconsistencies in the timing of revenues and expenses. It is not an acceptable method of accounting under GAAP.

13. Financial statements provide information about the risk of investing in a company. **Risk** is the uncertainty associated with the amount and timing of future returns. If the risk is considered high, then the investor expects a higher return. Investing as an owner is riskier than investing as a creditor because a company has a legal obligation to pay its creditors before its owners. Thus, an owner expects a higher return than a creditor via dividends and an increase in the stock price. A creditor can only expect to receive the agreed-upon interest and repayment of the principal.

14. The **current ratio** equals current assets divided by current liabilities. It is a measure of a company's short-term **liquidity**, or ability to meet its short-term obligations.

15. **Internal controls** are a company's policies and procedures to protect assets and minimize the risk of errors in the accounting system. **Preventive controls**, such as keeping cash locked up, are designed to prevent an error or irregularity (an intentional error). **Detective controls**, such as preparing cash reconciliations, are designed to find an error or irregularity. **Corrective controls**, such as requiring cashiers to make up any cash shortages, are designed to fix errors.

Featured Exercise

Part A: Show the effect of the following events on the accounting equations for each of the childcare companies, Tom's Tots, Inc. and Tiny Tim's, Inc.

Tom's Tots, Inc.		Assets =		Liabilities +	Shareholders' equity	
		Cash	All other assets		Contributed capital	Retained earnings
	May 1, 2012 beginning balances	$900	$600 Prepaid insurance 200 Supplies	$400 Note payable	$700 Common stock	$600 Retained earnings
1	Cares for 5 children for a fee of $300 per month for each child. Collects cash.					
2	Pays off the entire loan plus $4 interest.					
3	Pays $500 for May's rent.					
4	Determines that 1/3 of the insurance is used up.					
5	On May 31, only $50 of supplies are left.					

Tiny Tim's, Inc.		Assets =		Liabilities +	Shareholders' equity	
		Cash	All other assets		Contributed capital	Retained earnings
	May 1, 2012 beginning Balances	$900	$600 Prepaid insurance 200 Supplies	$400 Note payable	$700 Common stock	$600 Retained earnings
1	Cares for 5 children for a fee of $300 per month for each child, to be collected in June.					
2	Pays $4 interest on the loan.					
3	Pays $500 for May's rent.					
4	Determines that 1/3 of the insurance is used up.					
5	On May 31, only $50 of supplies are left.					

Part B: Using the information from Part A, prepare the four financial statements for both companies.

Tom's Tots, Inc. Income Statement For the Month Ended May 31, 2012	Tiny Tim's, Inc. Income Statement For the Month Ended May 31, 2012

Tom's Tots, Inc. Statement of Changes in Shareholder's Equity For the Month Ended May 31, 2012	Tiny Tim's, Inc. Statement of Changes in Shareholder's Equity For the Month Ended May 31, 2012

Tom's Tots, Inc. Balance Sheet May 31, 2012	Tiny Tim's, Inc. Balance Sheet May 31, 2012

Tom's Tots, Inc. Statement of Cash Flows For the Month Ended May 31, 2012	Tiny Tim's, Inc. Statement of Cash Flows For the Month Ended May 31, 2012

Part C: Answer the following questions using Parts A and B.

1. Are Tom's Tots and Tiny Tim's sole proprietorships, partnerships, or corporations? How can you tell?

2. Who should expect a higher return, the creditor who lent Tiny Tim's $400 or Tim, the owner of Tiny Tim's? Why?

3. Is Tom allowed to include his personal rent expense in Tom's Tots' income statement? Why or why not?

4. Which assumption requires that the items in the financial statements be measured in money, not inches or number of kids?

5. Describe and explain the revenue-recognition principle using the transactions from Tiny Tim's during the month ended May 31, 2012.

6. Describe and explain the matching principle using the adjusting entry for supplies during the month ended May 31, 2012.

7. Which company is more profitable for the month ended May 31, 2012? Would your answer be different if cash-basis accounting was used instead of accrual accounting? Explain.

8. Identify the internal controls that Tom's Tots uses to minimize the risk of errors in the accounting system as either preventive, detective, or corrective in each of the items below:
    a) The cash balance in the books is compared and reconciled to the bank statement balance.
    b) Tom's Tots requires all discrepancies be investigated and resolved.
    c) One person collects the cash and a different person, who has no access to the cash, records the cash in the accounting records.

Solution

Tom's Tots, Inc.		Assets	=	Liabilities	+	Shareholders' equity	
		Cash	All other assets			Contributed capital	Retained earnings
	May 1, 2012 beginning balances	$900	$600 Prepaid insurance 200 Supplies	$400 Note payable		$700 Common stock	$600 Retained earnings
1	Cares for 5 children for a fee of $300 per month for each child. Collects cash.	1,500					1,500 Revenue
2	Pays off the entire loan plus $4 interest.	(404)		(400) Note payable			(4) Interest expense
3	Pays $500 for May's rent.	(500)					(500) Rent expense
4	Determines that 1/3 of the insurance is used up.		(200) Prepaid insurance				(200) Insurance expense
5	On May 31, only $50 of supplies are left.		(150) Supplies				(150) Supplies expense
	May 31, 2012 balances	$1,496	400 Prepaid insurance 50 Supplies			$700 Common stock	$1,246 Retained earnings

Tiny Tim's, Inc.		Assets	=	Liabilities	+	Shareholders' equity	
		Cash	All other assets			Contributed capital	Retained earnings
	May 1, 2012 beginning Balances	$900	$600 Prepaid insurance 200 Supplies	$400 Note payable		$700 Common stock	$600 Retained earnings
1	Cares for 5 children for a fee of $300 per month for each child, to be collected in June.		1,500 Accounts receivable				1,500 Revenue
2	Pays $4 interest on the loan.	(4)					(4) Interest expense
3	Pays $500 for May's rent.	(500)					(500) Rent expense
4	Determines that 1/3 of the insurance is used up.		(200) Prepaid insurance				(200) Insurance expense
5	On May 31, only $50 of supplies are left.		(150) Supplies				(150) Supplies
	May 31, 2012 balances	$396	$1,500 Accounts Receivable 400 Prepaid insurance 50 Supplies	$400 Note payable		$700 Common stock	$1,246 Retained earnings

Part B:

Tom's Tots, Inc.
Income Statement
For the Month Ended May 31, 2012

Revenue		
Service fees earned		$1,500
Expenses		
Rent	$500	
Supplies	150	
Insurance	200	
Interest	4	
Total expenses		854
Net income		$ 646

Tom's Tots, Inc.
Statement of Changes in Shareholders' Equity
For the Month Ended May 31, 2012

Common stock		$ 700
Beginning retained earnings	$600	
Plus net income	646	
Less distributions to owners	0	
Ending retained earnings		1,246
Total shareholders' equity		$1,946

Tom's Tots, Inc.
Balance Sheet
May 31, 2012

Assets		Liabilities	$ 0
Cash	$1,496	Shareholders' equity	
Prepaid insurance	400	Common stock	700
Supplies	50	Retained earning	1,246
		Total liabilities	
Total assets	$1,946	and equity	$1,946

Tom's Tots, Inc.
Statement of Cash Flows
For the Month Ended May 31, 2012

Cash from operating activities		
Cash collected from customers	$1,500	
Cash paid for rent	(500)	
Cash paid for interest	(4)	
Total cash from operating activities		$996
Cash from investing activities		0
Cash from financing activities		
Repayment of loan	(400)	
Total cash from financing activities		(400)
Net change in cash		$596

Tiny Tim's, Inc.
Income Statement
For the Month Ended May 31, 2012

Revenue		
Service fees earned		$1,500
Expenses		
Rent	$500	
Supplies	150	
Insurance	200	
Interest	4	
Total expenses		854
Net income		$ 646

Tiny Tim's, Inc.
Statement of Changes in Shareholder's Equity
For the Month Ended May 31, 2012

Common stock		$ 700
Beginning retained earnings	$600	
Plus net income	646	
Less distributions to owners	0	
Ending retained earnings		1,246
Total shareholders' equity		$1,946

Tiny Tim's, Inc.
Balance Sheet
May 31, 2012

Assets		Liabilities	
Cash	$ 396	Note payable	$ 400
Accounts		Shareholders' equity	
receivable	1,500	Common stock	700
Prepaid		Retained earnings	1,246
insurance	400		
Supplies	50	Total liabilities	
Total assets	$2,346	and equity	$2,346

Tiny Tim's, Inc.
Statement of Cash Flows
For the Month Ended May 31, 2012

Cash from operating activities		
Cash paid for rent	$(500)	
Cash paid for interest	(4)	
Total cash from operating activities		$(504)
Cash from investing activities		0
Cash from financing activities		0
Net change in cash		$(504)

Part C:

1. Tom's Tots, Inc., and Tiny Tim's, Inc., are both corporations as indicated by the Inc. designation. Also, the shareholder's equity is separated into common stock and retained earnings. Sole proprietorships and partnerships combine contributed and earned capital into one amount called "capital."

2. Investing in a company as an owner is riskier than as a creditor. There is a legal obligation for a company to pay both interest and principal to its creditors. There is no legal obligation for a company to make any distributions to owners. There is a positive correlation between risk and return, thus an owner should expect a higher return.

3. The separate-entity assumption states that the owner's personal financial records and transactions should not be part of the company's. Only the company's rent expense should be on Tom's Tots' income statement.

4. The monetary-unit assumption requires financial statement items to be measured in monetary units.

5. The revenue recognition principle requires revenue to be recorded (recognized) when it is earned (*i.e.*, when goods or services have been delivered) without regard to when the cash is collected from customers. Tiny Tim's reported revenue of $1,500 on the income statement even though no cash has been received from its customers. Accounts receivable of $1,500, an asset on the balance sheet, will show the amount that has not yet been collected from customers. The statement of cash flows will show no cash collected from customers during the period. Thus, the three statements tell three important pieces of information about the sales to customers: 1) the income statement shows the amount of goods or services delivered (revenue); 2) the statement of cash flows shows the amount of cash received; and 3) the balance sheet links the two and shows the amount of revenue not yet collected (accounts receivable).

6. The matching principle requires expenses to be matched on the income statement with the revenue they helped generate. Only the supplies that are used to earn revenue during the period should be expensed. The unused supplies stay on the balance sheet as an asset until they are used.

7. Net income is a measure of profitability. Since both have the same net income, both are equally profitable. If cash-basis accounting were used instead of accrual accounting, Tom's Tots would be considered more profitable, which is misleading since both companies, in substance, performed equally well. The only difference is that Tiny Tim's did not collect cash from its customers. Accrual accounting better reflects the economic substance of the companies' activities during the month.

8. a) is a detective control; b) is a corrective control; c) is a preventive control.

Review Questions and Exercises

Completion Statements

Fill in the blank(s) to complete each statement.

1. A set of U.S. rules called _____ must be followed to help ensure the financial statements are useful.

2. GAAP must be followed when an amount is considered _____, *i.e.*, if it would affect someone's interpretation or decision.

3. Financial statements need to be _____ and _____ so that decision makers can compare the financial statements of one accounting period to other accounting periods and compare one company's financial statements with other companies'.

4. _____ means the information must be reported in a timely manner and _____ means the information must be accurate and truthful.

5. Before financial statements are prepared, the company must be sure to adjust all account balances to reflect accurate amounts. This process is called _____.

6. A _____ categorizes and lists assets as _____ if the assets will be turned into cash or used up within the year and _____ if the assets will be used for more than one year. It also lists as _____ the liabilities that will be satisfied during the year and _____ if the liabilities will not be satisfied within the year.

7. _____ is the uncertainty associated with the amount and timing of future returns. The higher the _____, the higher the _____.

8. _____ controls such as keeping cash locked up are designed to prevent an error or irregularity.

9. _____ controls such as preparing a cash reconciliation are designed to find an error or irregularity.

10. _____ controls such as denying future credit to slow paying or non-paying customers are designed to fix errors.

True/False

Indicate whether each statement is true (T) or false (F).

_____1. Financial statements prepared using cash-basis accounting will never have accounts receivable or accounts payable on the balance sheet.

_____2. Accrual accounting is GAAP; cash-basis accounting is not GAAP.

_____3. An owner of a corporation has the legal right to receive interest and dividends.

_____4. Investing as a creditor is riskier than investing as an owner and thus requires a higher return.

_____5. An accrual is recorded when the event occurs before the cash changes hands and a deferral is recorded when the cash changes hands before the event.

_____6. The going-concern assumption assumes a business is going to close in the near future and thus all its assets must be revalued to their current market values.

_____7. An example of a preventive control is to have the same person who has access to cash be the one who maintains the cash records in order to ensure accuracy.

_____8. Company A paid off its $400 note payable, as well as the related interest of $4, on the last day of the accounting period. Company B paid only the interest expense of $4 during the accounting period. As a result, Company A will show a lower net income during this accounting period than it would have had it not paid off the note.

Multiple Choice

Select the best answer for each question.

_____1. Rite-it-up, Inc. purchased land for $20,000 on May 1, 2012. On December 31, 2012, similar land sells for $25,000. Under U.S. GAAP, the land should be shown:
   A. on the balance sheet as a $25,000 asset.
   B. on the income statement as revenue of $5,000.
   C. on the balance sheet as a $20,000 asset.
   D. on the income statement as an expense of $20,000.

_____2. Ivan Rich is considering lending money to Kneady, Inc. As a potential creditor of Kneady, Inc., Ivan computed Kneady's current ratio in order to measure:
   A. Kneady's ability to replace current assets as they are used.
   B. Kneady's liquidity, *i.e.*, its ability to pay its current debts as they come due.
   C. Kneady's ability to convert its noncurrent assets into current assets.
   D. Kneady's profitability.
   E. The current ratio measures all of the above.

_____3. When an item is immaterial, it means:
   A. it is significant in amount.
   B. it is expressed in dollars instead of some other unit in preparing financial statements.
   C. companies are allowed to ignore recording the small dollar item in the accounting records.
   D. it can be recorded in the most convenient way even if it is not in accordance with GAAP.

_____4. Retained earnings can be found on:
   A. the income statement and statement of cash flows.
   B. the statement of changes in shareholders' equity only.
   C. the statement of changes in shareholders' equity and the balance sheet.
   D. the balance sheet only.

_____5. The owner of Shady Grove Company has the bookkeeper write company checks to pay for his personal items. This violates:
A. the matching principle.
B. the monetary-unit assumption.
C. the materiality concept.
D. the separate-entity assumption.

_____6. If you were told a company's net income was $100,000, what other information would be helpful in making this more meaningful?
A. The time period covered
B. The method used: accrual or cash-basis accounting
C. The amount of net income retained versus paid out in dividends
D. All of the above

_____7. A company in its first year of business earned revenues of $100,000 but collected only $80,000 in cash from its customers. Which of the following is correct?
A. The income statement will show Revenues of $100,000, the balance sheet will show Accounts receivable of $20,000, and the statement of cash flows will show Cash collected from customers of $80,000.
B. The income statement will show Revenues of $80,000, the balance sheet will show Accounts receivable of $100,000, and the statement of cash flows will show Cash collected from customers of $80,000.
C. The income statement will show Revenues of $100,000, the balance sheet will show Accounts receivable of $20,000, and the statement of cash flows will show Cash collected from customers of $100,000.
D. The income statement will show Revenues of $180,000, the balance sheet will show Accounts receivable of $100,000, and the statement of cash flows will show Cash collected from customers of $80,000.

_____8. During the year, ABC Company had revenues of $100,000 of which $90,000 has been collected from customers. It also had expenses of $60,000 of which $40,000 has been paid. The owners were paid $20,000 in dividends. Net income for the year equals:
A. $50,000   D. $20,000
B. $40,000   E. $10,000
C. $30,000

_____9. Which of the following statements about cash is true?
A. Cash is part of shareholders' equity.
B. Increases in cash and net income will be the same during an accounting period.
C. Revenue is earned only when cash is collected.
D. Expenses are recorded only when cash is paid.
E. None of the above is true.

_____10. Which of the following is not part of an internal control system?
A. Detective controls
B. Preventive controls
C. Liquidity controls
D. Corrective controls

Matching

From the list of concepts, principles, and assumptions, write the appropriate letter which best matches each item below.

A.	Accrual accounting	H.	Relevant
B.	Historical-cost principle	I.	Reliable
C.	Consistency	J.	Revenue recognition principle
D.	Comparable	K.	Conservatism
E.	Going-concern assumption	L.	Time-period assumption
F.	Matching principle	M.	Separate-entity assumption
G.	Materiality	N.	Monetary-unit assumption

1.	Which principle is violated when an owner of a company includes his personal expenses in the company's financial records?	
2.	ABC Company records revenues when the goods are delivered even though the cash will not be collected until a later accounting period.	
3.	Inventory is presented in dollars, not units, on the balance sheet.	
4.	Assumes companies are not going to liquidate in the near future and thus helps justify the use of historical cost rather than current cost in valuing assets.	
5.	The accounting information is provided in a timely fashion so that the information is still useful.	
6.	Assets are typically recorded at the amount paid for them.	
7.	Supplies are recorded as an asset and then expensed in the period they are used in helping generate revenue.	
8.	It is important for companies to use the same methods of measuring items on the financial statement each accounting period.	
9.	Comparing financial statements of different companies is more meaningful when the statements are prepared in accordance with GAAP.	
10.	The items on the financial statements should be accurate and truthful.	
11.	Financial statements can be prepared periodically in order to report the progress of the company over its life.	
12.	Accountants should anticipate losses and not gains. They also should not overstate assets.	
13.	Revenues are recorded when earned and expenses are recorded when incurred regardless of when the related cash changes hands.	
14.	Items that are too small to affect anyone's decision making can be recorded in a manner that is not necessarily in accordance with GAAP.	

Exercises

1. Fill in the accounting equation below for Tim's Ware, Inc.'s events that occurred during 2012, its first year of business:

Tim's Ware, Inc.		Assets =		Liabili-	Shareholders' equity	
		Cash	All other assets	ties +	Contrib. capital	Retained earnings
a.	Tim's Ware began operations by issuing $6,000 of common stock to its owners.					
b.	Tim's Ware purchased $3,000 of inventory and paid cash.					
c.	Tim's Ware purchased $400 of supplies and paid cash.					
d.	Tim's Ware made sales of $3,300 on account. The cost of the sales was $2,500.					
e.	Tim's Ware collected $2,700 of receivables during the year.					
f.	On July 1, 2012 Tim's Ware paid $2,400 in advance for an insurance policy that covers two years beginning July 1.					
g.	As of December 31, 2012, six months of insurance coverage has expired.					
h.	Supplies on hand as of December 31, 2012 amounted to $100.					

2. Tim's Ware's account titles:		Fill in the correct dollar amount:	Put an "X" in the column of the statement where the item will most likely appear:		
		Amount as of or for the year ended December 31	Income Statement	Balance Sheet	Statement of Cash Flows
a.	Stock issued for cash				
b.	Supplies expense				
c.	Supplies				
d.	Insurance expense				
e.	Prepaid insurance				
f.	Cash paid for insurance				
g.	Cash received from customers				
h.	Accounts receivable				
i.	Sales				
j.	Cost of goods sold				
k.	Inventory				

Solutions

Completion Statements

1. GAAP
2. material
3. Consistency; comparability
4. Relevant; reliable
5. adjusting the books
6. Classified balance sheet; current assets; noncurrent assets; current liabilities; noncurrent liabilities
7. Risk; risk; return
8. Preventive
9. Detective
10. Corrective

True/False

1. True   Revenues and expenses are recorded only when cash changes hands under the cash-basis accounting, which is not GAAP. Accounts receivable and accounts payable reflect the timing differences between when revenues and expenses are earned and incurred and when the cash later changes hands. These timing differences exist only under accrual accounting which is required under GAAP.
2. True   See 1. above.
3. False   Creditors have the legal right to receive interest and repayment of principal. Owners have no legal rights to receive dividends.
4. False   See 3. above. In the event of liquidation, creditor obligations must be paid before the owners can receive anything. Since owners are taking more risk, they expect to receive a higher return.
5. True   An example of an accrual is recording an account receivable when revenue is earned before cash is received. An example of a deferral is recording prepaid insurance as an asset when the cash changes hands and later recording the expense when the insurance is used.
6. False   The going-concern assumption assumes companies are not going to liquidate in the near future and thus helps justify valuing assets at their historical cost and not their current market values.
7. False   A preventive control would be to have these duties separated. Those who have access to cash should not do the record keeping. This separation of duties will help ensure that an employee does not pocket cash and then alter the books to conceal the theft.
8. False   The $400 payment of principal reduces assets (cash) and liabilities (notes payable); it does not decrease shareholders' equity. Both will have net income lowered by the same amount, the $4 interest expense.

Multiple Choice

1. C   U.S. GAAP require assets to be recorded at historical cost. (There are some exceptions that you will learn about later on in the text.)
2. B   The current ratio is a measure of liquidity and is calculated by dividing current assets by current liabilities.
3. D   Immaterial items can be recorded in a way that does not conform to GAAP as long as it does not have an effect on users' decisions. Immaterial items must be recorded just not in accordance with GAAP.
4. C   The statement of changes in shareholders' equity shows beginning retained earnings plus net income minus dividends to arrive at retained earnings at the end of the accounting period, which also is shown on the balance sheet.

5. D The owner's personal transactions and records must be kept separate from the company's transactions and records.

6. D Financial statements must state the time period covered, which could be a month, quarter, or year (A). GAAP require companies to use accrual accounting which typically results in a better measure of net income than cash-basis accounting (which is not GAAP) (B). It is useful to know how much of net income is retained and reinvested into the company versus paid out in dividends to owners; the statement of changes in shareholders' equity shows this amount (C).

7. A The activity can be summarized as follows:

Assets		Liabilities +	Shareholders' equity	
Cash	**All other assets**		**Contributed capital**	**Retained earnings**
	100,000 Accounts receivable (1)			100,000 Revenue (2)
80,000 (3)	(80,000) Accounts receivable (4)			

The balance sheet will show Accounts receivable of $20,000 or (1) + (4), the income statement will show Revenues of $100,000 (2), and the statement of cash flows will show Cash collected from customers as $80,000 (3) in the cash from operating activities section.

8. B Revenues ($100,000) minus expenses ($60,000) equals net income ($40,000). Accrual accounting requires revenues and expenses to be recorded when earned and incurred regardless of when the cash changes hands. Also, a dividend (which is shown on the statement of changes in shareholders' equity) is not an expense since it does not help generate revenues.

9. E Cash is an asset, not shareholders' equity. Net income and changes in Cash are typically different. Net income often includes revenues that may not have been collected and expenses that may not have been paid in the same accounting period as when the revenues were earned and the expenses incurred.

10. C Preventive, detective, and corrective controls are used to minimize the risk of errors in the accounting records.

Matching

1. M
2. J
3. N
4. E
5. H
6. B
7. F
8. C
9. D
10. I
11. L
12. K
13. A
14. G

Exercises

1. Tim's Ware, Inc.		Assets =		Liabili-ties +	Shareholders' equity	
		Cash	All other assets		Contrib. capital	Retained earnings
a.	Tim's Ware began operations by issuing $6,000 of common stock to its owners.	6,000			6,000 Common stock	
b.	Tim's Ware purchased $3,000 of inventory and paid cash.	(3,000)	3,000 Inventory			
c.	Tim's Ware purchased $400 of supplies and paid cash.	(400)	400 Supplies			
d.	Tim's Ware made sales of $3,300 on account. The cost of the sales was $2,500.		3,300 Accounts receivable (2,500) Inventory			3,300 Sales (2,500) Cost of goods sold
e.	Tim's Ware collected $2,700 of receivables during the year.	2,700	(2,700) Accounts receivable			
f.	On July 1, 2012 Tim's Ware paid $2,400 in advance for an insurance policy that covers two years beginning July 1.	(2,400)	2,400 Prepaid insurance			
g.	As of December 31, 2012, six months of insurance coverage has expired.		(600) Prepaid insurance			(600) Insurance expense
h.	Supplies on hand as of December 31, 2012 amounted to $100.		(300) Supplies			(300) Supplies expense

2. Tim's Ware's account titles:		Amount as of or for the year ended December 31	Select one for each line item:		
			Income Statement	Balance Sheet	Statement of Cash Flows
a.	Stock issued for cash	$6,000			X
b.	Supplies expense	$300	X		
c.	Supplies	$100		X	
d.	Insurance expense	$600	X		
e.	Prepaid insurance	$1,800		X	
f.	Cash paid for insurance	$2,400			X
g.	Cash received from customers	$2,700			X
h.	Accounts receivable	$600		X	
i.	Sales	$3,300	X		
j.	Cost of goods sold	$2,500	X		
k.	Inventory	$500		X	

CHAPTER 3
ACCRUALS AND DEFERRALS:
TIMING IS EVERYTHING IN ACCOUNTING

Chapter Overview

In Chapter 2, you learned about the difference between cash-basis and accrual-basis accounting. Often there is a difference in timing between a business event and the collection or payment of cash. Chapter 3 deals with accounting for the most common types of business events that involve these timing differences.

Chapter Highlights

1. **Net income** (or **net profit** or **net earnings**) is equal to **revenues** minus **expenses**. The life of a business is continuous, but we must be able to measure income for a shorter period of time, usually a year, quarter, or month. The **income statement**, also called the **statement of operations** or the **profit and loss statement**, reports income earned over a period of time. All revenues earned during the period and all expenses for the period must be included on the income statement. **Timing differences**, the difference between the time when business events take place and the time when cash changes hands, can make it difficult to measure income for a particular accounting period. Companies must make **adjustments** for these timing differences before financial statements can be prepared.

2. **Accruals**, business transactions in which the action takes place before the exchange of cash, can be either revenues or expenses. Accruals affect both the income statement and the balance sheet.

	Revenue	Expenses
Action first	Revenue earned must be on the income statement even though cash has not yet been collected.	Expenses incurred must be on the income statement even though cash has not yet been paid.

- Accrued revenues include sales of goods to customers on account. Other types of accrued revenue include interest earned on loans a company makes to others. When the loan is made, Other assets (not Accounts receivable from customers) is recorded.

Assets	Liab.	Shareholders' equity	
		Cont. Cap. +	Retained Earnings
+ Other assets - Cash			

At the end of the accounting period, the company must accrue the interest earned on the loan by showing this revenue on the current period's income statement, even though it has not yet been received in cash. The formula to calculate interest earned is **Interest = Principal** *times* **Rate** *times* **Time**. Interest rates are usually stated as annual percentages (a full twelve months), thus the correct fraction of a year must be used if the interest earned is for less than a full year.

Assets	Liab.	Shareholders' equity	
		Contrib. Cap. +	Retained Earnings
+ Interest receivable			+ Interest revenue

When cash is later collected (**realized**), the company will not record (**recognize**) revenue again. Instead, the company will record an increase in Cash and a decrease in Interest receivable.

Assets	Liab.	Shareholders' equity	
		Contrib. Cap. +	Retained Earnings
+ Cash - Interest receivable			

At the end of an accounting period, a company must look over its records to make sure that all revenues for services performed or goods delivered to customers are properly recorded. Revenue earned very late in the period may not even have been billed to the customers yet, but it still must be included as revenue on the income statement, and the related Accounts receivable must be shown as a current asset on the balance sheet. When cash is finally collected (**realized**) from these customers in the following accounting period, the company will not record (**recognize**) revenue again. Instead, the company will record an increase in Cash and a decrease in Accounts receivable.

- Expenses must be accrued at the end of each accounting period, too. A company must examine all of its business transactions to make sure that no expenses (and related liabilities) have been forgotten because the bills have not yet been received or paid.

- Interest expense, and the related liability Interest payable, must be accrued for all outstanding notes payable. Interest expense is the cost of using someone else's money for a period of time, and it must be shown as an expense on the income statement even though interest has not yet been paid in cash.

Assets	Liabilities	Shareholders' equity	
		Contrib. Cap. +	Retained Earnings
	+Interest payable		- Interest expense

If cash for this period's accrued interest expense is paid in the following accounting period, the interest expense will not be recorded again. Instead, the payment will reduce both Cash and Interest payable.

Assets	Liabilities	Shareholders' equity	
		Contrib. Cap. +	Retained Earnings
- Cash	-Interest payable		

- Salary expense is normally recorded when employees are paid. However, the last payday of the accounting period may not be the same as the last day of the accounting period. A company must accrue salary expense for work done by employees between the last payday and the financial statement date. Then the income statement will show the correct Salary expense for all work done by employees during the accounting period, and the balance sheet will show the related Salaries payable for amounts still owed to employees.

Assets	Liabilities	Shareholders' equity	
		Contrib. Capital +	Retained Earnings
	+ Salaries payable		- Salary expense

On the first payday of the following accounting period, the company must decrease Salaries payable for the amount of salary that was reported as a liability in the previous accounting period. It must also decrease Retained earnings for any additional salary expense incurred since the beginning of the new accounting period, and decrease Cash for the total amount paid to employees.

3. **Deferrals**, business transactions in which the dollars are exchanged before the business activity has occurred, can also be either revenues or expenses.

	Revenue	Expenses
Dollars first	Cash has been received from customers, but the company hasn't done its part to earn it.	Cash has been paid for services or goods not yet used.

- Sometimes a company collects cash from its customers before shipping merchandise to them or performing services for them. The company **defers revenue** when it receives these advance payments. It cannot record revenue yet because it has not done anything to earn the revenue. Instead, the company records the increase in Cash, and an increase in **Unearned revenue**, a liability.

Assets	Liabilities	Shareholders' equity	
		Contrib. Cap. +	Retained Earnings
+ Cash	+ Unearned revenue		

When the company finally ships the merchandise or performs the service for its customer, it decreases the liability, Unearned revenue, and records Sales revenue as an increase in Retained earnings.

Assets	Liabilities	Shareholders' equity	
		Contrib. Cap. +	Retained Earnings
	- Unearned revenue		+ Sales

- Four kinds of **expenses** are **deferred**, or paid for in advance. A company normally pays for many months of insurance in advance. When insurance coverage is paid for, no Insurance expense is recorded. Instead, the company decreases Cash and increases **Prepaid insurance**, an asset.

Assets	Liab.	Shareholders' equity	
		Contrib. Cap. +	Retained Earnings
+Prepaid insurance			
- Cash			

When financial statements are prepared, the company makes an adjusting entry to show the expired (used up) part of the insurance coverage as an expense. This adjustment decreases the asset, Prepaid insurance, and records Insurance expense, which decreases Retained earnings.

Assets	Liab.	Shareholders' equity	
		Contrib. Cap. +	Retained Earnings
-Prepaid insurance			-Insurance expense

After this adjusting entry is made, the asset, Prepaid insurance, will show the amount of insurance coverage still remaining for future months.

- Like insurance, rent is usually paid in advance. When a company pays cash for rent in advance, it records an increase in an asset, **Prepaid rent**, along with a decrease in Cash. When financial statements are prepared, an adjusting entry is made to decrease the asset Prepaid rent for the

amount of rent that has been used up. This adjustment also records Rent expense, which decreases Retained earnings.

- **Supplies** are miscellaneous items used in a business, and are not the same as **inventory**, which is merchandise purchased for resale. A company will usually buy and pay for supplies in advance. This purchase is recorded as a decrease in Cash and an increase in the asset, Supplies. As these supplies are used up day by day, no record is made of Supplies expense. Instead, at the end of an accounting period, the company counts the supplies that remain. An adjusting entry is made to decrease the asset account, Supplies, so that it equals the amount of supplies remaining. The amount of this decrease represents Supplies expense, the portion of supplies that have been used up. After this adjusting entry is made, the asset account on the balance sheet properly represents the amount of supplies left for future use. The income statement shows the expense of the supplies that have been used up.

- Often a company will buy an asset like equipment that benefits more than one future accounting period. The whole cost of the equipment is not treated as an expense in the period it is purchased. Instead, the matching principle requires that the cost be spread out over all of the accounting periods that benefit from using the equipment to earn revenue. This is called **depreciating** the asset and the expense reported in each accounting period is known as **Depreciation expense**.

When equipment is first purchased, the company decreases Cash and increases the asset, Equipment.

Assets	Liab.	Shareholders' equity	
		Contrib. Cap. +	Retained Earnings
+Equipment			
- Cash			

At the end of the accounting period, the company calculates Depreciation expense by dividing the cost of the equipment by the number of accounting periods it will be used. The adjusting entry records Depreciation expense, which decreases Retained earnings, and **Accumulated depreciation**, a **contra-asset**.

Assets	Liab.	Shareholders' equity	
		Contrib. Cap. +	**Retained Earnings**
-Accumulated depreciation			-Depreciation expense

Accumulated depreciation is considered to be an asset account, but it is subtracted from Equipment in the calculation of total assets on the balance sheet. The company's balance sheet will continue to show the cost of the equipment, but along with this cost the company will report Accumulated depreciation, the total depreciation that has been recorded for the equipment so far. Cost minus accumulated depreciation is the **book value** or **carrying value** of the equipment.

4. **Profit margin on sales** is equal to **net income** divided by **sales**. It measures how much of a company's sales revenue actually makes it to the bottom line, net income.

5. There are three significant risks associated with financial records and accounting information. The first risk is errors in recording and updating the accounting records. Input and processing controls are designed to make sure that only authorized transactions are entered in the accounting records. Reconciliation and control reports are designed to catch errors in the input and processing of accounting data. Computerized accounting systems can make sure that the accounting equation is in balance at every stage of data entry. Documentation can provide support for recorded transactions.

The second major risk is unauthorized access to accounting information, which exposes a company to leaks of confidential information and makes it possible for perpetrators to cover up theft by altering the accounting records. Accounting records should be kept in a secure location. Computerized systems have user ID's and passwords that limit access to the system. Firms should also carefully screen employees.

The third major risk is loss or destruction of accounting data. Computerized systems need to store backup data at a remote location.

Featured Exercise

For each question below, fill in the correct dollar amount and circle the correct financial statement on which it appears, using the following codes:

IS for the income statement for the year ended December 31, 2011
BS for the balance sheet at December 31, 2011
SOCF for the statement of cash flows for the year ended December 31, 2011

1. On September 1, 2011, Acme Enterprises borrowed $10,000 from the bank on a two-year, 9% note payable. All interest will be paid when the loan is repaid. On December 31, 2011, the correct adjusting entry was made for interest.

   a. Cash received from borrowing of $_____ appears on the: IS   BS   SOCF

   b. Interest payable of $_____ appears on the: IS   BS   SOCF

   c. Notes payable of $_____ appears on the: IS   BS   SOCF

   d. Interest expense of $_____ appears on the: IS   BS   SOCF

   e. Cash paid for interest of $_____ appears on the: IS   BS   SOCF

2. On October 1, 2011, Acme Enterprises loaned $100,000 to its CEO on a one-year, 12% note receivable. All interest will be received when the loan is collected. On December 31, 2011, the correct adjusting entry was made for interest.

   a. Notes receivable of $_____ appears on the: IS   BS   SOCF

   b. Interest receivable of $_____ appears on the: IS   BS   SOCF

   c. Interest revenue of $_____ appears on the: IS   BS   SOCF

   d. Cash received for interest of $_____ appears on the: IS   BS   SOCF

3. On December 30, 2011, Acme Enterprises completed a $2,000 consulting job for a client. Because most of the company employees are celebrating the New Year a little early, no one billed the customer when the job was finished. However, on December 31, 2011, the correct adjusting entry was made.

   a. Cash received from customers of $_____ appears on the: IS   BS   SOCF

   b. Accounts receivable of $_____ appears on the: IS   BS   SOCF

   c. Revenue of $_____ appears on the: IS   BS   SOCF

4. Acme Enterprises pays its employees every other Friday. The last payday was Friday, December 24, 2010, and the next payday will be Friday, January 7, 2011. Employees earned $3,500 in the last week of December, 2010. The correct adjusting entry was made on December 31.

    a. $_____ of this $3,500 appears as cash paid to employees on the: **IS   BS   SOCF**

    b. $_____ of this $3,500 appears as salary expense on the: **IS   BS   SOCF**

    c. Salaries payable of $_____ appears on the: **IS   BS   SOCF**

5. On August 1, 2011, Acme Enterprises received $6,000 in advance from a customer for services that Acme expected to perform over the next twelve months. The entire $6,000 was properly recorded as unearned revenue. On December 31, 2011, the correct adjusting entry was made.

    a. Revenue of $_____ appears on the: **IS   BS   SOCF**

    b. Unearned revenue of $_____ appears on the: **IS   BS   SOCF**

    c. Cash received from customers of $_____ appears on the: **IS   BS   SOCF**

6. On April 1, 2011, Acme Enterprises paid $1,200 for a 24-month insurance policy that went into effect the same day. On December 31, 2011, the correct adjusting entry was made.

    a. Cash paid for insurance of $_____ appears on the: **IS   BS   SOCF**

    b. Prepaid insurance of $_____ appears on the: **IS   BS   SOCF**

    c. Insurance expense of $_____ appears on the: **IS   BS   SOCF**

7. On January 1, 2011, Acme Enterprises had $1,000 of supplies in its supply room. During 2011, Acme paid $5,000 cash for more supplies. On December 31, 2011, Acme counted the supplies and found that only $800 of supplies remained. On December 31, 2011, the correct adjusting entry was made.

    a. Supplies of $_____ appears on the: **IS   BS   SOCF**

    b. Supplies expense of $_____ appears on the: **IS   BS   SOCF**

    c. Cash paid for supplies of $_____ appears on the: **IS   BS   SOCF**

8. On January 1, 2011, Acme Enterprises bought a delivery truck for $30,000 cash. The truck is expected to be used for six years. On December 31, 2011, the correct adjusting entry was made.

    a. Equipment of $_____ appears on the: **IS   BS   SOCF**

    b. Depreciation expense of $_____ appears on the: **IS   BS   SOCF**

    c. Cash paid for depreciation of $_____ appears on the: **IS   BS   SOCF**

    d. Accumulated depreciation of $_____ appears on the: **IS   BS   SOCF**

    e. Cash paid for equipment of $_____ appears on the: **IS   BS   SOCF**

Solution

1. a. Cash received from borrowing of **$10,000** appears on the **SOCF**.
   b. Interest payable of **$300** appears on the **BS**.
   c. Notes payable of **$10,000** appears on the **BS**.
   d. Interest expense of **$300** appears on the **IS**.
   e. Cash paid for interest of **$0** appears on the **SOCF**.

2. a. Notes receivable of **$100,000** appears on the **BS**.
   b. Interest receivable of **$3,000** appears on the **BS**.
   c. Interest revenue of **$3,000** appears on the **IS**.
   d. Cash received for interest of **$0** appears on the **SOCF**.

3. a. Cash received from customers of **$0** appears on the **SOCF**.
   b. Accounts receivable of **$2,000** appears on the **BS**.
   c. Revenue of **$2,000** appears on the **IS**.

4. a. **$0** of this $3,500 appears as cash paid to employees on the **SOCF**.
   b. **$3,500** of this $3,500 appears as salary expense on the **IS**.
   c. Salaries payable of **$3,500** appears on the **BS**.

5. a. Revenue of **$2,500** appears on the **IS**.
   b. Unearned revenue of **$3,500** appears on the **BS**.
   c. Cash received from customers of **$6,000** appears on the **SOCF**.

6. a. Cash paid for insurance of **$1,200** appears on the **SOCF**.
   b. Prepaid insurance of **$750** appears on the **BS**.
   c. Insurance expense of **$450** appears on the **IS**.

7. a. Supplies of **$800** appears on the **BS**.
   b. Supplies expense of **$5,200** appears on the **IS**.
   c. Cash paid for supplies of **$5,000** appears on the **SOCF**.

8. a. Equipment of **$30,000** appears on the **BS**.
   b. Depreciation expense of **$5,000** appears on the **IS**.
   c. Cash paid for depreciation of **$0** appears on the **SOCF**.
   d. Accumulated depreciation of **$5,000** appears on the **BS**,
   e. Cash paid for equipment of **$30,000** appears on the **SOCF**.

Review Questions and Exercises

Completion Statements

Fill in the blank(s) to complete each statement.

1. Profit margin on sales is _____ divided by _____.

2. The book value of equipment is _____ minus _____.

3. An asset that is subtracted from other assets to calculate total assets is called a _____.

4. The _____ principle requires that the cost of equipment be treated as an expense over all of the accounting periods the equipment is used.

5. Two financial statements, the _____ and the _____ are affected by adjusting entries.

6. Interest equals _____ times _____ times _____.

7. When a company receives payment in advance, it records _____, a liability.

8. Before financial statements can be prepared, _____ entries must be recorded for accruals.

True/False

Indicate whether each statement is true (T) or false (F).

_____ 1. The income statement is also known as a profit-and-loss statement.

_____ 2. Interest expense is recorded only after it is paid in cash.

_____ 3. Accruals involve business events that take place before cash is received or paid.

_____ 4. Supplies are part of a company's inventory.

_____ 5. Interest receivable must be accrued on notes payable.

_____ 6. Deferrals involve cash collected or paid before a business event takes place.

_____ 7. The cost of equipment is an expense of the period when it is purchased.

_____ 8. Most companies pay for insurance coverage in advance.

_____ 9. Controls can eliminate all business risks.

_____ 10. Depreciation expense is always the same amount as Accumulated depreciation.

Multiple Choice

Select the best answer for each question.

_____ 1. The adjusting entry to record an accrued expense also involves recording:
A. a revenue.
B. an asset.
C. a liability.
D. a decrease in Cash.

_____ 2. The adjusting entry to record an accrued revenue also involves recording:
A. an expense.
B. an asset.
C. a liability.
D. an increase in Cash.

_____ 3. When a company pays for six months of insurance in advance, it records:
A. prepaid insurance, an asset.
B. insurance expense, a liability.
C. prepaid insurance, an expense.
D. insurance expense, a decrease in Retained earnings.

_____ 4. When a company receives cash in advance for services it has not yet performed, it records:
A. Revenue earned.
B. Unearned service revenue, a liability.
C. Unearned service revenue, an asset.
D. This is a trick question. Nothing is recorded until services are performed.

_____ 5. ABC, Inc., shows $300 of Supplies expense on its income statement. ABC must have:
A. purchased $300 of supplies during the period.
B. paid cash for $300 of supplies during the period.
C. used $300 of supplies during the period.
D. The answer cannot be determined from the information given.

_____ 6. During June, Busy Beaver bought $5,000 of office supplies on account, and promised to pay the vendor the full amount in July. At the end of June, Busy Beaver estimated that there were $2,000 of office supplies left unused. How much Supplies expense should Busy Beaver report for June?
A. $5,000
B. $2,000
C. $3,000.
D. $ 0

_____ 7. During June, Busy Beaver performed $3,500 of services for clients on account. In June, $500 of this amount was collected in cash. The remaining $3,000 was collected in July. How much Service revenue should Busy Beaver report for June?
A. $ 0
B. $500
C. $3,000
D. $3,500

8. Salaries payable on a company's balance sheet indicates that:
A. the company is in serious financial difficulty. It doesn't even have enough cash to pay its employees.
B. the company's accountants are seriously confused. Salaries appear on the income statement, not the balance sheet.
C. employees had not received payment for the last few days of work because the last day of the accounting period was not a payday.
D. employees were overpaid and now owe the company money.

9. Accounts receivable appear on a company's balance sheet because:
A. the company collected cash when it sold merchandise to customers.
B. the company sold merchandise to customers but has not received payment yet.
C. the company bought merchandise on account.
D. the company paid for merchandise previously purchased on account.

10. The accountant for Ace Electronics forgot to make the adjusting entry for depreciation on the company's equipment. As a result of this mistake:
A. net income is too high.
B. total liabilities are too low.
C. net income is too low.
D. stockholders' equity is too low.

Matching

Adjusting entries affect both the income statement and the balance sheet. The left-hand column below lists revenue and expense accounts commonly used in adjusting entries. Match each of these income statement accounts with a related balance sheet account that would appear in an adjusting entry with the revenue or expense.

Income statement		**Balance sheet**	
_____	1. Subscription revenue	A.	Accumulated depreciation
_____	2. Interest revenue	B.	Supplies
_____	3. Interest expense	C.	Prepaid rent
_____	4. Depreciation expense	D.	Interest payable
_____	5. Supplies expense	E.	Salaries payable
_____	6. Insurance expense	F.	Interest receivable
_____	7. Salary expense	G.	Prepaid insurance
_____	8. Rent expense	H.	Unearned revenue

Exercises

Show the effect on the accounting equation of each of the events described. This company has a fiscal year that ends on December 31.

1		Assets =	Liabilities +	Shareholders' Equity
a	On December 31, made an adjusting entry to accrue $3,000 of sales revenue earned that has not yet been billed to a customer.			
b	On January 2, billed the customer for $3,000.			
c	On January 15, collected all $3,000 in cash.			

2		Assets =	Liabilities +	Shareholders' Equity
a	On October 31, paid $2,400 for six months' rent in advance.			
b	Made the adjusting entry required on December 31.			

3		Assets =	Liabilities +	Shareholders' Equity
a	On June 1, borrowed $10,000 for two years at 9% interest. Interest will be paid when the loan is repaid.			
b	Made the adjusting entry required on December 31.			

4		Assets =	Liabilities +	Shareholders' Equity
a	On August 1, loaned $20,000 for two years at 12% interest. Interest will be collected when the loan is repaid.			
b	Made the adjusting entry required on December 31.			

5		Assets =	Liabilities +	Shareholders' Equity
a	On December 30, the last working day of the year, employees have earned $1,800. They will not be paid for another week. Make the adjusting entry required on December 31.			
b	Paid employees $4,000 for work done in December and January.			

6		Assets =	Liabilities +	Shareholders' Equity
a	Noticed that only $100 of office supplies remain in the back room. Bought $700 more office supplies on account.			
b	Paid the vendor for the office supplies purchased in (6a) above.			
c	On December 31, $200 of office supplies are left in the back room. Made the adjusting entry required on December 31.			

7		Assets =	Liabilities +	Shareholders' Equity
a	On June 21, paid $9,000 for rent for the six months beginning August 1.			
b	Made the adjusting entry required on December 31.			
c	On December 21, paid $10,000 for rent for the six months beginning February 1 of next year.			
d	Made the adjusting entry required on December 31.			

8		Assets =	Liabilities +	Shareholders' Equity
a	On December 28, received a $75 bill for electric service used in December. Payment is not due until January 10.			
b	On January 10, paid December's $75 electric bill.			
c	On December 31, the company still had not received the December bill from the gas company. This bill usually runs about $225 for winter months.			
d	December's gas bill for $230 arrived on January 3. The bill was paid on January 15.			

9		Assets =	Liabilities +	Shareholders' Equity
a	On January 1, bought a $3,600 copy machine, which is expected to last for three years.			
b	Made the adjusting entry required on December 31.			

Solutions

Completion Statements

1. net income, net sales
2. cost, accumulated depreciation
3. contra-asset
4. matching
5. income statement, balance sheet
6. principal, rate, time
7. unearned revenue
8. adjusting

True/False

1. True
2. False: Interest expense must be accrued for notes payable.
3. True
4. False: Supplies are miscellaneous items used in a business. Inventory is merchandise purchased for resale.
5. False: Interest expense and Interest **payable** must be accrued on notes payable.
6. True
7. False: The matching principle requires that the cost of equipment be treated as an expense over all of the accounting periods when the equipment is used, not just the period when it is purchased.
8. True
9. False: Internal controls will help to mitigate, not eliminate, business risks.
10. False: Depreciation expense is just the current period's depreciation. Accumulated depreciation is all of the depreciation expense that has ever been recorded for a particular asset. In the first accounting period an asset is used, Accumulated depreciation will be the same as Depreciation expense. In later accounting periods, Accumulated depreciation will be more than Depreciation expense for the period.

Multiple Choice

1. C Expenses are accrued because something has been used up to earn revenue, but cash has not been paid yet. The liability to make future payment for something already used up must be recorded as well.
2. B Revenues are accrued because they have been earned and should appear on the income statement. However, cash has not yet been received in exchange for goods or services already delivered. The right to receive cash in the future from this revenue is an asset.
3. A In exchange for payment for six months of future insurance coverage, the company gets an asset, Prepaid insurance, because the company will receive future benefit from the insurance policy. Adjusting entries are needed to turn the asset into an expense as the coverage is used up.
4. B The company has not done anything yet to earn the advance payment it has received. The company should record a liability because it owes its customer services now that it has accepted payment in advance.
5. C Supplies are an expense when they are used to earn revenue. Purchasing supplies creates an asset called Supplies which the company has on hand to use in the future. Payment for supplies removes a liability to pay for items already received.

6. C Supplies become an expense when they are used in the business to earn revenue. This company started with $5,000 of supplies, but has only $2,000 left unused. The missing $3,000 of supplies must have been used up, and should be reported as an expense.

7. D Revenue is recorded when it is earned by performing services for clients. It doesn't matter when cash is collected.

8. C The last payday of the accounting period rarely is the same as the date of the financial statements. However, the income statement must show as an expense all that employees earned for the period. Any amounts that have not been paid in cash yet are shown as Salaries payable, a liability on the balance sheet. Almost every company will routinely show Salaries payable because of timing differences. So it doesn't mean a company is unable to pay its employees. (However, if Salaries payable are very large when compared with Salary expense for the year, it might mean the company has some financial problems.)

9. B Accounts receivable are created when a company earns revenue and has the right to receive cash from customers.

10. A The missing entry would record Depreciation expense and Accumulated depreciation. Depreciation expense, like all expenses, decreases net income, retained earnings, and total stockholders' equity. Without the missing expense, net income, retained earnings, and total stockholders' equity are all too high, not too low. Accumulated depreciation is a contra-asset that decreases total assets. Neither Depreciation expense nor Accumulated depreciation has any effect on liabilities.

Matching

H 1. Subscription revenue/ Unearned revenue
F 2. Interest revenue/ Interest receivable
D 3. Interest expense/ Interest payable
A 4. Depreciation expense/ Accumulated depreciation
B 5. Supplies expense/ Supplies
G 6. Insurance expense/ Prepaid insurance
E 7. Salary expense/ Salaries payable
C 8. Rent expense/ Prepaid rent

Exercises

1		Assets =	Liabilities +	Shareholders' Equity
a	On December 31, made an adjusting entry to accrue $3,000 of sales revenue earned that has not yet been billed to a customer. *The income statement must show all revenue earned during the year.*	3,000 Accounts receivable		3,000 Sales
b	On January 2, billed the customer for $3,000. *No entry is required because revenue has already been recorded in the previous accounting period.*	No entry	No entry	No entry
c	On January 15, collected all $3,000 in cash. *Revenue is recorded in December, when it is earned, not when cash is collected.*	3,000 Cash (3,000) Accounts receivable		

2		Assets =	Liabilities +	Shareholders' Equity
a	On October 31, paid $2,400 for six months' rent in advance. *This prepayment is an asset because it will provide future benefit. No expense will be recorded until the rent is used up.*	(2,400) Cash 2,400 Prepaid rent		
b	Made the adjusting entry required on December 31. *Two months of rent have been used up. ($2,400/6) x 2 months = $800*	(800) Prepaid rent		(800) Rent expense

3		Assets =	Liabilities +	Shareholders' Equity
a	On June 1, borrowed $10,000 for two years at 9% interest. Interest will be paid when the loan is repaid. *No interest expense is recorded until the company has used the $10,000 for a period of time.*	10,000 Cash	10,000 Notes payable	
b	Made the adjusting entry required on December 31. *The company has used the borrowed cash for seven months. $10,000 x .09 x (7/12) = $525*		525 Interest payable	(525) Interest expense

4		Assets =	Liabilities +	Shareholders' Equity
a	On August 1, loaned $20,000 for two years at 12% interest. Interest will be collected when the loan is repaid. *Interest is earned as time goes by. However, on the date of the loan, no time has elapsed so no interest is recorded yet.*	20,000 Notes receivable (20,000) Cash		
b	Made the adjusting entry required on December 31. *The loan has earned interest for 5 months. $20,000 x .12 x (5/12) = $1,000*	1,000 Interest receivable		1,000 Interest revenue

5		Assets =	Liabilities +	Shareholders' Equity
a	On December 30, the last working day of the year, employees have earned $1,800. They will not be paid for another week. Make the adjusting entry required on December 31. *Expenses are recorded when they are used to earn revenue.*		1,800 Salaries payable	(1,800) Salary expense
b	Paid employees $4,000 for work done in December and January. *$1,800 of the cash has already been recorded as an expense in December.* *$4,000 – 1,800 = $2,200*	(4,000) Cash	(1,800) Salaries payable	(2,200) Salary expense

6		Assets =	Liabilities +	Shareholders' Equity
a	Noticed that only $100 of office supplies are left in the back room. Bought $700 more office supplies on account. *The supplies will be used in the future, so they are recorded as an asset.*	700 Supplies	700 Other payables	
b	Paid the vendor for the office supplies purchased in (6a) above. *No expense is recorded when cash is paid for a liability.*	(700) Cash	(700) Other payables	
c	On December 31, $200 of office supplies are left in the back room. Made the adjusting entry required on December 31. *Supplies used are an expense.* *$100 + 700 – 200 = $600*	(600) Supplies		(600) Supplies expense

7		Assets =	Liabilities +	Shareholders' Equity
a	On June 21, paid $9,000 for rent for the six months beginning August 1. *This rent will be used in the future, so it is recorded as an asset.*	9,000 Prepaid rent (9,000) Cash		
b	Made the adjusting entry required on December 31. *Five month's rent has been used up.* *($9,000/6 months) x 5 months = $7,500*	(7,500) Prepaid rent		(7,500) Rent expense
c	On December 21, paid $10,000 for rent for the six months beginning February 1 of next year.	10,000 Prepaid rent (10,000) Cash		
d	Made the adjusting entry required on December 31. *No entry is required because none of the rent prepaid on December 21 has expired yet.*	no entry	no entry	no entry

8		Assets =	Liabilities +	Shareholders' Equity
a	On December 28, received a $75 bill for electric service used in December. Payment is not due until January 10. *The electricity was used to earn revenue in December, so it should be an expense in December even though it has not been paid in cash.*		75 Other payables	(75) Utilities expense
b	On January 10, paid December's $75 electric bill. *The $75 was expensed in December and thus should not be expensed again when the liability is paid.*	(75) Cash	(75) Other payables	
c	On December 31, the company still had not received the December bill from the gas company. This bill usually runs about $225 for winter months. *December's estimated utility expense must be recorded and included on the income statement in December.*		225 Other payables	(225) Utilities expense
d	December's gas bill for $230 arrived on January 3. The bill was paid on Jan. 15. *Most of the December bill was accrued as an expense in December, and should not be expensed in January, too. The December estimate was $5 too low, so January's income statement will include $5 extra expense. Estimates are never perfect, but this $5 is immaterial.*	(230) Cash	(225) Other payables	(5) Utilities expense

9		Assets =	Liabilities +	Shareholders' Equity
a	On January 1, bought a $3,600 copy machine which is expected to last for three years. *The equipment is an asset because it will benefit future accounting periods.*	3,600 Equipment (3,600) Cash		
b	Made the adjusting entry required on December 31. *The cost of the equipment must be spread out over all the years it will be used.* $3,600 / 3 years = $1,200	(1,200) Accumulated depreciation		(1,200) Depreciation expense

CHAPTER 4
PAYMENT FOR GOODS AND SERVICES: CASH AND ACCOUNTS RECEIVABLE

Chapter Overview

Chapter 4 will help you to understand how to account for cash and accounts receivable and how this information is reported in the financial statements.

Chapter Highlights

1. Internal controls surrounding cash are important to help safeguard it and ensure that sales and cash collections are properly recorded. Controls include limiting access to the cash; **segregation of duties**, so that cash recordkeeping is not done by someone who has access to the cash; and monitoring cash by preparing a **bank reconciliation**. A bank reconciliation, also known as a cash reconciliation, is a crucial control that compares the **bank statement** balance with the cash balance on the company's accounting records (books) and helps determine the company's true cash balance to be shown in the financial statements.

- A cash reconciliation is prepared as follows:

Balance per bank statement	XX
+ Deposits in transit	XX
+ Bank errors in bank's favor	XX
- Bank errors in company's favor	(XX)
- Outstanding checks	(XX)
= True (correct) cash balance	XX

Balance per books	XX
+ Notes collected by bank	XX
+ Interest earned	XX
+ Company errors in bank's favor	XX
- Company errors in company's favor	(XX)
- NSF checks	(XX)
- Bank charges	(XX)
= True (correct) cash balance	XX

A bank reconciliation is prepared properly only if the correct (true) cash balances are the same going from the bank statement to the books and from the books to the bank

statement. Any discrepancies must be investigated.

- The bank reconciliation is a worksheet that does not directly affect the company's accounting records. Adjusting entries are required for all items needed to make the balance per books equal to the true cash balance.

2. **Cash equivalents** are highly liquid investments with a maturity of three months or less that can easily be converted into a known amount of cash. "Cash and cash equivalents" is the first asset listed on the balance sheet and represents the amount on hand at the balance sheet date. The statement of cash flows explains the change in cash from one balance sheet date to the next.

3. **Accounts receivable**, also called receivables, are current assets arising from credit sales to customers. Unfortunately a company cannot expect to collect 100% of its receivables. There are always some customers who do not pay. GAAP requires a company to estimate its uncollectible accounts. This estimated **bad debts expense** is matched with the related sales in the same accounting period. This is called the **allowance method**. The adjusting entry required is:

Assets	Liab.	Shareholders' equity	
		CC	Retained earnings
- Allowance for un-collectible accounts			- Bad debts expense

The **allowance for uncollectible accounts** is a contra-asset account. Accounts receivable is not reduced directly because at the time of the adjusting entry the company is unable to identify exactly which accounts are not going to be collected. The allowance account represents only an estimate of uncollectible accounts. Accounts receivable minus the allowance for uncollectible accounts is called **net realizable value**, or the carrying value, or book value, of accounts receivable, and represents the amount the company believes it will actually collect from its customers.

4. Under the allowance method, there are two ways to estimate the amount of uncollectible accounts, the percentage of sales method, and the accounts receivable method. The accounts affected are the same regardless of which method is used. It is the amount of the estimate that may differ.

- The **percentage of sales method** focuses on the income statement. Management estimates bad debts expense as a percentage of credit sales. The sales method ignores the unadjusted balance in the allowance for uncollectible accounts in estimating bad debts expense.

- The **accounts receivable method**, sometimes called the aging or percent of accounts receivable method, focuses on the balance sheet. Management analyzes accounts receivable by preparing an **aging schedule** of receivables. Based on this schedule, management estimates the percentage of accounts receivable that will not be collected. The amount already in the allowance for uncollectible account is adjusted so that it equals this percentage of accounts receivable. This method is more involved than the sales method because the amount of the adjustment depends on the unadjusted balance already in the allowance for uncollectible accounts.

5. The entry and the dollar amount to write off a specific customer's account will be the same regardless of which method is used.

Assets	Liab.	Shareholders' equity
+ Allowance for un-collectible accounts - Accounts receivable, J. Doe		

Notice the write-off of a specific account does not affect net accounts receivable or total assets,

since both the allowance and accounts receivable are reduced by the same amount. The entry is reclassifying a previously "unnamed" uncollectible account to a "named" uncollectible account. Since bad debts expense is only an estimate, each period bad debts expense usually contains a little adjustment for the over- or under-estimate from the previous period's entry, represented by the unadjusted balance in the allowance account remaining from the previous accounting period.

6. The allowance method (using either the percentage of sales or accounts receivable method) results in a better, more realistic measure of net income and accounts receivable than if the company were to wait until specific customers' accounts were determined to be uncollectible. Companies may ignore the allowance method only if their uncollectible accounts are very small. If they are immaterial, GAAP allows companies to use the **direct write-off method**. The company waits to write off a specific customer's account instead of making an adjusting entry for estimated bad debts in the same period as the related sales. This method violates the matching principle because the sale and the write-off of the uncollectible account may occur in different accounting periods. The direct write-off is recorded as:

Assets	Liab.	Shareholders' equity	
		CC	Retained earnings
- Accounts receivable, J. Doe			- Bad debt expense

7. Credit card sales are not as risky as credit sales and are recorded as:

Assets	Liab.	Shareholders' equity	
		CC	Retained earnings
+ Accounts receivable (credit card company)			+ Sales - Credit card expense

The credit card company, for a fee, will pay the company daily (or weekly):

Assets	Liab.	Shareholders' equity	
		CC	Retained earnings
+ Cash - Accounts receivable (credit card company)			

The company must compare the credit card fees with the benefits of credit card sales such as having the credit card company pursue late and non-paying customers.

8. **Promissory notes**, or notes receivable, are promises by **makers** to pay a specified amount plus interest to the **payees** on specific dates. Interest is calculated as:

Interest = Principal x Rate x Time

Since the interest rate is an annual rate, the time must be expressed as a fraction of a year if the note is a short-term note or if the period covered by the financial statements is less than a year. The entry to record the collection of a note receivable is:

Assets	Liabilities	Shareholders' equity	
		CC	Retained earnings
+ Cash - Note receivable			+Interest revenue

9. Financial statements and related footnotes provide sales and accounts receivable information to help users assess a company's ability to collect its receivables and pay its obligations. The **current ratio** helps to measure a company's liquidity, or its ability to meet its short-term obligations:

$$\frac{\text{Current assets}}{\text{Current liabilities}}$$

The **accounts receivable turnover ratio** measures a company's ability to collect cash from its credit customers.

$$\frac{\text{net credit sales}}{\text{average net accounts receivable}}$$

This ratio can also be expressed as the average number of days it takes to collect accounts receivable:

$$\frac{\text{365 days}}{\text{accounts receivable turnover ratio}}$$

10. Important internal controls are needed to help safeguard cash, accounts receivable, and other assets and to ensure the financial records are accurate and reliable. Employees who have physical access to the assets should not have access to the accounting records. These employees should be given clear assignments of their responsibilities for physically controlling the assets. The procedures to be followed should be well documented. Lastly, the accounting data should be independently verified internally. For instance, requiring cashiers to give receipts to customers provides an independent verification of the sale.

Featured Exercise

Part A. Fill in the accounting equation below for Tina's Ware, Inc.'s events that occurred during 2012.

Tina's Ware, Inc.		Assets =		Liabilities +	Shareholders' equity	
		Cash	All other assets		Contribut. capital	Retained earnings
	Beginning balances, January 1, 2012	$500	Accounts receivable $7,500 Allowance for uncollectible accounts (450) Inventory 5,000 Prepaid insurance 600 Truck (net) 16,000	Accounts payable $6,000 Interest payable 700 Notes Payable 7,000	Common Stock $6,000	Retained earnings $9,450
a	Purchased $32,000 of inventory on account.					
b	Made sales of $55,000 on account. The cost of the sales was $35,000.					
c	$49,000 of receivables were collected. A $1,000 account receivable was late and reclassified as a 3-month note receivable.					
d	Wrote off $400 of specific customer accounts considered uncollectible.					
e	Paid $34,000 of its accounts payable.					
f	Paid $2,400 in advance for an insurance policy that covers two years beginning July 1.					
g	One year of insurance coverage has expired.					
h	Adjusting entries are $5 interest on the note receivable, $4,000 for depreciation, and $700 for interest owed.					
i.	Tina's Ware uses the accounts receivable allowance method and estimates that 5% of its accounts receivable will be uncollectible.					

Part B: Tina's Ware's financial statement line items:		Fill in the correct dollar amount:	Put an "X" in the column of the statement where the item will most likely appear:		
		Amount as of or for the year ended December 31	**Income Statement**	**Balance Sheet**	**Statement of Cash Flows**
a.	Cash paid to suppliers				
b.	Accounts payable				
c.	Inventory				
d.	Cost of goods sold				
e.	Sales				
f.	Cash received from customers				
g.	Accounts receivable				
h.	Allowance for uncollectible accounts				
i.	Bad debts expense				
j.	Notes receivable				
k.	Interest receivable				

Part C:

1. Assume Tina's Ware uses the sales method instead of the accounts receivable method to estimate bad debts expense. It believes 1% of its sales are uncollectible. What would be the adjusting entry?

Assets	Liabilities	Shareholders' equity	
		CC	Retained earnings

2. Calculate Tina's Ware's 2011 (not 2012) current ratio. The notes payable and related interest payable are due in 2013.

3. Calculate Tina's Ware's 2012 (not 2011) accounts receivable turnover ratio. Do not include the $1,000 note receivable in the calculation.

4. When the bank statement is received each month, the cashier is required to adjust the cash balance in the accounting records to agree with the bank balance. Discuss the risk associated with this practice and suggest some internal controls that Tina's Ware should have in place.

Solution Tina's Ware, Inc.		Assets =		Liabilities +	Shareholders' equity	
		Cash	**All other assets**		**CC**	**RE**
	Beginning balances, January 1, 2012	500	Accounts receivable $7,500 Allowance for uncollectible accounts (450) Inventory 5,000 Prepaid insurance 600 Truck (net) 16,000	Accounts payable 6,000 Interest payable 700 Notes payable 7,000	Common stock $6,000	Retained earnings 9,450
a	Purchased $32,000 of inventory on account.		32,000 Inventory	32,000 Accounts payable		
b	Made sales of $55,000 on account. The cost of the sales was $35,000.		55,000 Accounts receivable (35,000) Inventory			55,000 Sales (35,000) Cost of goods sold
c	$49,000 of receivables were collected. A $1,000 account receivable was late and reclassified as a 3-month note receivable.	49,000	(50,000) Accounts receivable 1,000 Notes receivable			
d	Wrote off $400 of specific customer accounts considered uncollectible.		400 Allowance for uncollectible accounts (400) Accounts receivable			
e	Paid $34,000 of its accounts payable.	(34,000)		(34,000) Accounts payable		
f	Paid $2,400 in advance for an insurance policy that covers two years beginning July 1.	(2,400)	2,400 Prepaid insurance			
g	One year of insurance coverage has expired.		(1,200) Prepaid insurance			(1,200) Insurance expense
h	Adjusting entries are $5 interest on the note receivable, $4,000 for depreciation and $700 for interest owed.		5 Interest receivable (4,000) Accumulated depreciation	700 Interest payable		5 Interest revenue (4,000) Depr. expense (700) Interest expense
i.	Tina's Ware uses the accounts receivable allowance method and estimates that 5% of its accounts receivable will be uncollectible.		(555) Allowance for uncollectible accounts (see * below)			(555) Bad debts expense

* $7,500 + 55,000 - 50,000 - 400 = $12,100 Accounts receivable;

$12,100 x (5%) = $(605) adjusted Allowance for uncollectible accounts; $(450)+ 400 + X = $(605); X = (555)

Solution

Part B. Tina's Ware, Inc.'s financial statement line items:		Fill in the correct dollar amount:	Put an "X" in the column of the statement where the item will most likely appear:		
		Amount as of or for the year ended December 31	**Income Statement**	**Balance Sheet**	**Statement of Cash Flows**
a.	Cash paid to suppliers	$(34,000)			X
b.	Accounts payable	$4,000		X	
c.	Inventory	$2,000		X	
d.	Cost of goods sold	$35,000	X		
e.	Sales	$55,000	X		
f.	Cash received from customers	$49,000			X
g.	Accounts receivable	$12,100		X	
h.	Allowance for uncollectible accounts	$(605) =$12,100 x (5%)		X	
i.	Bad debts expense	$555	X		
j.	Notes receivable	$1,000		X	
k.	Interest receivable	$5		X	

Part C:

1. **Assets**	**Liabilities**		**Shareholders' equity**
		CC	Retained earnings
(550) Allowance for uncollectible accounts *(1%) x $55,000 = $(550)*			(550) Bad debts expense

2. Current ratio = $\dfrac{\text{current assets}}{\text{current liabilities}}$ = $\dfrac{\text{cash + accounts receivable (net) + inventory + prepaid insurance}}{\text{accounts payable}}$
   (2011)

   = $\dfrac{\$500 + (7,500 - 450) + 5,000 + 600}{\$6,000}$ = 2.2

3. A/R turnover = $\dfrac{\text{Net sales}}{\text{Average net AR}}$ = $\dfrac{\$55,000}{((\$7,500-450)+(12,100-605))/2}$ = 5.9 times
   (2012)

4. The cashier could steal cash and then change the cash balance in the accounting records without being detected. An important internal control is the segregation of duties. The cashier, who handles the cash, should not have access to the accounting records. The record keeper should not have access to the cash. A bank reconciliation done correctly is a verification of the cash balance and should be performed by someone other than the cashier and record keeper. All the procedures and responsibilities of the employees should be well documented.

Review Questions and Exercises

Completion Statements

Fill in the blank(s) to complete each statement.

1. A _____ involves comparing the cash balance in the accounting records and the bank statement cash balance for the month.

2. Deposits made on the last day of the bank statement that did not reach the bank's recordkeeping department in time to be included in the bank statement and are added to the bank balance are called deposits in _____.

3. _____ are highly liquid investments with a maturity of three months or less that a firm can easily convert into a known amount of cash.

4. GAAP requires companies to use the _____ method to account for bad debts of customers instead of the direct write-off method.

5. The two allowance methods of estimating bad debts expense are the _____ and the _____ methods.

6. The _____ represents the amount the company believes it will collect from its customers. This is also called the _____ value or _____ value of accounts receivable.

7. An _____ is an analysis of the amounts owed to a firm by the length of time they have been outstanding.

8. A difference between an account receivable and a note receivable is the note receivable requires the maker to pay both _____ and _____.

9. The _____ principle requires that bad debts expense be recorded in the same period as the related sales.

10. The _____ ratio measures the company's ability to collect cash and is calculated by dividing credit sales by average net accounts receivable.

True/False

Indicate whether each statement is true (T) or false (F).

_____1. The adjusting entry for bad debts is the same whether a company uses the direct write-off method or the sales method.

_____2. The current ratio is a measure of a company's ability to pay its short-term obligations.

_____3. The lower the accounts receivable turnover ratio, the longer it takes the company to collect its credit sales on average.

_____4. The adjusting entry to estimate bad debt expense is recorded in the same period as the related sale instead of in a later period when the customer is identified as a non-paying customer.

_____5. The direct write-off method is better than the allowance method because it results in a better matching of bad debts expense with the related sales.

_____6. When using the sales method, bad debts expense equals the net sales times the percentage management considers uncollectible plus any balance already in the unadjusted allowance for uncollectible accounts.

_____7. Bad debts expense will be higher for a company that accepts major credit cards rather than selling to customers on account using its own credit card.

_____8. An effective internal control procedure is to have the cashier count the cash in the cash drawer and record the sales in the accounting records.

_____9. The collection of an account receivable will cause the current ratio to increase.

_____10. The matching principle requires bad debts expense be estimated and recorded in the period in which the sale is made, not in the period in which a specific receivable is later written off.

Multiple Choice

Select the best answer for each question.

_____1. The Allowance for uncollectible accounts on the balance sheet shows:
   A. how much a company wrote off as uncollectible during the period.
   B. how much a company recorded as bad debts expense during the period.
   C. the amount of receivables that a company believes it will not collect.
   D. the accumulation of all the uncollectible accounts since the beginning of the business.

_____2. Using the accounts receivable method, a company determines the Allowance for uncollectible accounts should have an adjusted balance of $(1,000). Using the sales method, the company determines bad debt expense should equal $1,000. If the unadjusted balance of the Allowance for uncollectible accounts is $(100), which allowance method would result in a larger decrease in shareholders' equity?
   A. Accounts receivable method
   B. Sales method
   C. Both will result in the same decrease in shareholders' equity.
   D. Neither will result in a decrease in shareholders' equity.

_____3. Rite On, Inc., uses the allowance method and decided to write off an account receivable from I.M. Broke that is considered uncollectible. When Rite On writes off the account:
   A. total assets will increase.
   B. total assets will decrease.
   C. total assets will remain unchanged.
   D. retained earnings will decrease.
   E. Both B and D are correct.

_____4. Which method will result in an Allowance for uncollectible accounts account?
  A. Accounts receivable method
  B. Direct write-off method
  C. Sales method
  D. Both A and C are correct.

_____5. Which method ignores the unadjusted balance in Allowance for uncollectible accounts when recording the adjusting entry for bad debts expense?
  A. Accounts receivable method
  B. Direct write-off method
  C. Sales method
  D. Both B and C are correct.

_____6. Which of the following is an effective segregation of duties in controlling cash? The employee who has access to cash should not:
  A. take the deposits to the bank.
  B. prepare the cash reconciliation.
  C. open the mail since it often includes checks.
  D. take sales orders from customers.
  E. All of the above are proper segregation of duties.

_____7. Collectibles, Inc., estimated that $20,000 of its receivables will be uncollectible based on an aging of its accounts receivable. Why, then, did Collectibles, Inc., record bad debts expense of only $18,000?
  A. Collectibles, Inc., purposely understated its expenses.
  B. Collectibles, Inc., had already written off $2,000 of its accounts receivable during the year.
  C. Collectibles, Inc., already had a $(2,000) balance in its Allowance for uncollectible accounts.
  D. Collectibles, Inc., had underestimated its bad debts expense in the prior year.

_____8. The matching principle requires a company to:
  A. record the bad debts expense in the same period as the related sale.
  B. write off an uncollectible account in the period the account is found to be uncollectible.
  C. match the balance in the Allowance for uncollectible accounts with the Bad debts expense.
  D. match the Allowance for uncollectible accounts with the net realizable value of accounts receivable.

_____9. Which one of the following items from a cash reconciliation does the company need to record in its accounting records?
  A. Deposits in transit
  B. NSF checks
  C. Outstanding checks
  D. None of the above since the company already has recorded these items prior to preparing its cash reconciliation.

_____10. Which of the following is true for a company that accepts credit cards?
  A. The company is more assured of collecting credit card sales.
  B. The company must compare the cost of the credit company's fees with the benefit of receiving cash sooner and the benefit of not needing to pursue non-paying customers.
  C. The company records a credit card expense when it records the related sale.
  D. All of the above are true.

Exercises

1. Complete the May 31, 2012 bank reconciliation for Well Balanced, Inc. given the following:

   a. Outstanding checks: No. 975 for $1,260; No. 991 for $300; No. 1073 for $1,300
   b. Check no. 1018 (for repair expense) was written for $483 but erroneously recorded in Well Balanced's records as $843.
   c. Deposits in transit: $3,370
   d. NSF check from I.M. Broke: $440
   e. Bank service charge: $20

Well Balanced, Inc. Bank Reconciliation, May 31, 2012					
Balance per bank statement	$15,700		Balance per books	$16,310	
Add:			Add:		
Deduct:			Deduct:		
True cash balance			True cash balance		

2. Which of the above reconciling items (a-e) require adjusting entries in Well Balanced's records?

3. Liquidators, Inc. uses the sales method in estimating bad debts expense and has found that such expense has consistently approximated 1% of net sales. At December 31 of the current year, Accounts receivable has a $100,000 balance and the Allowance for uncollectible accounts has a $(300) balance prior to adjustment. Net sales for the current year were $800,000. The appropriate adjusting entry is:

Assets	Liabilities	Shareholders' equity	
		Contributed capital	Retained earnings

4. Macrohard, Inc., after aging its accounts receivable, estimated that 2% of its $125,000 receivables on hand would probably prove uncollectible. The Allowance for uncollectible accounts contained a balance of $(300) prior to adjustments. The appropriate adjusting entry is:

Assets	Liabilities	Shareholders' equity	
		Contributed capital	Retained earnings

5. A customer used a credit card to purchase a $100 battery from Chargemup, Inc. What entry should Chargemup, Inc., record if the credit card company charges a 4% fee for its service?

Assets	Liabilities	Shareholders' equity	
		Contributed capital	Retained earnings

For Exercises 6-8, show the effect on the accounting equation by circling either increase, decrease, or no effect in each column.

6. The adjusting entry to record the estimate for bad debts expense is:

Assets	Liabilities	Total shareholders' equity
Increase	Increase	Increase
Decrease	Decrease	Decrease
No effect	No effect	No effect

7. The entry to record the collection of an account receivable is:

Assets	Liabilities	Total shareholders' equity
Increase	Increase	Increase
Decrease	Decrease	Decrease
No effect	No effect	No effect

8. The writing-off of a specific account receivable for a company that uses the allowance method is:

Assets	Liabilities	Total shareholders' equity
Increase	Increase	Increase
Decrease	Decrease	Decrease
No effect	No effect	No effect

9. Cycles, Inc.'s net credit sales for the current year are $6,000,000. Net accounts receivable at the beginning of the year was $700,000 and at the end was $800,000. Calculate the accounts receivable turnover. Also calculate the average number of days its takes Cycles to collect its receivables (assume 365 days to a year).

Solutions

Completion Statements

1. bank reconciliation
2. transit
3. Cash equivalents
4. allowance
5. sales, accounts receivable
6. net realizable value, carrying, book
7. aging schedule
8. principal, interest
9. matching
10. accounts receivable turnover

True/False

1. False   The direct write-off method violates GAAP (and the matching principle) because no adjusting entry for bad debts expense is recorded in the period the related sales were recorded. The sales method is an acceptable method and is in accordance with GAAP because an adjusting entry for estimated bad debts expense is recorded in the same period as the related sales.

2. True

3. True

4. True

5. False   The allowance method (GAAP) is better than the direct write-off method (not GAAP).

6. False   The sales method estimates bad debts expense as net sales times the percentage management considers uncollectible. The balance left in the unadjusted Allowance for uncollectible accounts is not part of the calculation. (However, it is part of the calculation of bad debts expense when a company uses the accounts receivable method).

7. False   The credit card company charges a fee because it takes on the risk of non-paying customers, relieving the company of bad debts expense.

8. False   Employees who have access to cash should not have any recordkeeping responsibilities. Otherwise an employee could steal cash and manipulate the bank reconciliation to conceal the theft.

9. False   The current ratio will not be affected because both cash and accounts receivable are in the numerator. When accounts receivable is exchanged for cash the numerator is unchanged.

10. True

Multiple Choice

1. C   The Allowance for uncollectible accounts, a contra-asset on the balance sheet, is subtracted from accounts receivable to show the net realizable value (the amount the company believes it will collect from its customers).

2. B   The accounts receivable method requires bad debts expense (which reduces shareholders' equity) to be only $900 since there is already a $(100) balance in the allowance account. The sales method does not consider what is left in the allowance account and thus the bad debts expense is the entire $1,000 estimate.

3. C   The write-off of a specific account receivable has no effect on the net realizable value of receivables (accounts receivable minus allowance for uncollectible accounts) or on total assets:

Assets	Liabilities	Shareholders' equity	
		Contributed capital	Retained earnings
- Accounts receivable + Allowance for uncollectible accounts			

4. D   The direct write-off method, which violates the matching principle, does not require an allowance account since no attempt is made to record the estimated amount of bad debts expense in the same period as the related sales. Accounts receivable are written off (expensed) in the period the receivables are considered uncollectible.

5. D   The sales method's bad debts expense equals the percentage of sales that management believes to be uncollectible times the credit sales; the adjusting amount is not dependent on the balance in the allowance account. The direct write-off method's bad debts expense is the actual amount of the specific accounts receivable written off; there is no allowance account needed with this method.

6. B   Employees who have access to cash should not have any recordkeeping responsibilities. Otherwise an employee could steal cash and manipulate the cash reconciliation to conceal the theft.

7. C   Management based its estimate on an aging of its accounts receivable and thus uses the accounts receivable method. The estimated $20,000 is the balance needed in the Allowance for uncollectible accounts, not Bad debts expense. The Bad debts expense amount is dependent on the unadjusted balance in the Allowance for uncollectible accounts which must have had a $(2,000) unadjusted balance since the expense was only $18,000.

8. A   The matching principle is extremely important for companies to follow since it results in net income being a more realistic, consistent, and comparable measure of profitability.

9. B   The items in a bank reconciliation that require adjustment to the company's books are the items added or subtracted from the cash per the company's books to arrive at the true cash balance. These reconciling items include NSF checks and errors made by the company, collections made by the bank on the company's behalf, bank charges and interest earned.

10. D   Credit card companies typically pay for credit card sales daily or weekly. The credit card company takes on the risk of non-paying customers, relieving the company of bad debts expense. The cost of the credit card sales is a fee that is recorded as an expense at the same time as the related credit card sale.

Exercises

1. Well Balanced, Inc. Bank Reconciliation, May 31, 2012				
Balance per bank statement	$15,700		Balance per books	$16,310
Add:			Add:	
Deposits in transit	3,370		Correction of an error ($843-483)	360
Deduct:			Deduct:	
Check: no. 975	(1,260)		NSF check	(440)
Check no. 991	(300)		Bank service charge	(20)
Check no. 1073	(1,300)			
True cash balance	$16,210		True cash balance	$16,210

2. Which of the above reconciling items (a-e) require adjusting entries in Well Balanced's records?

The error the company made (b), the NSF check (d), and the bank service charge (e) are all reconciling items that need to be recorded in Well Balanced's accounting records.

3. Assets	Liabilities	Shareholders' equity	
		Contrib. cap.	Retained earnings
(8,000) Allowance for uncollectible accounts			(8,000) Bad debts expense *(1% x $800,000)*

4. Assets	Liabilities	Shareholders' equity	
		Contrib. cap.	Retained earnings
(2,200) Allowance for uncollectible accounts *(2% x $125,000) + $300*			(2,200) Bad debts expense

5. Assets	Liabilities	Shareholders' equity	
		Contrib. cap.	Retained earnings
96 Accounts receivable			100 Sales (4) Credit card expense

	Assets	Liabilities	Total shareholders' equity
6.	Decrease	No effect	Decrease
7.	No effect	No effect	No effect
8.	No effect	No effect	No effect

9. $$\text{AR turnover} = \frac{\text{Net sales}}{\text{Average net AR}} = \frac{\$6,000,000}{(\$700,000 + 800,000)/2} = 8 \text{ times per year}$$

$$\frac{365 \text{ days}}{\text{AR turnover}} = \frac{365}{8} = 45.6 \text{ days}$$

CHAPTER 5
THE PURCHASE AND SALE OF INVENTORY

Chapter Overview

Chapter 4 focuses on the **operating cycle** for a merchandising company: starting with cash, the company buys inventory, sells the inventory, and collects cash from customers. In this chapter you will learn how a company accounts for the purchase and sale of inventory and how this information is reported in the financial statements.

Chapter Highlights

1. The acquisition process is well controlled when a company requires the use of the following documents and procedures. A purchase requisition, a document requesting goods or services needed by someone in the company, should be sent to the company's purchasing agent who obtains the required authorizations and determines the best place to obtain the goods or services. The purchasing agent specifies what is needed in a **purchase order** sent to the selected vendor, the receiving department, and the accounts payable department. The receiving department will let the accounts payable department know when the goods have arrived. Accounts payable will pay for the goods when it has a vendor invoice to match with the purchase order.

2. When a company uses a **perpetual inventory system**, every purchase of inventory is recorded as an increase in the inventory account. Each time an item is sold, the company moves the cost of the inventory sold from the inventory account to cost of goods sold. So at any given point in time, the balance in the inventory account represents the **cost of goods available for sale.**

3. If the terms of purchase are **FOB shipping point**, then the buyer pays the shipping cost. Freight paid by the purchasing company is called freight-in and is included in the buyer's inventory cost. If the terms are **FOB destination**, then the seller pays the shipping cost. Delivery expense for the seller is called freight-out and is an operating expense on the seller's income statement.

4. **Purchase returns and allowances** reflect the amount of goods the purchasing company returned to the vendor and cost reductions the vendor allowed for defective goods kept by the company. Purchase returns and allowances decrease the cost of inventory.

5. **Purchase discounts**, offered by vendors for prompt payment, also reduce the cost of inventory. Discounts are expressed in terms such as 2/10, n/30, which means that the buyer gets a 2% discount if the bill is paid within 10 days. Otherwise, no discount will be given and the full amount of the bill is due within 30 days. Buyers should always take cash discounts, since missing the discount adds 2% to their cost, but gives them only a 20-day extension in time to pay. This amounts to a 36% annual interest rate in a 360-day year.

If a company purchases $300 of inventory on account, terms 1/10, n/30, the $300 is recorded as an increase in both inventory and accounts payable. If the purchasing company takes the 1% cash discount, it reduces the amount of cash the company pays and the value of its inventory:

Assets	Liabilities	Share. Eq.	
		CC	RE
300 Inventory	300 AP		
(297) Cash	(300) AP		
(3) Inventory			

6. Sales revenue is recognized either when the goods are shipped (FOB shipping point) or when they are delivered (FOB destination). **Sales returns and allowances** and **sales discounts** are **contra-revenue** accounts that are subtracted from sales on the income statement to calculate **net sales**.

7. Most retail firms must collect a percentage of sales as sales tax for the state government. Sales tax increases the amount of cash or accounts receivable, but not the amount of sales

revenue. Instead, sales taxes payable is recorded as a current liability.

8. Some companies still use a **periodic inventory system** rather than a perpetual system. With a periodic system, cost of goods sold can be calculated only after a physical count of inventory is taken. The inventory account does not show a running balance of the cost of goods available for sale, but is updated only at the end of the accounting period. With advances in technology, many companies are now able to use a perpetual inventory system instead, which has the advantage of providing current information about inventory and cost of goods sold at all times. It also allows a company to identify inventory shrinkage by comparing its perpetual records with a physical count of inventory.

9. In calculating cost of goods sold on the income statement, companies do not have to track the actual cost of each specific inventory item sold. This would be too time-consuming and expensive for companies that make many purchases at continually changing costs. GAAP allows companies to select one of several inventory cost flow assumptions when determining the cost of goods sold. The method used does not have to be consistent with the actual physical flow of goods. Since the various methods can result in significantly different amounts, GAAP requires companies to disclose the amounts and methods used in the notes to the financial statements. The four basic methods used to calculate cost of goods sold and the cost of ending inventory are:

- **Specific identification method**. The cost of goods sold equals the actual cost of the specific goods that have been sold. This method is the only method where the cost flow is consistent with the physical flow of goods. This method is typically used by companies that purchase a small quantity of easily-identifiable luxury items.

- **Weighted-average cost method**. An average unit cost is calculated by dividing the total cost of goods available for sale by the total number of units available for sale. The average unit cost is then multiplied 1) by the

number of units sold to arrive at cost of goods sold on the income statement and 2) by the number of units remaining unsold to arrive at ending inventory on the balance sheet.

- **First-in, first-out method (FIFO)**. Regardless of which specific items are sold, FIFO assumes the first goods purchased are the first goods sold. Cost of goods sold is the cost of the older items available for sale and ending inventory is the cost of the more recent purchases.

- **Last-in, first-out method (LIFO)**. Regardless of which specific items are sold, LIFO assumes the most recently purchased goods are sold first. Cost of goods sold is the cost of the newer items available for sale and ending inventory is the cost of the older items.

10. A company has to decide not only which inventory cost flow method to use, but also when to record its cost of goods sold. A company will use one of two options:

- A **perpetual inventory** system records cost of goods sold and updates the inventory account after every sale, when two entries are required: one to record the sale and the other to record the cost of the sale.

Assets	Liab.	Shareholders' Eq.	
		CC	RE
60 AR or Cash			60 Sales
(25) Inventory			(25) COGS

With a perpetual system, careful attention must be paid to the dates of purchases and sales.

- A **periodic inventory** system records cost of goods sold and updates the inventory balance only after a physical count of inventory at the end of each accounting period. When a sale is made only one entry is recorded.

Assets	Liab.	Shareholders' Eq.	
		CC	RE
60 AR or Cash			60 Sales

After a physical inventory count at the end of the accounting period, cost of goods sold and ending inventory are determined, using weighted-average, FIFO, or LIFO.

11. The choice of inventory method affects the amounts shown for cost of goods sold on the income statement and inventory on the balance sheet. A company might choose a method used by other companies in the same industry, in order to make its financial statements comparable. Or it might choose the method which results in lower income taxes and higher cash flows.

When prices are rising, LIFO, which uses the newer, higher prices as cost of goods sold, will report a higher cost of goods sold, lower income, and lower ending inventory. Lower reported income means lower income taxes and higher cash from operating activities because less cash is used to pay taxes. Since the IRS requires that companies using LIFO for tax purposes must also use LIFO for financial reporting (the **LIFO conformity rule**), many companies choose to use LIFO.

On the other hand, a manager whose bonus is tied to reported profits might choose to use FIFO, which uses lower, older prices as cost of goods sold. Lower cost of goods sold means higher reported net income and a higher bonus for the manager.

IFRS do not allow the use of LIFO. Currently, many international companies use LIFO for their inventory in the U.S. and a different method for their operations outside of the U.S. As GAAP converges with IFRS, LIFO may no longer be used in the U.S.

12. GAAP requires inventory to be valued on the balance sheet using the **lower-of-cost-or-market (LCM) rule** to help prevent inventory from being overstated. Market value is the inventory's **replacement cost**, which is the cost to buy similar inventory. If the market value is lower than the historical cost of inventory, then the value of the inventory must be reduced. Firms that deal in cutting-edge technology are most likely to have inventory that becomes obsolete and declines in value.

13. A company's **gross profit ratio** shows the percentage of sales dollars a company has left after covering its cost of goods sold. It should be large enough to cover a company's other operating expenses and have something left over for profit.

$$\text{Gross profit ratio} = \frac{\text{Sales} - \text{Cost of goods sold}}{\text{Sales}}$$

Retailers are particularly concerned with their gross profit ratios. Companies that sell a high volume of merchandise generally have lower gross profit ratios than companies with low sales volumes.

The **inventory turnover ratio** shows how quickly a company is selling and replacing its inventory.

$$\text{Inventory turnover ratio} = \frac{\text{Cost of goods sold}}{\text{Average inventory}}$$

The inventory turnover ratio varies significantly from one industry to another. Managers can calculate the **average days in inventory** by dividing 365 days by the inventory turnover ratio.

14. There are significant risks associated with inventory that can be reduced by good internal control policies and procedures. In addition to controls such as selecting a reliable vendor and making sure that the items received are the ones that were ordered, companies should limit access to inventory by using locked storage rooms. Segregation of duties means that those who keep the inventory records should not have physical access to inventory. Inventory should also be monitored for obsolescence and written-off so as not to overstate inventory and earnings.

15. (Appendix 5A) An error in ending inventory will affect both cost of goods sold and net income.

Beginning inventory
+Purchases
=Cost of goods available for sale
-Ending inventory
=Cost of goods sold

If ending inventory is too high, too much is subtracted from the cost of goods available for sale and cost of goods sold will be too low. This makes net income on the income statement too high. If, on the other hand, ending inventory is too low, then too little is subtracted from the cost of goods available for sale and cost of goods sold will be too high. This makes net income on the income statement too low.

If the error is not discovered before the next year's financial statements are prepared, then this year's incorrect ending inventory becomes next year's incorrect beginning inventory. If this year's ending inventory is too high, then next year's beginning inventory will also be too high. Both cost of goods available for sale and cost of goods sold will be too high next year. Net income will be understated. On the other hand, if this year's ending inventory is too low, then next year's beginning inventory will also be too low. Both cost of goods available for sale and cost of goods sold will be too low next year. Net income will be overstated.

Total income for the two years combined will be correct, but it is important that each year's income statement be correct as well.

16. (Appendix 5B) The **gross profit method** allows companies to estimate inventory rather than actually count it. A company may use this method to estimate inventory for monthly or quarterly financial statements or to estimate lost inventory for insurance claims. Estimated inventory is calculated by first calculating the company's typical gross profit percentage (gross profit divided by sales) from prior periods. Second, the company multiplies the sales for the period by the estimated gross profit percentage to arrive at an estimated gross profit. Third, the sales minus the estimated gross profit equals the estimated cost of goods sold. Fourth, the ending inventory can then be determined by subtracting the estimated cost of goods sold from the goods available for sale (beginning inventory plus purchases).

Featured Exercise

The Ultimate Snowboard Shop's records showed the following information about its beginning inventory, purchases, and sales of snowboards for January:

	Units	Unit Price
Beginning inventory, January 1	10	$200
Purchase, January 15	10	$210
Purchase, January 18	20	$220
Sale, January 20	36	$450
Purchase, January 23	10	$230

For each question below, fill in the correct dollar amount and circle the correct financial statement on which it appears, using the following code:

IS for the income statement for the month ended January 31
BS for the balance sheet at January 31
SOCF for the statement of cash flows for the month ended January 31

1. Assume Ultimate uses a **LIFO perpetual** inventory system.

   a. Cost of goods sold of $_____ appears on the: **IS**   **BS**   **SOCF**

   b. Inventory of $_____ appears on the: **IS**   **BS**   **SOCF**

   c. Sales of $_____ appears on the: **IS**   **BS**   **SOCF**

   d. Gross profit of $_____ appears on the   **IS**   **BS**   **SOCF**

2. Assume Ultimate uses a **LIFO periodic** inventory system.

   a. Cost of goods sold of $_____ appears on the: **IS**   **BS**   **SOCF**

   b. Inventory of $_____ appears on the: **IS**   **BS**   **SOCF**

   c. Sales of $_____ appears on the: **IS**   **BS**   **SOCF**

   d. Gross profit of $_____ appears on the   **IS**   **BS**   **SOCF**

3. Assume Ultimate uses a **FIFO perpetual** inventory system.

   a. Cost of goods sold of $_____ appears on the: **IS**   **BS**   **SOCF**

   b. Inventory of $_____ appears on the: **IS**   **BS**   **SOCF**

   c. Gross profit of $_____-_____ appears on the   **IS**   **BS**   **SOCF**

4. Assume Ultimate uses a **FIFO periodic** inventory system.

    a. Cost of goods sold of $_____ appears on the: **IS**   **BS**   **SOCF**

    b. Inventory of $_____ appears on the: **IS**   **BS**   **SOCF**

    c. Gross profit of $_____ appears on the   **IS**   **BS**   **SOCF**

5. Assume Ultimate uses a **weighted average periodic** inventory system.

    a. Cost of goods sold of $_____ appears on the: **IS**   **BS**   **SOCF**

    b. Inventory of $_____ appears on the: **IS**   **BS**   **SOCF**

    c. Gross profit of $_____ appears on the: **IS**   **BS**   **SOCF**

6. Which method, LIFO or FIFO, results in the following?

    a. Higher net income?

    b. Lower taxes?

    c. Higher inventory turnover rate?

    d. Higher current ratio?

    e. Higher gross profit ratio?

Solution

1. LIFO perpetual:
    a. (20 x $220) + (10 x $210) + (6 x $200) = $7,700; IS
    b. (4 x $200) + (10 x $230) = $3,100; BS
    c. 36 x $450 = $16,200; IS
    d. $16,200 - 7,700 = $8,500; IS

2. LIFO periodic:
    a. (10 x $230) + (20 x $220) + (6 x $210) = $7,960; IS
    b. (10 x $200) + (4 x $210) = $2,840; BS
    c. 36 x $450 = $16,200; IS
    d. $16,200 - 7,960 = $8,240; IS

3. FIFO perpetual:
    a. (10 x $200) + (10 x $210) + (16 x $220) = $7,620; IS
    b. (10 x $230) + (4 x $220) = $3,180; BS
    c. $16,200 - 7,620 = $8,580; IS

4. FIFO periodic: same answers as in FIFO perpetual (3. above).

5. Weighted average cost periodic = $\dfrac{\text{cost of goods available for sale}}{\text{total snowboards available for sale}}$

$$= \dfrac{(10 \times \$200) + (10 \times \$210) + (20 \times \$220) + (10 \times \$230)}{10 + 10 + 20 + 10} = \dfrac{\$10{,}800}{50} = \$216 \text{ per snowboard}$$

   a. 36 snowboards x $216 = $7,776; IS
   b. (50 – 36) x $216 = $3,024; BS
   c. $16,200 - 7,776 = $8,424; IS

6. a. FIFO   The cost of snowboards has been rising. The FIFO method assumes the older, less expensive items are part of cost of goods sold. A lower cost of goods sold results in higher net income.
   b. LIFO   The cost of snowboards has been rising. The LIFO method assumes the newer, more expensive items are part of cost of goods sold. A higher cost of goods sold results in lower net income and lower income taxes.
   c. LIFO   Inventory turnover equals cost of goods sold divided by inventory. The cost of goods sold in the numerator is higher using LIFO, which assumes the newer, more expensive items are sold first, and the inventory in the denominator is smaller since the older, less expensive items are left in inventory.
   d. FIFO   The current ratio equals current assets divided by current liabilities. Inventory is a current asset. FIFO results in a higher inventory balance in times of rising prices than the other methods, because with FIFO the newer, more expensive items are left in inventory. Accounts payable is a current liability and would be the same balance, for the amount owed to the vendors, regardless of which method is used.
   e. FIFO   The gross profit ratio equals the gross profit (or sales minus cost of goods sold) divided by sales. In times of rising prices, the FIFO method assumes the older, less expensive items are part of cost of goods sold. A lower cost of goods sold results in a higher gross margin. Since sales in the denominator is the same regardless of which inventory method is used, FIFO will result in the higher ratio.

Review Questions and Exercises

Completion Statements

Fill in the blank(s) to complete each statement.

1. A purchase _____ is a record of the company's request to a vendor for goods or services.

2. Purchase _____ and _____ reflect the amount of goods the company returned and price reductions the vendor allowed for defective goods kept by the company.

3. If the terms of purchase are _____, then the buyer pays the shipping cost. _____ is the cost paid by the purchasing company and is included in the buyer's cost of the goods.

4. If the terms of purchase are _____, then the seller pays the shipping cost. _____ is the delivery expense to the seller and is an operating expense on the seller's income statement.

5. When using the _____ method, the cost of goods sold equals the exact cost of the actual goods that have been sold. This method is the only method where the cost flow is the same as the physical flow of the goods.

6. When using the _____ method, a unit cost is calculated by dividing the total cost of goods available for sale by the total number of units available for sale.

7. The _____ method assumes the first goods purchased are sold first. Thus, the cost of goods sold is the cost of the older items and ending inventory is the cost of the more recent purchases.

8. The _____ method assumes the more recently purchased goods are sold first. Thus, the cost of goods sold is the cost of the newer items and ending inventory is the cost of the older items.

9. A _____ system records cost of goods sold and updates the inventory balance after every sale.

10. A _____ system records cost of goods sold and updates the inventory balance only at the end of each accounting period.

11. The formula for calculating the gross profit ratio is _____.

12. (Appendix 5B) The _____ provides a means of estimating inventory instead of actually counting the inventory. A company may use this method to estimate inventory for monthly or quarterly financial statements or to estimate lost inventory for insurance claims.

True/False

Indicate whether each statement is true (T) or false (F).

_____1. The purchase of inventory is recorded as an expense called cost of goods sold.

_____2. A company that uses the last-in, first-out method of valuing cost of goods sold must sell its newer inventory before selling any of its older inventory, even though some of the older items may be perishable.

_____3. A company that uses a perpetual inventory system must calculate cost of goods sold each time it records a sale.

_____4. IFRS does not allow the use of LIFO.

_____5. In a time of rising prices, a company that uses FIFO will have higher cash flow from operating activities than a company that uses LIFO.

_____6. Goods available for sale equals beginning inventory minus cost of goods sold.

_____7. A company has a gross profit ratio of 40%. This means that for every $1 of sales the company's cost of goods sold is $0.40.

_____8. A car dealership will have a lower inventory turnover than a grocery store.

_____9. (Appendix 5A) Cost of goods sold can be expressed as goods available for sale minus ending inventory.

_____10. (Appendix 5B) The gross profit method is used to estimate cost of goods sold and ending inventory when the actual amounts are not available.

Multiple Choice

Select the best answer for each question.

_____1. Inventory would be found in:
  A. the current liabilities section of the balance sheet.
  B. the current assets section of the statement of financial position.
  C. the operating section of the statement of operations.
  D. the noncurrent assets section of the balance sheet.

_____2. Which of the following accounting treatments violates the matching principle?
  A. A grocery store uses the LIFO cost flow method.
  B. Inventory is expensed in the period when it is sold.
  C. Inventory is expensed in the period when it is purchased.
  D. More than one of the above violates the matching principle.

_____3. The lower-of-cost-or-market rule requires a company to:
  A. use the LIFO method in times of rising prices.
  B. adjust the inventory balance downward if its replacement cost is lower than its historical cost.
  C. adjust the cost of goods sold downward if the inventory's replacement cost is lower than its historical cost.
  D. use this method if its inventory has been destroyed or lost.

_____4. The gross profit ratio for Proffits, Inc., increased from 45% in 2010 to 50% in 2011. Which of the following is **true**?
  A. Proffits made more sales in 2011 than in 2010.
  B. Proffits' net income was greater in 2011 than in 2010.
  C. Proffits' cost of sales was lower relative to sales in 2011 than in 2010.
  D. Proffits' markup on its goods was less in 2011 than in 2010.

_____5. The excess of sales over cost of goods sold is:
  A. net income.
  B. income before taxes.
  C. operating income.
  D. gross profit.

_____6. Redux, Inc., purchased $2,500 of inventory on account with terms of 2/10, n/30 and paid the bill within the discount period. How much did Redux pay?
  A. $2,500
  B. $2,450
  C. $2,300
  D. $2,250

_____ 7. FOB shipping point means:
  A. the purchaser pays the shipping costs and records an expense called freight-in.
  B. the purchaser pays the shipping costs and records the cost as a part of inventory.
  C. the seller pays the shipping costs and records an expense called freight-out.
  D. the seller pays the shipping costs and records a contra-revenue account called freight-out.

_____ 8. Which of the following problems might explain an unusually high inventory turnover ratio?
  A. The inventory may be too low, causing goods to be out of stock and sales to be lost.
  B. The inventory may not be selling as quickly as it was in the past.
  C. The inventory may have been bought in quantities that are too large, causing goods to be on hand for too long.
  D. More than one of the above may be the cause of a high inventory turnover ratio.

_____ 9. In a time of rising prices, which inventory valuation method will report higher cost of goods sold?
  A. LIFO
  B. FIFO
  C. Weighted average cost
  D. This is a trick question. The choice of inventory valuation method has nothing to do with cost of goods sold.

_____ 10. In a time of **falling** prices, which inventory valuation method will report higher net income?
  A. LIFO
  B. FIFO
  C. Weighted average cost
  D. This is a trick question. The choice of inventory valuation method has nothing to do with net income.

_____ 11. (Appendix 5A) With a periodic inventory system, an undiscovered error that overstates the 2010 year-end inventory will cause:
  A. an overstatement of 2010 net income and an understatement of 2011 net income.
  B. an understatement of assets on the 2010 balance sheet.
  C. an overstatement of 2010 cost of goods sold.
  D. An overstatement of 2010 net income, but have no effect on 2011 net income.

_____ 12. (Appendix 5B) If a company's inventory was destroyed by fire but the accounting records were saved, the method that would probably be used to estimate the amount of inventory lost would be:
  A. the LIFO method.
  B. the weighted average cost method.
  C. the gross profit method.
  D. the specific identification method.

Exercises

For exercises 1. – 4., show the effect on the accounting equation. Include the proper account titles. Assume the company uses a perpetual inventory system.

1. On January 8, the company purchased $500 of inventory on account.

Assets	Liabilities	Shareholders' Equity	
		CC	Retained earnings

2. On February 8, the company paid the $500 invoice for merchandise previously purchased.

Assets	Liabilities	Shareholders' Equity	
		CC	Retained earnings

3. On February 9, the company sold merchandise to a customer on account for $400. The cost of the merchandise sold was $300.

Assets	Liabilities	Shareholders' Equity	
		CC	Retained earnings

4. On March 9, the company collected $400 of its accounts receivable.

Assets	Liabilities	Shareholders' Equity	
		CC	Retained earnings

5. Put an "X" in the column that indicates the best place to find each of the following items:

		Balance Sheet	Statement of Cash Flows	Income Statement	Notes to the Financial Statements
a.	The cost of inventory sold				
b.	The amount of merchandise on hand				
c.	The amount paid for inventory				
d.	The amount owed for inventory				
e.	The gross profit				
f.	The inventory method used				

6. Calculate the gross profit ratio and the inventory turnover ratio for the year ended December 31, 2011:

For the year ended	December 31, 2011	December 31, 2010
Inventory	$20,000	$30,000
Sales	$400,000	$380,000
Cost of goods sold	$180,000	$170,000

7. Stockit, Inc., has the following inventory information available from a recent month:

Date	Description	Units	Unit Cost / Price	Total
12/1	Beginning inventory	10	$10	$100
12/6	Purchase	20	$12	$240
12/18	Purchase	30	$16	$480
12/20	Sale	55	$30	$1,650
12/24	Purchase	10	$18	$180

Use the information above to complete the following table:

	Cost flow method:	Cost of goods sold	Ending inventory
a.	Perpetual LIFO		
b.	Periodic LIFO		
c.	Perpetual FIFO		
d.	Periodic FIFO		
e.	Periodic weighted average (round the unit cost to the nearest cent)		

8. (Appendix 5A) Put an "X" in the column that indicates whether the item is overstated, understated, or correctly stated as a result of a company overstating its December 31, 2010 inventory balance.

		Overstated	Understated	Correctly stated
a.	Inventory, January 1, 2010			
b.	Purchases during 2010			
c.	Goods available for sale in 2010			
d.	Inventory, December 31, 2010			
e.	Cost of goods sold in 2010			
f.	Net income in 2010			
g.	Retained earnings, December 31, 2010			
h.	Purchases during 2011			
i.	Goods available for sale in 2011			
j.	Inventory, December 31, 2011			
k.	Cost of goods sold in 2011			
l.	Net income in 2011			
m.	Retained earnings, December 31, 2011			

9. (Appendix 5B) S. Mates, Inc., filed an insurance claim for inventory destroyed by a storm. The inventory at the beginning of the year was $20,000. Purchases were $140,000 and sales were $240,000 for the year up to the storm. The gross profit ratio has historically been 45%. How much inventory should this company claim was lost?

Solutions

Completion Statements

1. order
2. returns, allowances
3. FOB shipping point, Freight-in
4. FOB destination, Freight-out
5. specific identification
6. weighted-average
7. First-in, first-out (FIFO)
8. Last-in, first-out (LIFO)
9. perpetual
10. periodic
11. gross profit / sales or (sales – cost of goods sold) / sales
12. gross profit method

True/False

1. False   Inventory is a current asset until it is sold. When the inventory is sold, the cost of the sale is matched with the related sale in the same accounting period (the matching principle).
2. False   GAAP allows companies to select one of several inventory cost flow assumptions when determining the amount of cost of goods sold. The method used does not have to be consistent with the actual physical flow of the goods. Thus, a company that uses the LIFO method can physically sell its older inventory before its newly purchased items.
3. True
4. True
5. False   If a company uses FIFO, the oldest costs are used as cost of goods sold. When prices are rising, these old cost will be relatively low, resulting in a low cost of goods sold. Low cost means high income and high income taxes, which must be paid in cash. So a company that uses FIFO will pay more taxes and have less cash from operating activities.
6. False   Cost of goods available for sale equals beginning inventory **plus** purchases.
7. False   The gross profit ratio of 40% means that for every $1 of sales, the cost of goods sold is $0.60 and the gross profit is $0.40.
8. True
9. True
10. True

Multiple Choice

1. B Inventory is a current asset since it should be sold within the year. Another name for the balance sheet is the statement of financial position.

2. C Inventory is an asset until it is sold. The matching principle requires the cost of the goods sold be reported in the same period as the related sale. The cost flow assumptions, such as LIFO and FIFO, are used to estimate the amount of cost of goods sold. GAAP allows companies to use estimates instead of tracking the actual physical flow and actual cost of each item sold.

3. B Companies are required by GAAP to reduce the inventory balance downward if the historical cost of the inventory is higher than its market value, which is defined as replacement cost. This rule helps to prevent companies from overstating their inventory.

4. C The gross profit ratio is calculated by dividing gross profit (or sales minus cost of goods sold) by sales. When the cost of goods sold is lower relative to sales, than the percentage increases since the numerator, gross profit, is larger. Choice A is incorrect because sales can increase at the same rate as cost of goods sold, causing the gross profit to remain the same. Choice B is incorrect because other operating expenses may have increased, offsetting any increase in the gross profit. Choice D is incorrect because a higher gross profit results when a company increases its markup on goods.

5. D Sales minus cost of goods sold (or cost of sales) is the gross profit. It represents the markup on a company's goods.

6. B The discount term, 2/10, n/30, means the buyer will receive a 2% discount if the invoice is paid within 10 days, otherwise the entire amount is due within 30 days. A 2% discount on $2,500 is $50. The buyer will pay $2,450 ($2,500 − 50).

7. B FOB (free on board) shipping point means the purchaser pays the shipping costs. The shipping cost is considered part of the cost of buying the inventory and is included in inventory along with the purchase price. If the terms were FOB destination, then the seller would pay and record the cost as an expense, freight-out.

8. A The inventory turnover equals cost of goods sold divided by average inventory. If the inventory is low, the result would be a high turnover, which is typically good. However, if inventory is too low, the result would be loss of sales if the goods are temporarily out of stock. A low inventory turnover is usually not good and may be a result of not being able to sell the goods quickly enough and/or having too much inventory on hand.

9. A If prices are rising, LIFO will use the most recent, high prices as cost of goods sold.

10. A LIFO uses the more recent prices as cost of goods sold. If prices are falling, LIFO will use the more recent, lower prices as cost of goods sold. Lower cost of goods sold means higher income.

11. A Cost of goods sold is calculated by subtracting ending inventory from goods available for sale. If too much is subtracted, cost of goods sold will be too low. Low cost of goods sold results in high net income for 2010. In 2011, the high amount of beginning inventory increases the cost of goods available for sale. If the correct ending inventory for 2011 is subtracted from a number that is too large, cost of goods sold is too high for 2011 and net income is too low. Choice B is incorrect because assets on the balance sheet will be too large at the end of 2010. Choice C is incorrect because cost of goods sold in 2010 is too low, not too high. Choice D is incorrect because the error in 2010 ending inventory also has an effect on the income reported in 2011.

12. C The gross profit method is the only method that can be used to calculate inventory without knowing the actual number of units in ending inventory. For both choices A and B, the number of units in inventory must be multiplied by the appropriate prices to calculate inventory cost. For Choice D, both the number of units and the actual cost of those units must be known.

Exercises

The effects of Exercises 1. – 4. on the accounting equation:

	Assets	Liabilities	CC	Shareholders' Equity Retained earnings
1.	500 Inventory	500 Accounts payable		
2.	(500) Cash	(500) Accounts payable		
3.	400 Accounts receivable (300) Inventory			400 Sales (300) Cost of goods sold
4.	400 Cash (400) Accounts receivable			

5.		Balance Sheet	Statement of Cash Flows	Income Statement	Notes to the Financial Statements
a.	The cost of inventory sold			X	
b.	The amount of merchandise on hand	X			
c.	The amount paid for inventory		X		
d.	The amount owed for inventory	X			
e.	The gross profit			X	
f.	The inventory method used				X

6.

$$\text{Gross profit ratio:} \quad \frac{\text{gross profit}}{\text{sales}} = \frac{\$400,000 - 180,000}{\$400,000} = .55 \text{ or } 55\%$$

$$\text{Inventory turnover} = \frac{\text{Cost of goods sold}}{\text{Average inventory}} = \frac{\$180,000}{((\$20,000 + \$30,000)/2)} = 7.2 \text{ times}$$

7.	Cost flow method:	Cost of goods sold	Ending inventory
a.	Perpetual LIFO	(30 x $16) + (20 x $12) + (5 x $10) = $770	(5 x $10) + (10 x $18) = $230
b.	Periodic LIFO	(10 x $18) + (30 x $16) + (15 x $12) = $840	(10 x $10) + (5 x $12) = $160
c.	Perpetual FIFO	(10 x $10) + (20 x $12) + (25 x $16) = $740	(10 x $18) + (5 x $16) = $260
d.	Periodic FIFO	(10 x $10) + (20 x $12) + (25 x $16) = $740	(10 x $18) + (5 x $16) = $260
e.	Periodic weighted average $\frac{(\$100 + 240 + 480 + 180)}{(10 + 20 + 30 + 10)} =$ $\frac{\$1,000 \text{ cost of goods available}}{70 \text{ units available for sale}}$ = $14.29 per unit (rounded)	55 x $14.29 = $785.95	$1,000 Cost of goods available for sale - $785.95 Cost of goods sold = $214.05

8.		Overstated	Understated	Correctly stated
a.	Inventory, January 1, 2010			X
b.	Purchases during 2010			X
c.	Goods available for sale in 2010			X
d.	Inventory, December 31, 2010	X		
e.	Cost of goods sold in 2010		X	
f.	Net income in 2010	X		
g.	Retained earnings, December 31, 2010	X		
h.	Purchases during 2011			X
i.	Goods available for sale in 2011	X		
j.	Inventory, December 31, 2011			X
k.	Cost of goods sold in 2011	X		
l.	Net income in 2011		X	
m.	Retained earnings, December 31, 2011			X

9. First estimate cost of goods sold:

Sales	100%	$240,000
- Cost of goods sold	- 55%	132,000 ((100%-45%) x $240,000)
Gross profit	45%	$108,000

Then estimate inventory:

Beginning inventory	$ 20,000
+Purchases	140,000
=Cost of goods available for sale	$160,000
-Estimated cost of goods sold	(132,000) (see cost of goods sold above)
=Estimated ending inventory	$ 28,000

CHAPTER 6
ACQUISITION AND USE OF LONG-TERM ASSETS

Chapter Overview

A business acquires long-term (or fixed) assets such as property, plant, and equipment that will be used in the business. From Chapter 6, you should understand how to account for the purchase, use, and sale of these long-term assets.

Chapter Highlights

1. There are two types of long-term assets. **Tangible assets** are assets used in the business to help generate revenue. They can be seen and touched and include property, plant, equipment, and natural resources. **Intangible assets**, whose true value resides in the rights and privileges given to their owners, include **copyrights** (legal protection for authors), **patents** (property rights for inventors), **trademarks** (legal rights to a symbol, word, phrase or logo), and **franchises** (authorization to sell a company's goods or services in a certain area).

2. The **historical cost principle** requires that a long-term asset be recorded at its purchase price plus any costs necessary to get the asset in place and ready to use. Such additional costs may include freight-in, transportation insurance, installation costs, commissions, architect and attorney fees, construction costs, and the costs of renovating, repairing, or preparing the asset for use.

3. Two or more long-term assets are sometimes bought for a single price. These assets may depreciate at different rates or not at all (land). Thus the assets must be recorded separately. The **relative fair market value method** is used to assign separate costs to each individual asset using the individual asset's market values or appraisal value at the time of purchase. The fair market value of a single asset is divided by the sum of the assets' fair market values to arrive at a percentage. This percentage is then multiplied by the total cost to get an asset's individual cost.

4. When a long-term asset is purchased, its cost is **capitalized**. **Capitalizing** a cost means to record the cost as an asset on the balance sheet. Any expenditure that will benefit more than one accounting period is called a **capital expenditure**. As the asset is used to generate revenue, the matching principle requires the cost of the asset to be allocated to expense on the income statement over the periods it is used. This process of **expensing (writing off** the cost of a long-term asset to expense) is called **depreciation** for plant and equipment, **depletion** for natural resources, and **amortization** for intangible assets. Land is the only long-term asset that remains on the books at cost.

5. Depreciation is a systematic, rational allocation of the cost of a fixed asset to expense over the periods benefited and does not measure the actual physical deterioration or decrease in market value of the asset. The **book value (or carrying value)** of an asset is the cost of the asset minus **accumulated depreciation** (all the depreciation taken to date). GAAP allows three common methods of depreciation for financial statements.

- **Straight-line depreciation** is a simple method in which depreciation expense is the same amount each accounting period. Depreciation expense equals the depreciable base divided by the estimated useful life of the asset. The **depreciable base** equals the cost of the asset minus its salvage value. The **salvage value** (or residual value) is what the company estimates it can sell the asset for when it is done using it. The **estimated useful life** is the number of periods the company estimates it will benefit from the use of the asset.

- **Activity depreciation**, also called **units-of-production depreciation**, calculates depreciation rate by dividing the depreciable base by the estimated total units of activity the asset will provide. This depreciation rate is then multiplied by the actual number of units used or produced during an accounting period. The activity and straight-line methods differ in that the activity method

1) uses units (not time) in the denominator, 2) requires multiplying the number of actual units used or produced during the accounting period by the depreciation rate, and 3) may result in different depreciation expense each period depending on the amount of use.

- **Declining balance depreciation** is an **accelerated method** that allows for more depreciation expense in the early years and less in the later years of an asset's life. A common rate used is 200% and is called **double-declining balance** because the rate at which an asset is depreciated is 200% or twice that of the straight-line rate. For example, if the life of an asset is 5 years, the straight-line rate is 1/5 or 20% and the double-declining balance rate is twice that, 2/5 or 40%. Depreciation expense for the period is calculated by multiplying the asset's book value (*not its cost*) by the double-declining balance rate. Since the book value is cost minus accumulated depreciation, the book value will become smaller every period the asset is depreciated. Thus, each later period's depreciation expense is smaller than the prior period's expense. Since salvage value is not built into the double-declining balance calculation, depreciation will need to be adjusted to ensure the net book value equals the salvage value by the end of the asset's useful life.

6. The effect of the adjusting entry to record depreciation (or use of an asset) during an accounting period is the same regardless of the method used:

Assets	Liab.	Shareholders' equity	
		CC	Retained earnings
- Accumulated depreciation			- Depreciation expense

The income statement will show depreciation expense for the accounting period. Depreciation expense will be closed into Retained earnings at the end of each accounting period. Accumulated depreciation, unlike depreciation expense, accumulates over time, so its balance equals all the depreciation taken to date, not just the current period's depreciation.

The balance sheet will show:
Cost
Minus accumulated depreciation
Net book value

The net book value is the amount of undepreciated historical cost.

7. **Depletion** is the systematic write-off of the cost of natural resources, *e.g.* forests, oil, and mineral deposits. It is similar to the activity depreciation method. A depletion rate is found by dividing the cost of the natural resource, minus its salvage value, by the estimated total units to be produced over its life. The units of the natural resource produced are board feet of lumber, barrels of oil, tons of ore, etc. The depletion rate per unit is then multiplied by the actual number of units produced in a given accounting period.

8. **Amortization** of intangible assets such as copyrights, patents, franchises, etc., is similar to straight-line depreciation. An intangible asset is amortized over the shorter of its useful life or legal life. If an intangible asset has an indefinite useful life, it is not amortized, but the firm will periodically evaluate it for any permanent decline in value and write it down if necessary.

Goodwill results from one company purchasing another company at a price that is greater than the market value of net assets. The purchased assets are recorded at their market values, and goodwill is recorded as an intangible asset. Goodwill is not amortized, but must be evaluated regularly and written down if it has declined in value.

Research and development (R&D) costs must be expensed immediately (*i.e.*, not capitalized) since it is too uncertain that the costs will result in future benefit. Software development costs are considered R&D expenses until they result in a product that is technologically feasible, after which additional costs from that time on may be capitalized.

9. Every time it prepares financial statements, a company must review its long-term assets for **impairment**, the permanent reduction of market value below book value.

10. Expenditures that have no future benefit beyond the current accounting period (revenue expenditures) are to be expensed on the income statement. The matching principle requires **expensing** the cost in the same period as the related revenue. Companies usually have policies that dictate whether a cost is a capital expenditure (an asset) or an expense.

- For the sake of efficiency, the materiality principle allows companies to expense certain small-dollar capital expenditures rather than capitalizing them and later having to depreciate them over time. An example would be the purchase of a $10 wastebasket.

- Costs to repair or remodel a long-term asset are capital expenditures if they increase the useful life, efficiency, or productivity of the asset. These costs are added to the historical cost of the asset, and future depreciation expense is revised based on the new book value of the improved asset, its salvage value, and its remaining useful life.

- Ordinary repairs to keep an asset in good operating condition are expensed because they are routine and do not significantly increase the life or efficiency of an asset. Examples include painting, tune-ups for vehicles, and cleaning and lubricating equipment.

11. The asset's useful life and salvage value are estimates made by managers that may later need to be revised because of additional information. Revising an estimate is not treated as correcting an error; it does not require restating previous records and financial statements. The revision is used only for future periods by adjusting the depreciation formula using the net book value (cost minus accumulated depreciation) and the new residual value or useful life.

- For example, an asset cost $1,000, had a salvage value of $100 and a useful life of three years. Its net book value at the end of the first year using straight-line is $700. At the end of the second year, management decided to revise the salvage value to $200 and the useful life to five years. The revised depreciation for the second year will equal the net book value minus the revised salvage value divided by the remaining useful life of four years or ($700-200)/4 years.

12. When a company finally sells an asset at the end of its useful life, the price often differs from the net book value. The result is a gain if the amount received is greater than the net book value or a loss if the amount received is less than the net book value. Both the asset and its accumulated depreciation must be removed from the company's books.

- A machine that originally cost $1,000 with accumulated depreciation of $800 at the end of its useful life has a net book value equal to its estimated residual value of $200. If the **proceeds** (or price the asset sells for) are $300, then a gain is recorded:

Assets	Liab.	Sh. equity	
		CC	Retained earnings
300 Cash (1,000) Machine 800 Accumulated depreciation			100 Gain on sale of machine

If the machine sold for only $150, then a loss would be recorded:

Assets	Liab.	Sh. equity	
		CC	Retained earnings
150 Cash (1,000) Machine 800 Accumulated depreciation			(50) Loss on sale of machine

- Gains or losses from sales of assets not sold in the ordinary course of business are reported on the income statement, usually below the subtotal "operating income."

13. The financial statements provide useful information for decision makers about long-term assets. The balance sheet reports the cost, the accumulated depreciation (depletion or amortization), and the net book value of long-term assets that reflects the future usefulness of the assets. The income statement includes depreciation (depletion and amortization) expense (not necessarily as separate line items). The expense reflects the use of the asset during the current accounting period matched with the related revenue the asset helped to generate. Finally, the notes to the financial statements provide additional useful information such as the depreciation methods used and the useful lives of the long-term assets. The investing activities section of the statement of cash flows shows cash paid for long-term assets and cash received from selling long-term assets.

IFRS allow a choice of valuing long-term assets at fair values or historical cost. IFRS also allow impairment losses to be reversed if an asset's condition improves; U.S. GAAP does not.

14. A ratio that measures how well a company is using its assets to generate revenue is **return on assets** (or ROA) and equals net income divided by average total assets. ROA is meaningful only when compared with ROA from other years or other companies.

15. Another ratio that evaluates a firm's use of assets is the **asset turnover ratio**: net sales divided by average total assets. This ratio varies significantly from one industry to another, so it is important to compare only firms in the same industry.

16. Safeguarding assets is one of the main purposes of an internal control system in order to minimize the risk of theft or damage. Physical controls that limit access to assets are important and can be as simple as locks on doors. Complete and reliable record keeping is also an important control. **Segregation of duties** is vital, so those responsible for record keeping are different from those who have physical custody of the assets. The assets and related records and controls should be monitored on an on-going basis, often by a company's own internal auditors.

17. (Appendix) GAAP are the rules followed in preparing financial statements. The Internal Revenue Code dictates the legal rules used for preparing federal tax returns. A significant difference in the rules is the method of depreciating assets. A common method on tax returns that is not allowed on GAAP financial statements is the **Modified Accelerated Cost Recovery System (MACRS)**. This method results in assets being written off very quickly. The high deduction for depreciation results in lower taxable income and lower federal income taxes. Lower taxes (which must be paid in cash) should increase a company's cash flow for the year, giving it more cash to invest in the purchase of additional assets, which in turn will help it to earn additional revenue.

Featured Exercise

On January 1, 2010, the San Diego Sea World purchased Arco the whale from the Washington Coast Aquarium. Arco cost $500,000 plus 5% sales tax. The transportation costs included $4,000 for an 11-ton truck and crane, $100,000 for airfare, and $1,000 in transportation insurance premiums. The San Diego Sea World paid $50,000 in fish food, $6,000 annual insurance premiums, and $20,000 in training and maintenance costs for Arco during 2010. Arco's estimated useful life is 10 years and 8,000 performances. The residual value for Arco is 5,000 pounds at $2 per pound. Arco performed in 750 shows during 2010 and 820 during 2011.

Required:

Part A: Identify which costs the San Diego Sea World should capitalize (*i.e.*, capital expenditures) and which costs should be expensed (*i.e.*, revenue expenditures) for the year ended December 31, 2010.

Part B: What is the effect of depreciation on San Diego Sea World's accounting equation?

Assets	Liabilities	Shareholders' equity	
		CC	**Retained earnings**

Part C: Calculate the depreciation expense, accumulated depreciation, and the net book value of Arco the whale using the three depreciation methods (straight-line, activity, and double-declining balance methods) for the years ended December 31, 2010 and 2011.

Straight-line method	Depreciation expense	Accumulated depreciation	Net book value
Year ended December 31, 2010			
Year ended December 31, 2011			

Activity method	Depreciation expense	Accumulated depreciation	Net book value
Year ended December 31, 2010			
Year ended December 31, 2011			

Double-declining balance method	Depreciation expense	Accumulated depreciation	Net book value
Year ended December 31, 2010			
Year ended December 31, 2011			

Part D: Show the effect of the sale of Arco for $14,000 at the end of his useful life assuming a net book value of $10,000 at the time of sale.

Assets	Liabilities	Shareholders' equity	
		CC	Retained earnings

Solution

Part A: The costs to get Arco in place and ready to perform that should be capitalized:

Whale	$500,000
Sales tax (0.05 x $500,000)	25,000
Truck and crane rental	4,000
Airfare	100,000
Transportation insurance	1,000
Total cost of whale	$630,000

The costs that are revenue expenditures are as follows:

Fish food	$ 50,000
Insurance premiums	6,000
Training and maintenance	20,000
Depreciation	(amount depends on method used)

Part B:

Assets	Liabilities	Shareholders' equity	
		CC	Retained earnings
-Accumulated depreciation			-Depreciation expense

Part C:

Straight-line method:

Year ended	Depreciation expense	Accumulated depreciation	Net book value
December 31, 2010	$62,000	$(62,000)	$568,000
December 31, 2011	$62,000	$(124,000)	$506,000

Depreciation expense on the income statement for the year ended December 31, 2010 is $62,000.

$$\frac{\text{Cost - residual value}}{\text{Estimated useful life}} = \frac{\$630,000 - (\$2 \times 5,000 \text{ pounds})}{10 \text{ years}} = \$62,000$$

Accumulated depreciation on the balance sheet at December 31, 2010 is $(62,000)

The net book value of Arco on the balance sheet at December 31, 2010 is $568,000 or the cost minus accumulated depreciation ($630,000 - 62,000).

Depreciation expense on the income statement for the year ended December 31, 2011 is $62,000.

$$\frac{\text{Cost - residual value}}{\text{Estimated useful life}} = \$62,000 \text{ (same for each year)}$$

Accumulated depreciation (a contra asset) on the balance sheet at December 31, 2011 is $(124,000) or $(62,000) for each of the two years combined.

The net book value of Arco on the balance sheet at December 31, 2011 is $506,000 or the cost minus accumulated depreciation ($630,000 - 124,000).

Activity method:

Year ended	Depreciation expense	Accumulated depreciation	Net book value
December 31, 2010	$58,125	$(58,125)	$571,875
December 31, 2011	$63,550	$(121,675)	$508,325

Depreciation expense on the income statement for the year ended December 31, 2010 is $58,125.

$$\text{Depreciation rate} = \frac{\text{Cost - residual value}}{\text{Estimated total performances}} = \frac{\$630,000 - 10,000}{8,000} = \$77.50 \text{ per performance}$$

Depreciation expense = Depreciation rate x performances in 2010 = $77.50 x 750 = $58,125.

Accumulated depreciation on the balance sheet at December 31, 2010 is $(58,125).

The net book value of Arco on the balance sheet at December 31, 2010 is $571,875 or the cost minus accumulated depreciation ($630,000 - 58,125).

Depreciation expense on the income statement for the year ended December 31, 2011 is $63,550.

Depreciation rate x performances in 2011 = $77.50 x 820 = $63,550.

Accumulated depreciation on the balance sheet at December 31, 2011 is $(121,675) or $(58,125) beginning accumulated depreciation plus $(63,550) accumulated depreciation for 2010.

The net book value of Arco on the balance sheet at December 31, 2011 is $508,325 or the cost minus accumulated depreciation ($630,000 - 121,675).

Double-declining balance method:

Year ended	Depreciation expense	Accumulated depreciation	Net book value
December 31, 2010	$126,000	$(126,000)	$504,000
December 31, 2011	$100,800	$(226,800)	$403,200

Depreciation expense on the income statement for the year ended December 31, 2010 is $126,000.

$$\text{Net book value} \times \frac{2}{\text{Estimated useful life}} = (\$630,000 - 0) \times \frac{2}{10} = \$126,000.$$

Accumulated depreciation on the balance sheet at December 31, 2010 is $(126,000).

The net book value of Arco on the balance sheet at December 31, 2010 is $504,000 or the cost minus accumulated depreciation ($630,000 - 126,000).

Depreciation expense on the income statement for the year ended December 31, 2011 is $100,800.

$$\text{Net book value} \times \frac{2}{\text{Estimated useful life}} = (\$630,000 - 126,000) \times \frac{2}{10} = \$100,800.$$

Accumulated depreciation on the balance sheet at December 31, 2011 is $(226,800) or $(126,000) beginning accumulated depreciation plus (100,800) accumulated depreciation for 2011.

The net book value of Arco on the balance sheet at December 31, 2011 is $403,200 or the cost minus accumulated depreciation ($630,000 - 226,800).

Part D: Proceeds minus net book value = $14,000 - 10,000 = $4,000 gain on sale of Arco.

Assets	Liabilities	Shareholders' equity	
		CC	Retained earnings
14,000 Cash			4,000 Gain on sale of whale
(630,000) Whale			
620,000 Accumulated depreciation			

Review Questions and Exercises

Completion Statements

Fill in the blank(s) to complete each sentence.

1. _____ can be seen and touched and include property, plant, equipment, and natural resources.

2. _____, whose true value resides in the rights and privileges given to the owners, include copyrights, patents, franchises, trademarks, and goodwill.

3. When a long-term asset is purchased, its cost is _____ *i.e.*, is recorded as an asset rather than an expense.

4. The _____ is a common method used to assign the joint costs to the individual assets using the individual assets' market values, or appraisal values, at the time of purchase.

5. The cost of an asset minus its accumulated depreciation is called _____.

6. Depreciation expense using the straight-line method equals _____.

7. Depreciation expense using the activity method equals _____.

8. _____ is an_____ that allows for more depreciation expense in the early years and less in the later years of an asset's life.

9. _____ allow a choice of valuing long-term assets at fair values or historical cost and also allow impairment losses to be reversed if assets' conditions improve; U.S. GAAP does not.

10. The formula for calculating asset turnover is _____.

True/False

Indicate whether each statement is true (T) or false (F).

_____1. Capital expenditures are costs that are found on the balance sheet as assets.

_____2. Depreciation expense will always be higher in the first year of an asset's life when the double-declining balance method is used instead of the straight-line method.

_____3. A gain on the sale of a long-term asset will result when the salvage value is greater than the proceeds.

_____4. A basket purchase allocation is required when the costs are less than their relative fair market values.

_____5. Despite the method of depreciation chosen by a company, the amount of accumulated depreciation will be the same at the end of the asset's useful life.

_____6. Despite the method of depreciation chosen by a company, the amount of depreciation expense will be the same each accounting period.

_____7. Despite the method of depreciation chosen by a company, the effect on the accounting equation is to decrease assets and decrease shareholders' equity.

_____8. The return on assets will increase if a company purchases inventory on account instead of paying cash.

_____9. Internal controls surrounding the safeguarding of assets include monitoring the assets by comparing the physical assets to what is recorded in the information system.

_____10. (Appendix) MACRS is a depreciation method used only for financial reporting, not tax reporting.

Multiple Choice

Select the best answer for each question.

_____1. Which of the following should be recorded as an intangible asset?
  A. Research and development costs on a new project
  B. Cost of advertising a new product
  C. Cost of employee education
  D. Cost to obtain exclusive rights to manufacture a unique product

_____2. Which financial statement shows how much cash was paid for newly acquired property, plant, and equipment?
  A. Statement of financial position
  B. Statement of operations
  C. Statement of cash flows
  D. Statement of changes in shareholders' equity

_____3. Which of the following accounting treatments violates the matching principle?
  A. A capital expenditure is recorded as an asset when acquired and expensed as it generates revenue.
  B. Repairs on a long-term asset are recorded as expenses.
  C. A long-term asset is expensed over its useful life using one of the depreciation methods in accordance with GAAP.
  D. None of the above violates the matching principle.

_____4. The bookkeeper did not record depreciation expense for the period. As a result:
  A. assets will be understated.
  B. liabilities will be understated.
  C. shareholders' equity will be overstated.
  D. There is no effect on the accounting equation because accumulated depreciation is a contra asset account that offsets depreciation expense.

_____5. The bookkeeper recorded a capital expenditure as an asset. As a result:
  A. assets will be understated.
  B. liabilities will be understated.
  C. shareholders' equity will be overstated.
  D. There is no effect on the accounting equation because capital expenditures should be recorded as assets, not expenses.

_____6. The net book value (or carrying value) of an asset is:
  A. increased when the market value of the asset increases.
  B. the original cost of the asset minus its salvage value minus its accumulated depreciation.
  C. the amount for which the asset could be sold.
  D. the original cost of the asset minus its accumulated depreciation.

_____7. E-buy, Inc. purchased a mainframe computer for $500,000 plus state sales tax of $20,000. It cost $1,000 to transport, $5,000 to install, and $10,000 to test the computer. Six months later the computer was cleaned for $500 and a programmer was paid $300 to make adjustments to the programs that back up the accounting information system. The proper treatment in recording these events is to:

A. capitalize $500,000 as an asset on the balance sheet and show $36,800 as expenses on the income statement.

B. capitalize $520,000 as an expense on the balance sheet and $16,800 as an asset on the balance sheet.

C. capitalize $536,000 as an asset on the balance sheet and show $800 as expenses on the income statement.

D. capitalize $536,800 as an asset on the balance sheet.

_____8. The process of expensing the cost of an intangible asset over its useful life is called:

A. amortization.

B. depreciation.

C. depletion.

D. accumulated depreciation.

E. None of the above. An intangible asset is not expensed over its useful life.

_____9. The process of expensing the cost of a natural resource over its useful life is called:

A. amortization.

B. depreciation.

C. depletion.

D. accumulated depreciation.

E. None of the above. Natural resources are not expensed over their useful lives.

_____10. Fair Market, Inc. purchased land, a warehouse, and a delivery truck for $450,000. The appraised values for the items are $300,000, $150,000, and $50,000, respectively. Fair Market should record this purchase:

A. as an expense of $450,000 on the income statement.

B. as assets on the balance sheet: $270,000 for the land, $135,000 for the building, and $45,000 for the delivery truck.

C. as assets on the balance sheet: $300,000 for the land, $150,000 for the building, and $50,000 for the delivery truck.

D. as assets on the balance sheet: $500,000 for basket purchase minus $50,000 accumulated depreciation.

Exercises

For Exercises 1-4: Fill in the correct dollar amount and put an "X" in the column of the financial statement where the item will most likely be found.

1. On April 1, 2011, AAA, Inc. paid $36,000 cash for a truck. AAA plans to use the truck for 5 years and then sell it for $6,000. The straight-line depreciation method was used. Give the adjusting journal entry required at the end of April and at the end of May.

Financial statement line item:	Amount as of or for the month ended April 30	Select one for each line item:		
		Income Statement	Balance Sheet	Statement of Cash Flows
a. Cash paid for truck				
b. Depreciation expense				
c. Accumulated depreciation				
d. Truck (net of accumulated depreciation)				

Financial statement line item:	Amount as of or for the month ended May 31	Select one for each line item: (if applicable)		
		Income Statement	Balance Sheet	Statement of Cash Flows
e. Cash paid for truck				
f. Depreciation expense				
g. Accumulated depreciation				
h. Truck (net of accumulated depreciation)				
i. Cash paid for depreciation expense				

2. On January 1, 2010, E-commerce began operations and purchased a truck for $25,000 cash. This truck has an estimated useful life of 4 years and a salvage value of $5,000. The straight-line depreciation method was used.

Financial statement line item:	Amount as of or for the year ended December 31, 2010	Select one for each line item:		
		Income Statement	Balance Sheet	Statement of Cash Flows
a. Depreciation expense				
b. Accumulated depreciation				
c. Truck (net of accumulated depreciation)				

Financial statement line item:	Amount as of or for the year ended December 31, 2011	Select one for each line item:		
		Income Statement	Balance Sheet	Statement of Cash Flows
d. Depreciation expense				
e. Accumulated depreciation				
f. Truck (net of accumulated depreciation)				

On January 1, 2012, E-commerce sold the truck (in 2 above) for $12,000.

Financial statement line item:	Amount as of or for the year ended December 31, 2012	Select one for each line item:		
		Income Statement	Balance Sheet	Statement of Cash Flows
g. Gain (loss) on sale of truck				
h. Proceeds from sale of truck				

3. On January 1, 2010, Slippery Slope, Inc. purchased equipment for $400,000 cash. This equipment has an estimated useful life of 10 years and a salvage value of $20,000. The **double-declining depreciation method** was used.

Financial statement line item:	Amount as of or for the year ended December 31, 2010	Select one for each line item:		
		Income Statement	Balance Sheet	Statement of Cash Flows
a. Depreciation expense				
b. Accumulated depreciation				
c. Equipment (net of accumulated depreciation)				

Financial statement line item:	Amount as of or for the year ended December 31, 2011	Select one for each line item:		
		Income Statement	Balance Sheet	Statement of Cash Flows
d. Depreciation expense				
e. Accumulated depreciation				
f. Equipment (net of accumulated depreciation)				

4. On January 1, 2010, Tons-of-Coal, Inc. purchased mining equipment for $70,000, which had an estimated useful life of five years or 200,000 tons of coal and an estimated residual value of $10,000. Tons-of-Coal used the activity method of depreciation and the machine produced 35,000 tons in 2010 and 40,000 in 2011.

Financial statement line item:	Amount as of or for the year ended December 31, 2010	Select one for each line item:		
		Income Statement	Balance Sheet	Statement of Cash Flows
a. Depreciation expense				
b. Accumulated depreciation				
c. Machinery (net of accumulated depreciation)				

Financial statement line item:	Amount as of or for the year ended December 31, 2011	Select one for each line item:		
		Income Statement	Balance Sheet	Statement of Cash Flows
d. Depreciation expense				
e. Accumulated depreciation				
f. Machinery (net of accumulated depreciation)				

5. Show the effect on the accounting equation for each of the following:

	Assets	Liab.	Shareholders' equity CC	Retained earnings
a. On January 1, 2011, Ridof, Inc. sold its van for $1,000 cash. The van had cost $20,000 and had $18,000 in accumulated depreciation. Record the sale of the van.				
b. Changes, Inc. revised its truck's estimated useful life from 5 years to 4 years at the beginning of its 3rd year. Record depreciation for year 3 using the straight-line method given that the truck cost $60,000 and had accumulated depreciation of $20,000 and a residual value of $10,000.				
c. Safety, Inc. paid $200 for a special insurance policy to cover the delivery of a new machine.				
d. Fixit, Inc. paid $100 for routine repairs of its copy machine.				
e. Expand, Inc. built a $50,000 addition to its building by borrowing from the bank.				
f. Expand, Inc. paid $500 in architect fees related to the addition to its building in (e) above.				
g. Tops, Inc. paid $3,000 for a newly shingled roof.				
h. Accume, Inc. recorded $1,000 amortization on its copyright.				
i. Accume, Inc. recorded $3,000 depreciation on its fixed assets.				
j. Rand, Inc. spent $800,000 on research and development during the year.				

6. Calculate the 2011 return on assets and asset turnover ratio for Rachio, Inc. given the selected information from its financial statements:

As of or for the year ended	December 31, 2011	December 31, 2010
Current assets	$18,000	$20,000
Long-term assets	$27,000	$35,000
Current liabilities	$10,000	$10,000
Long-term liabilities	$15,000	$15,000
Sales	$100,000	$90,000
Net income	$4,000	$5,000

Solutions

Completion Statements

1. Tangible assets
2. Intangible assets
3. capitalized
4. relative fair market value method
5. net book value (or carrying value)
6. (Cost – salvage value) / estimated useful life
7. ((Cost – salvage value) / estimated total units) times the units produced or used during the period.
8. Declining-balance method, accelerated method
9. International Financial Reporting Standards (IFRS)
10. Net sales divided by average total assets

True/False

1. True
2. True
3. False   A gain on the sale of a long-term asset will result when the net book value is less than the proceeds.
4. False   A basket purchase allocation is needed when the items are purchased together for a single price. The costs must be separated and can be allocated based on their relative fair market values.
5. True
6. False   Depreciation expense may differ depending on the method of depreciation used. Straight-line will result in the same expense each accounting period; depreciation expense using the activity method will vary depending on the level of activity; and depreciation expense using the declining-balance method will be higher in the early periods compared with the later years of the asset's life.
7. True
8. False   The return on assets will decrease if a company purchases inventory on account because the increase in inventory (an asset) will cause average total assets, the denominator, to increase while net income, the numerator, remains the same.
9. True
10. False   MACRS is a depreciation method used only for tax reporting. The accelerated method used for financial reporting is the declining balance method.

Multiple Choice

1. D   Due to uncertainty, research and development costs, employee education and training costs, and advertising are all expensed, not capitalized.
2. C   The cash flow from the investing activities section of the statement of cash flows shows how much cash was spent on purchases of long-term assets. The balance sheet shows the balances of long-term assets net of their related accumulated depreciation (depletion or amortization), i.e., their net book value. The income statement shows the depreciation (depletion or amortization) expense for the period.
3. D   The matching principle requires costs to be expensed in the period the items help generate revenue. Capital expenditures and long-term assets are assets until they will help to generate

revenues in the future. Repairs are expensed in the current period since they benefit the current period.

4. C The adjusting entry to record depreciation (depletion and amortization) is to reduce assets and reduce shareholders' equity. Shareholders' equity and the assets were not properly reduced, so they will be overstated.

5. D A capital expenditure should be recorded as an asset since it will provide future benefit.

6. D The net book value of an asset is found on the balance sheet and represents the undepreciated balance (or cost minus accumulated depreciation).

7. C All costs incurred to get an asset in place and ready to use are capitalized. Once the asset is in place and being used, the costs for ordinary repairs and upkeep are expensed.

8. A The process of expensing the cost of an intangible asset is amortization, the cost of expensing a fixed asset (except land) is depreciation, and the cost of expensing natural resources is depletion.

9. C The process of expensing the cost of an intangible asset is amortization, the cost of expensing a fixed asset (except land) is depreciation, and the cost of expensing natural resources is depletion.

10. B The relative fair market value method allocates the cost as follows:
Land: ($300,000/($300,000 + 150,000 + $50,000)) x $450,000 = $270,000
Warehouse: ($150,000/($300,000 + $150,000 + $50,000)) x $450,000 = $135,000
Truck: ($50,000/($300,000 + $150,000 + $50,000)) x $450,000 = $45,000.

Exercises

1. Financial statement line item:	Amount as of or for the month ended April 30	Income Statement	Balance Sheet	Statement of Cash Flows
a. Cash paid for truck	$36,000			X
b. Depreciation expense	$\frac{\$36,000 - 6,000}{60 \text{ months}} = \$500$	X		
c. Accumulated depreciation	$500		X	
d. Truck (net of accumulated depreciation)	$36,000 - 500 = $35,500		X	

1. Financial statement line item:	Amount as of or for the month ended May 31	Income Statement	Balance Sheet	Statement of Cash Flows
e. Cash paid for truck	$0			Not shown
f. Depreciation expense	$\frac{\$36,000 - 6,000}{60 \text{ months}} = \$500$	X		
g. Accumulated depreciation	$1,000		X	
h. Truck (net of accumulated depreciation)	$36,000 - 1,000 = $35,000		X	
i. Cash paid for depreciation expense	$0			Not shown

The second table header note: Select one for each line item: (if applicable)

2. Financial statement line item:	Amount as of or for the year ended December 31, 2010	Select one for each line item:		
		Income Statement	Balance Sheet	Statement of Cash Flows
a. Depreciation expense	$25,0000 - 5,000 = $5,000 / 4 years	X		
b. Accumulated depreciation	$5,000		X	
c. Truck (net of accumulated depreciation)	$25,000 - 5,000 = $20,000		X	

2. Financial statement line item:	Amount as of or for the year ended December 31, 2011	Select one for each line item:		
		Income Statement	Balance Sheet	Statement of Cash Flows
d. Depreciation expense	$25,000 - 5,000 = $5,000 / 4 years	X		
e. Accumulated depreciation	$5,000 + 5,0000 = $10,000		X	
f. Truck (net of accumulated depreciation)	$25,000 - 10,000 = $15,000		X	

2. Financial statement line item:	Amount as of or for the year ended December 31, 2012	Select one for each line item:		
		Income Statement	Balance Sheet	Statement of Cash Flows
g. Gain (loss) on sale of truck	$12,000 - 15,000 = ($3,000)	X		
h. Proceeds from sale of truck	$12,000			X

3. Financial statement line item:	Amount as of or for the year ended December 31, 2010	Select one for each line item:		
		Income Statement	Balance Sheet	Statement of Cash Flows
a. Depreciation expense	$400,000 x 2/10 = $80,000	X		
b. Accumulated depreciation	$80,000		X	
c. Equipment (net of accumulated depreciation)	$400,000 - 80,000 = $320,000		X	

3. Financial statement line item:	Amount as of or for the year ended December 31, 2011	Select one for each line item:		
		Income Statement	Balance Sheet	Statement of Cash Flows
d. Depreciation expense	$320,000 x 2/10 = $64,000	X		
e. Accumulated depreciation	$80,000 + 64,000 = $144,000		X	
f. Equipment (net of accumulated depreciation)	$400,000 - 144,000 = $256,000		X	

4. Financial statement line item:	Amount as of or for the year ended December 31, 2010	Select one for each line item: Income Statement	Balance Sheet	Statement of Cash Flows
a. Depreciation expense	(($70,000 - 10,000)/200,000 tons) x 35,000 tons = $10,500	X		
b. Accumulated depreciation	$10,500		X	
c. Machinery (net of accumulated depreciation)	$70,000 - 10,500 = $59,500		X	

4. Financial statement line item:	Amount as of or for the year ended December 31, 2011	Select one for each line item: Income Statement	Balance Sheet	Statement of Cash Flows
d. Depreciation expense	(($70,000 - 10,000)/200,000 tons) x 40,000 tons = $12,000	X		
e. Accumulated depreciation	$10,500 + 12,000 = $22,500		X	
f. Machinery (net of accumulated depreciation)	$70,000 - 22,500 = $47,500		X	

5.	Assets	Liabilities	Shareholders' equity CC	Retained earnings
a.	1,000 Cash (20,000) Van 18,000 Accumulated depreciation			(1,000) Loss on sale of van
b.	(15,000) Accumulated depreciation or $60,000 - 20,000 - 10,000 = $15,000 2 years			(15,000) Depreciation expense
c.	200 Machine (200) Cash			
d.	(100) Cash			(100) Repairs expense
e.	50,000 Building	50,000 Note payable		
f.	500 Building (500) Cash			
g.	(3,000) Cash 3,000 Building			
h.	(1,000) Copyright			(1,000) Amortization expense
i.	(3,000) Accumulated depreciation			(3,000) Depreciation expense
j.	(800,000) Cash			(800,000) R&D expense

6. ROA = Net income/Average total assets = $4,000/(($55,000 + 45,000)/2) = 0.08 or 8%
    Asset turnover ratio = Net sales/Average total assets = $100,000/(($55,000 + 45,000)/2) = 2.0

CHAPTER 7
ACCOUNTING FOR LIABILITIES

Chapter Overview

This chapter discusses how companies use financing from creditors, both current and long-term, to buy assets and services. You will learn about accounting for payroll, estimated liabilities, and long-term installment notes. You will also learn about bonds, which are a special type of long-term borrowing available to large companies.

Chapter Highlights

1. A liability is recorded in the accounting records when an obligation is incurred. Liabilities can be classified into two types. **Definitely determinable liabilities**, such as accounts payable, can be measured exactly, while **estimated liabilities**, such as warranty payable, have some uncertainty in the amount.

2. Payroll is a common business expense that creates definitely determinable, current liabilities. The amount an employee earns (gross pay) is larger than his take-home pay (net pay or net wages). The difference is the taxes withheld from the employee's gross pay. The company is required by law to act as an agent for the government and send the money withheld to the proper authorities. These taxes include federal income taxes (FIT), Social Security taxes (FICA, currently 6.2% of gross pay) and Medicare taxes (currently 1.45% of gross pay). The employer is also required to match the amount of Social Security taxes and Medicare taxes withheld from the employee and record the matching amount as payroll tax expense.

3. An employee's paycheck affects a company's accounting equation as follows:

Assets	Liabilities	Sh. Equity	
		CC	RE
- Cash (net pay)	+ FIT payable + FICA payable + Medicare taxes payable		- Salary expense (gross pay)

When the company pays these taxes and also records and pays matching FICA and Medicare taxes, the effect on the accounting equation is:

Assets	Liabilities	Sh. Equity	
		CC	RE
- Cash	- FIT payable - FICA payable - Medicare taxes payable		- Payroll tax expense

4. A line of credit allows a company to borrow from a bank for 60 to 90 days to pay routine operating expenses when there is a predictable, temporary short-term shortage of cash. A line of credit should not be used to finance long-term assets.

5. When a company sells products under warranty, the matching principle requires that it recognize an estimated warranty expense in the same accounting period that the sale is recorded, even though the amount of future warranty costs is unknown. This creates an estimated warranty liability, which is similar in some ways to the allowance for uncollectible accounts:

Assets	Liabilities	Sh. Equity	
		CC	RE
	+ Estimated warranty liability		- Warranty expense

When repairs are later made under warranty, the liability is decreased (the cost is written-off against the reserve) but no additional expense is recorded:

Assets	Liabilities	Sh. Equity	
		CC	RE
- Cash	- Estimated warranty liability		

6. Short-term notes are debts that are due in one year or less. **Long-term notes** like car loans and mortgages are usually repaid with a series of equal installments over the life of the note. Some

of each payment is interest and some is repayment of principal.

- Part of each installment payment decreases the outstanding principal of the loan. As the balance of the loan gets smaller, the interest for the next period gets smaller, too. Since the total amount of the installment payment stays the same, more of the next payment is used to repay loan principal because less of it is needed to cover interest. An **amortization schedule** is a chart that shows the amount of interest included in each loan payment.

- A **mortgage** is a special type of long-term note used to purchase property. It gives the lender a claim against the property until the loan is repaid. Payments on installment notes are calculated using the time value of money, which is discussed in the appendix to Chapter 7.

7. Suppose you buy property by signing a $100,000, three-year, 8% mortgage note, with annual payments to be made at the end of each year. When the first installment payment of $38,803.35 is made, the interest component of this payment is $8,000 (**Interest = principal x rate x time**, or $100,000 x .08 x 1 year). The payment's effect on the accounting equation is:

Assets	Liabilities	Sh. Equity	
		CC	RE
(38,803.35) Cash	(30,803.35) Mortgage payable		(8,000) Interest expense

For the second year of the loan, the balance now owed on the mortgage is $69,196.65 ($100,000 – 30,803.35). When the second installment payment of $38,803.35 is made, the interest component of the payment is $5,535.73 ($69,196.65 x .08 x 1 year). The remaining $33,267.62 of the payment is applied to the loan principal, reducing the principal to $35,929.03 ($69,196.65 – 33,267.62).

When the final installment payment of $38,803.35 is made, the interest component of the payment is $2,874.32 ($35,929.03 x .08 x 1 year). The remaining $35,929.03 of the payment

is applied to the loan principal, reducing the principal to zero.

Look at the amortization schedule in Exhibit 7-4 of your text. Each year the interest component of the loan payment is smaller because the loan principal is smaller, and more of each payment is used to repay principal.

8. Firms that need to borrow a lot of money may issue (*i.e.*, sell) **bonds**, which are written agreements to pay interest and to repay the buyers of the bonds (the lenders) at the end of the bonds' term. Companies issue bonds rather than borrow from a bank because: 1) firms can borrow more money with bonds than with bank loans, 2) the time period for bonds may be 20 or 30 years, longer than the term usually available from banks, and 3) the interest rate on bonds is also usually lower than the interest rate on bank loans.

Bond owners are creditors who have priority over stockholders, who are the owners of the business. Bondholders may also get extra protection from **covenants** that are included in the bond agreement, such as limits on the issuing company's future borrowing or a requirement that the company maintain a particular current ratio.

9. The principal amount of a bond is also called the face amount, face value, stated value, or par value. Most bonds are issued in multiples of $1,000. The length of the loan period is the bonds' maturity. Most bonds pay the face value to bondholders at the maturity date. In the United States, bonds usually make annual or semiannual interest payments based on the stated rate, which is the interest rate quoted on the face of the bonds.

10. There are different types of bonds. **Secured bonds** give the bondholder a claim to a specific company asset if there is a default (failure to meet the bond's obligations). Unsecured bonds, called **debentures**, are backed by the general credit of the company. **Term bonds** all mature on the same date. **Serial bonds** mature over a period of years. **Convertible** bonds can be exchanged for common stock whenever bondholders want. **Callable** bonds allow the

issuing company to buy back a bond at any time before maturity at a price specified in the bond agreement. Some bonds, called **zero-interest** or **zero coupon bonds**, do not make regular interest payments to bondholders because the stated rate of interest on these bonds is 0%. Instead, they make only a single payment of the bonds' face value at maturity. These bonds sell at a big (deep) discount. **Junk bonds** are risky bonds that have been downgraded below investment grade to BB or below.

11. When a company issues (sells) bonds, it receives cash **proceeds**. The selling price of a bond depends on the **market rate of interest**, which is the rate investors can earn on investments of similar risk. When market interest rates increase, a bond's selling price falls (and *vice versa*). This is because the bond's stated rate is fixed. If market interest rates have gone up and investors can earn a higher return elsewhere, the bond will be an unattractive investment unless the price of the bond goes down. Similarly, if the bond's stated interest rate is higher than the prevailing market rate of interest, investors will find the bond attractive and will bid up the price.

Bond prices are quoted as a percentage of face value.

- **Bonds issued at par** sell at 100, which stands for 100% of face value.
- **Bonds issued at a discount** sell for an amount less than face value and have a price below 100.
- **Bonds issued at a premium** sell for an amount greater than face value and have a price above 100.

Bonds can be bought and sold in the secondary market between investors just as stocks can be sold. Prices of bonds change with changes in interest rates, the economy, and the risks associated with a particular firm's bonds. Bond quotes in the financial press include the current selling price as a percentage of face value, the coupon rate (stated rate), the maturity date, the current yield (the interest rate investors will actually earn), and a bond rating (an indication of risk).

12. When a company issues bonds, it records the cash received and the liability to repay the face value of the bonds, called Bonds payable. The periodic interest payments are calculated using the face amount of the bonds times the stated interest rate times the fraction of a year that has elapsed, even if the bonds sold for some amount other than the face value. The effect on the accounting equation is:

Assets	Lia.	Shareholders' equity	
		CC	**RE**
- Cash			- Interest expense

- Bonds sell at par only if the stated rate of interest is the same as the market rate of interest.

- When the stated interest rate is higher than the market rate of interest, the bonds will sell at a premium.

- When the stated interest rate is lower than the market rate of interest, the bonds will sell at a discount.

13. If a $1,000, 6-year bond with annual interest payments of 5% was issued for $951 because the market rate of interest was approximately 6%, the issuing company would record the $49 difference as a **discount on bonds payable**, a separate, negative liability called a contra-liability. The effect on the accounting equation is:

Assets	Liabilities		Sh. Eq.	
			CC	**RE**
951 Cash	951	Bonds payable (net)		

The balance sheet will show a long-term liability, Bonds payable, at its net value or **carrying value**, which is face value minus the related discount.

If a $1,000, 6-year bond with annual interest payments of 5% was issued for $1,052 because the market rate of interest was approximately 4%, the issuing company would record the difference as a **premium on bonds payable**, a

Copyright © 2011 Pearson Education, Inc. Publishing as Prentice Hall separate liability, called an adjunct liability, which will be added to Bonds payable on the balance sheet. The effect on the accounting equation is:

Assets	Liabilities	Sh. Eq.	
		CC	RE
1,052 Cash	1,052 Bonds payable (net)		

14. Bond premiums and discounts are amortized, written off (reduced to zero) over the life of the bond issue. Interest expense shown on the company's annual income statement will not be the same amount as the cash interest payments made to bondholders.

Using the **effective interest method**, interest expense is calculated by multiplying the carrying value of the bond times the market rate of interest in effect when the bond was issued times the appropriate fraction of a year. If a bond was issued at a discount, its carrying value, also called its net value or book value, is the amount of Bonds payable minus the related Discount on bonds payable. The difference between this interest expense and the actual interest payment made to bondholders (which is based on the face value, not the carrying value, and the stated interest rate, not the market interest rate) is the amount of the premium or discount to be amortized for the period.

Continue to use the example above of a $1,000, 6-year bond with annual interest payments of 5% that was issued for $951 because the market rate of interest was approximately 6%. Interest expense for the first year would be:

$951 x 6% x 1 year = $57.06

However, the annual cash interest payment is:

$1,000 x 5% x 1 year = $50.00

The $7.06 difference between interest expense and the cash payment is the amount of the bond discount to be amortized.

The effect of the interest payment and discount amortization on the accounting equation is:

Assets	Liabilities	Sh. equity	
		CC	RE
(50) Cash	7.06 Bonds payable (net)		(57.06) Interest expense

As the bond discount is amortized it becomes smaller. For the first year, $(49) + 7.06 = $(41.94). This means that less will be subtracted from the $1,000 balance in Bonds payable and the carrying value of the bond increases ($1,000 − 41.94 = $958.06). At maturity, the discount will be zero and the carrying value of the bond will be equal to its $1,000 face value.

With the effective interest method, the interest expense shown on the income statement is based on the actual cash loaned to the company, $951, not the $1,000 face value of the bond. Interest expense also reflects the market rate of interest that investors demand, approximately 6%, not the 5% stated rate. The cash interest payment made to bondholders, however, is less than the interest expense. The difference increases the carrying value of the bond, so that interest expense will be calculated for the second year on a greater principal amount, compounding interest on interest.

At maturity, bondholders receive the $1,000 face value of the bond, not the $951 they loaned the company. The difference between the two, the original unamortized discount of $49, can be thought of as extra interest that bondholders earn over the life of the bond issue, so that in effect they earn 6% on $951 rather than 5% on $1,000.

15. Bond premiums can also be amortized using the effective interest method. Go back to the earlier example of a $1,000, 6-year bond with annual interest payments of 5% issued for $1,052 when the market rate of interest was approximately 4%. Interest expense in the first year would be:

$1,052 x 4% x 1 year = $42.08

However, the annual cash interest payment is:

$1,000 x 5% x 1 year = $50.00

The $7.92 difference between interest expense and the cash payment is the amount of the bond premium to be amortized. The effect of the interest payment and premium amortization on the accounting equation is:

Assets	Liabilities	Sh. equity	
		CC	RE
(50) Cash	(7.92) Bonds payable (net)		(42.08) Interest expense

As the bond premium is amortized, it becomes smaller. For the first year, $52 - 7.92 = $44.08. This means that less will be added to the $1,000 balance in Bonds payable and the carrying value of the bond decreases ($1,000 + 44.08 = $1,044.08). At maturity, the premium will be zero and the carrying value of the bond will be equal to its $1,000 face value.

16. A second way to calculate the dollar amount of premium or discount to be amortized is to use the straight-line method. Simply divide the total premium or discount by the number of interest payment periods. An equal amount of premium or discount will be amortized each period. Straight-line amortization is easy, but it is not GAAP. However, it is allowed if the resulting interest expense and carrying value of bonds payable are not significantly different from those calculated using the effective interest method.

17. A company's **capital structure** is the mix of debt and equity that it uses to finance its assets. Borrowing money is a good idea for a company if the benefit to the company is greater than the cost of borrowing. This means the company has positive **financial leverage**, which is using borrowed money to increase earnings.

The **debt-to-equity ratio** compares the value of creditors' claims to the value of owners' claims. It is calculated as:

$$\frac{\text{Total liabilities}}{\text{Total shareholders' equity}}$$

A debt-to-equity ratio around 100% (half debt and half equity) is common. A company with a high ratio is referred to as highly-leveraged. Details about a company's long-term debt are usually found in the notes to its financial statements.

18. Debt carries risk for both the issuing company and its creditors, which is the risk that the company will not meet its obligations. A company can reduce its risk by 1) a thorough cost-benefit analysis of any intended long-term borrowing to determine if it will earn more than it costs, and 2) studying the characteristics such as interest rates, borrowing terms, and ease of obtaining money for different types of borrowing available.

19. Off-balance-sheet financing occurs when a firm structures a transaction so that debt does not appear on its balance sheet. It is not always unethical or a violation of GAAP, but some major frauds, such as Enron, have involved off-balance-sheet financing.

20. (Appendix) Simple interest is calculated on only the principal of a loan. Compound interest is calculated on the principal plus any interest that has been earned but not yet collected or paid. Money invested at compound interest grows much faster than money invested at simple interest, because with compound interest the amount on which interest is calculated gets bigger each year.

21. A dollar received today is worth exactly $1. A dollar received a year ago is worth more than $1 today. It is worth the original dollar plus the interest that has been earned for the year gone by. A dollar received one year in the future is worth less than a dollar today. The $1 future receipt includes interest to compensate you for waiting. When you remove the interest, called **discounting** the future payment to calculate its value to you today (its **present value**), you have less than $1 today. The interest rate used in present value problems of this type is called the **discount rate**.

You can find the present value of a single sum using the formula:

$$PV = FV_n \quad \text{x} \quad \frac{1}{(1+i)n}$$

You can also find the present value of a future amount using the *Present Value of $1 Table* at the end of the appendix to Chapter 7 of your textbook. The interest rate used in present value problems is called the **discount rate**. There are also instructions in this appendix for finding the present value of a single amount using a financial calculator.

22. An **annuity** is a series of payments where the dollar amount of each payment is the same, and the time period between payments is also the same. With an **ordinary annuity** the investor receives payments at the end of each time period.

Interest rates quoted by lenders are usually annual interest rates. If interest is compounded more than once a year, both the interest rate (i) and the number of periods (n) must be adjusted. If 6% interest is compounded monthly (12 times a year) for three years, then use a 0.5% interest rate (6% divided by 12 compoundings per year) for 36 periods (three years times 12 payments per year).

- You can calculate the present value of an annuity by finding the present value of each payment separately, then adding them together.

- You can use the *Present Value of an Annuity Table* found at the end of the appendix to Chapter 7 of your textbook.

- You can use a financial calculator, following the instructions in this same appendix.

23. The present value of a series of installment loan payments is the same as the principal amount. To calculate the dollar amount of installment payments, first make sure that the annual interest rate and number of time periods are adjusted to fit the payment schedule. If payments are made monthly, the annual interest rate must be divided by 12 and the number of years must be multiplied by 12. The amount being borrowed, the loan's present value, is equal to the unknown future installment payments times the appropriate factor from the *Present Value of an Annuity Table*. Divide the loan principal by the appropriate factor from the table and your answer is the amount of each installment payment.

24. The price at which a bond is issued is equal to the present value of the future cash flows to be received by the bondholder, discounted at the market rate of interest:

- First calculate the amount of the periodic interest payments: face value of the bond times the stated interest rate of the bond times the appropriate fraction of a year.

- Next calculate the present value of these future cash interest payments (the present value of an annuity).

- Then calculate the present value of the future payment of the bond's face value (the present value of a single amount).

- Finally add the two present values together to determine the amount of cash the company will receive when the bond is issued.

Featured Exercise

A company needs to borrow $1,000,000 to finance a major expansion. One financing alternative is a ten-year bank loan with an annual interest rate of 8%. Annual payments will be $149,029.52.

Part A: Prepare an amortization schedule for the loan.

Mortgage balance		Annual payment	Interest portion of payment	Amount of mortgage reduction
Beginning balance $1,000,000	1st			
After 1st payment	2nd			
After 2nd payment	3rd			
After 3rd payment	4th			
After 4th payment	5th			
After 5th payment	6th			
After 6th payment	7th			
After 7th payment	8th			
After 8th payment	9th			
After 9th payment	10th			
After 10th payment 0				

Part B: Now assume that the company decides instead to issue $1,000,000 of ten-year, 6.5% mortgage bonds to finance the expansion. The bonds will pay interest annually.

1. If the market rate of interest is 7%, these bonds will sell at (circle one):
    a premium   a discount   par

2. How much cash will the company pay on each interest payment date? _____

3. How much cash will the company pay when the bonds mature? Assume the last interest payment has already been made separately. _____

4. Complete the amortization schedule for the first four years of the bond issue using the effective interest method, assuming that the bonds were sold for $964,882.70.

	Beginning carrying value	Cash payment	Interest expense	Amortization of discount	Ending carrying value
Year 1					
Year 2					
Year 3					
Year 4					

5. At maturity, the unamortized discount on the bonds will be _____ and the carrying value of the bonds will be _____.

6. If the market rate of interest is 6%, these bonds will sell at (circle one):
   a premium   a discount   par

7. How much cash will the company pay on each interest payment date? _____

8. How much cash will the company pay when the bonds mature? Assume the last interest payment has already been made separately. _____

9. Complete the amortization schedule for the first four years of the bond issue using the effective interest method, assuming the bonds were sold for $1,036,795.85.

	Beginning carrying value	Cash payment	Interest expense	Amortization of premium	Ending carrying value
Year 1					
Year 2					
Year 3					
Year 4					

10. At maturity, the unamortized premium on the bonds will be _____ and the carrying value of the bonds will be _____.

Solution

Mortgage balance			Annual payment	Interest portion of payment	Amount of mortgage reduction
Beginning balance $1,000,000		1st	$149,029.52	$80,000.00 *1,000,000 x .08*	$69,029.52 *149,029.52 – 80,000.00*
After 1st payment	930,970.48 *1,000,000 – 69,029.52*	2nd	149,029.52	74,477.64 *930,970.48 x .08*	74,551.88 *149,029.52 – 74,477.64*
After 2nd payment	856,418.60 *930,970.48 - 74,551.88*	3rd	149,029.52	68,513.49 *856,418.60 x .08*	80,516.03 *149,029.52 – 68,513.49*
After 3rd payment	775,902.57 *856,418.60 - 80,516.03*	4th	149,029.52	62,072.21 *775,902.57 x .08*	86,957.31 *149,029.52 – 62,072.21*
After 4th payment	688,945.26 *775,902.57- 86,957.31*	5th	149,029.52	55,115.62 *688,945.26 x .08*	93,913.90 *149,029.52 – 55,115.62*
After 5th payment	595,031.36 *688,945.26 - 93,913.90*	6th	149,029.52	47,602.51 *595,031.36 x .08*	101,427.01 *149,029.52 – 47,602.51*
After 6th payment	493,604.35 *595,031.36 - 101,427.01*	7th	149,029.52	39,488.35 *493,604.35 x .08*	109,541.17 *149,029.52 – 39,488.35*
After 7th payment	384,063.18 *493,604.35 - 109,541.17*	8th	149,029.52	30,725.05 *384,063.18 x .08*	118,304.47 *149,029.52 – 30,725.05*
After 8th payment	265,758.71 *384,063.18 - 118,304.47*	9th	149,029.52	21,260.70 *265,758.71 x .08*	127,768.82 *149,029.52 – 21,260.70*
After 9th payment	137,989.89 *265,758.71 - 127,768.82*	10th	149,029.08*	11,039.19 *137,989.89 x .08*	137,989.89
After 10th Pmt.	0				

* The final payment is adjusted to equal the balance due on the mortgage plus the last year's interest ($137,989.89 + 11,039.19)

Part B:
1. a discount
2. $65,000 ($1,000,000 x .065 x 1 year)
3. $1,000,000

4.	Beginning carrying value	Cash payment	Interest expense	Amortization of discount	Ending carrying value
1	$964,882.70	$65,000.00 *1,000,000 x .065*	$67,541.79 *964,882.70 x .07*	$2,541.79 *67,541.79 – 65,000*	967,424.49 *964,882.70 + 2,541.79*
2	967,424.49	65,000.00	67,719.71 *967,424.49 x .07*	2,719.71 *67,719.71 – 65,000*	970,144.20 *967,424.49 + 2,719.71*
3	970,144.20	65,000.00	67,910.09 *970,144.20 x .07*	2,910.09 *67,910.09 – 65,000*	973,054.29 *970,144.20 + 2,910.09*
4	973,054.29	65,000.00	68,113.80 *973,054.29 x .07*	3,113.80 *68,113.80 – 65,000*	976,168.09 *973,054.29 + 3,113.80*

5. At maturity, the unamortized discount on the bonds will be $0 and the carrying value of the bonds will be $1,000,000.
6. a premium

7. $65,000 ($1,000,000 x .065 x 1 year)
8. $1,000,000

9.	Beginning carrying value	Cash payment	Interest expense	Amortization of premium	Ending carrying value
1	$1,036,795.85	$65,000.00 *1,000,000 x .065*	$62,207.75 *1,036,795.85 x .06*	$2,792.25 *65,000 – 62,207.75*	$1,034,003.60 *1,036,795.85 - 2,792.25*
2	1,034,003.60	65,000.00	62,040.22 *1,034,003.60 x .06*	$2,959.78 *65,000 - 62,040.22*	1,031,043.82 *1,034,003.60 - 2,959.78*
3	1,031,043.82	65,000.00	61,862.63 *1,031,043.82 x .06*	3,137.37 *65,000 - 61,862.63*	1,027,906.45 *1,031,043.82 - 3,137.37*
4	1,027,906.45	65,000.00	61,674.39 *1,027,906.45 x .06*	3,325.61 *65,000 - 61,674.39*	1,024,580.84 *1,027,906.45- 3,325.61*

10. At maturity, the unamortized premium on the bonds will be $0 and the carrying value of the bonds will be $1,000,000.

Review Questions and Exercises

Completion Statements

Fill in the blank(s) to complete each statement.

1. There are two types of liabilities: _____, such as accounts
    payable, can be measured exactly; _____, such as warranty payable,
    have some uncertainty in the amount.

2. The amount an employee earns is called _____. His/her take-home pay is
    called _____.

3. Employers are required by law to withhold _____, _____,
    and _____ from their employees.

4. A _____ is a special type of long-term note used to purchase property. It
    gives the lender a claim against the property until the loan is repaid.

5. Bondholders may get extra protection from _____ included in the bond
    agreement. These might place limits on the issuing company's future borrowing or require the
    company to maintain a particular current ratio.

6. Most bonds pay the face value to bondholders at the _____.

7. Unsecured bonds, called _____, are backed by the general credit of the company.

8. _____ bonds all mature on the same date, while _____ bonds
    mature over a period of years.

9. The formula for calculating the debt-to-equity ratio is _____.

10. Financial _____ is the use of borrowed funds to increase earnings.

11. (Appendix) A series of payments where the dollar amount of each payment is the same and the time
    period between payments is also the same is called an _____.

12. (Appendix) Removing the interest from a future payment to calculate its present value is called
    _____. The interest rate used in present value problems of this type is called the
    _____.

True/False

Indicate whether each statement is true (T) or false (F).

_____ 1. Employers are required to match the amount of social security they withhold from their employees.

_____ 2. Employers are required to match the amount of federal income tax they withhold from their employees.

_____ 3. Gross pay is larger than net pay.

_____ 4. If the market rate of interest is higher than a bond's stated rate, the bond will sell at a premium.

_____ 5. A low times-interest-earned ratio may mean a company is having difficulty making its interest payments.

_____ 6. A company that is highly leveraged has very little debt.

_____ 7. If a company issues bonds at a discount, interest paid to bondholders during the period will be more than the interest expense shown on the company's income statement.

_____ 8. The carrying value of a bond sold at a premium is the face value of the bond plus the related premium.

_____ 9. Assume that a long-term note payable will be repaid with five equal annual installment payments. Interest expense reported from this loan will be the same for each of the five years.

_____ 10. At maturity, the discount on a bond sold below par is zero.

Multiple Choice

_____ 1. Bonds sell at par when the stated rate is _____ the market rate of interest.
   A. higher than
   B. lower than
   C. the same as
   D. The answer cannot be determined from the information given.

_____ 2. _____ bonds can be exchanged for common stock whenever bondholders want.
   A. Convertible
   B. Callable
   C. Serial
   D. Term

USE THE FOLLOWING INFORMATION TO ANSWER THE NEXT SEVEN QUESTIONS:
On January 1, 2012, Debtor Corporation issued $2,000,000 of 20-year, 8% bonds at 96, when the market rate of interest was 8.5%. The bonds pay interest annually on December 31. The company uses the effective interest method of amortization.

_____ 3. These bonds sold at:
    A. a premium.
    B. a discount.
    C. par.

_____ 4. How much cash did Debtor Corporation receive when the bonds were issued?
    A. $960,000
    B. $1,920,000
    C. $2,000,000
    D. $1,840,000
    E. $1,830,000

_____ 5. How much cash will bondholders receive when the bonds mature? (Assume that the final payment of interest has already been made separately.)
    A. $60,000
    B. $1,920,000
    C. $2,000,000
    D. $1,840,000
    E. $1,830,000

_____ 6. How much cash will bondholders receive on December 31, 2012, the first interest payment date?
    A. $160,000
    B. $170,000
    C. $153,600
    D. $163,200

_____ 7. How much interest expense will Debtor Corporation report on its income statement for the year ended December 31, 2012?
    A. $160,000
    B. $170,000
    C. $153,600
    D. $163,200

_____ 8. With each annual payment of bond interest, the net value (or carrying value) of the bonds will:
    A. increase.
    B. decrease.
    C. remain the same.
    D. change in a way that cannot be predicted because it depends on the market rate of interest in effect at the end of each year.

_____ 9. With each annual payment of bond interest, the interest expense reported for the year will:
    A. increase.
    B. decrease.
    C. remain the same.
    D. change in a way that cannot be predicted because it depends on the market rate of interest in effect at the end of each year.

_____ 10. Bonds that make no annual interest payments to investors, but instead pay only the face value of the bonds at maturity, are:
- A. convertible bonds.
- B. serial bonds.
- C. premium bonds.
- D. zero-interest or zero-coupon bonds.

Exercises

1. On January 1, a company borrowed $40,000 at 11% interest. The loan will be repaid with four equal annual installment payments of $2,893 made on the last day of each year.

   Complete the amortization schedule for the loan. Round your answers to the nearest dollar.

Mortgage balance		Annual payment	Interest portion of payment	Amount of Mortgage reduction
Beginning balance $40,000	1st			
After 1st payment	2nd			
After 2nd payment	3rd			
After 3rd payment	4th			
After 4th payment 0				

2. Check your answers for the amortization table above, then answer the questions below. Fill in the correct dollar amount and circle the statement on which it appears, using the following codes:
   IS is the income statement for the year described
   BS is the balance sheet at the end of the year described
   SOCF is the statement of cash flows for the year described

   a. For Year 1, Interest expense of $_____ appears on the: **IS   BS   SOCF**

   b. For Year 1, Cash paid for interest of $_____ appears on the: **IS   BS   SOCF**

   c. For Year 1, Notes payable of $_____ appears on the: **IS   BS   SOCF**

   d. For Year 1, Cash paid for loan principal of $_____ appears on the: **IS   BS   SOCF**

   e. For Year 2, Cash paid for loan principal of $_____ appears on the: **IS   BS   SOCF**

   f. For Year 2, Notes payable of $_____ appears on the: **IS   BS   SOCF**

   g. For Year 2, Interest expense of $_____ appears on the: **IS   BS   SOCF**

   h. For Year 2, Cash paid for interest of $_____ appears on the: **IS   BS   SOCF**

3. On January 21, 2012, the company's gross payroll for the pay period is $8,000. The taxes withheld include federal income taxes withheld of $1,600, Social Security taxes of 6.2%, and Medicare taxes of 1.45%. The company will not deposit payment for these taxes until February. Show the effect on the accounting equation, including both account titles and dollar amounts.

Assets	Liabilities	Shareholders' Equity	
		CC	Retained earnings

4. On February 1, 2013, the company recorded its payroll tax expense and payment of taxes owed from 3 above. Show the effect on the accounting equation, including both account titles and dollar amounts.

Assets	Liabilities	Shareholders' Equity	
		CC	Retained earnings

5. (Appendix) The company issued $10,000,000 of 20-year, 5.5% bonds on January 1, when the market rate of interest was 5%. Calculate the proceeds of the bond issue.

Solutions

Completion Statements

1. definitely determinable, estimated
2. gross pay, net pay
3. federal income tax (FIT), Social Security (FICA), Medicare tax
4. mortgage
5. covenants
6. maturity date
7. debentures
8. Term, serial
9. Total liabilities divided by Total shareholders' equity
10. leverage
11. annuity
12. discounting, discount rate

True/False

1. True
2. False — Only Social Security and Medicare are matched by the employer.
3. True
4. False — If the market rate of interest is higher for other investments, investors will refuse to buy the bond unless the price is less than face value. The bond will sell at a discount.
5. True
6. False — Financial leverage is using borrowed money to increase earnings. A highly-leveraged company has a lot of debt.
7. False — If the bond was sold at a discount, the stated interest rate on the bond must be lower than the market rate of interest in effect when the bond was issued. Using the effective interest method, interest expense on the income statement will reflect the higher, market interest rate, and be more (not less) than the cash paid for interest. Part of the current period's interest expense is paid to bondholders in cash, and the remainder is added to the carrying value of the discounted bond, to be paid to bondholders at maturity.
8. True
9. False — Part of each of the five installment payments is interest and part is principal. Since each of the payments makes the principal smaller, interest expense will be calculated on a smaller principal amount each period. Interest expense decreases with each successive payment, even though the total amount of the payment stays the same.
10. True

Multiple Choice

1. C — The law of supply and demand determines prices in the bond market. If the stated interest rate is higher than the market interest rate, the rate investors can earn elsewhere, they will see the bond as a good investment and drive the price up above par. If the stated interest rate is lower than the market interest rate, investors will not buy the bond unless the price is less than face value.
2. A — If the bonds are convertible, bondholders can exchange their bonds for stock at any time. The issuing company is allowed to buy back callable bonds whenever it wants. Term bonds all mature on the same date, while serial bonds mature over a period of years.
3. B — The price at which the bonds were issued is 96, which means 96% of face value. Since investors could earn the 8.5% market rate of interest elsewhere, they will not buy the bonds unless the price drops below par.
4. B — 96% x $2,000,000 = $1,920,000
5. C — Bondholders receive the full $2,000,000 face value of the bonds at maturity, regardless of the price that they paid for the bonds.
6. A — Interest payments are determined by the terms of the bond contract ($2,000,000 x .08 x 1 year).
7. D — Using the effective interest method, interest expense is based on the carrying value (or net value) of the bond, times the effective interest rate when the bonds were issued, times the appropriate fraction of a year ($1,920,000 x .085 x 1 year).
8. A — Each year the Discount on bonds payable will decrease by the difference between interest expense and the cash paid for interest. As the Discount on bonds payable becomes smaller, less is subtracted from the face value of the bonds, and the net value becomes larger.
9. A — Using the effective interest method, interest expense is based on the carrying value (or net value) of the bond, times the effective interest rate when the bonds were issued (not the rate in effect at the end of each year). As the carrying value of the bonds increases from year to year, the interest expense will increase, too.

10. D Since the annual interest payment is based on the stated interest rate times the face value of the bond, a zero-coupon bond, which has a stated interest rate of 0%, does not make annual interest payments to bondholders.

Exercises

1.	**Mortgage balance**			**Annual payment**	**Interest portion of payment**	**Amount of Mortgage reduction**
Beginning balance	$40,000	1st		$12,893	$4,400 *40,000 x .11*	$8,493 *12,893 - 4,400*
After 1st payment	31,507 *40,000 - 8,493*	2nd		12,893	3,466 *31,507 x .11*	9,427 *12,893 – 3,466*
After 2nd payment	22,080 *31,507 - 9,427*	3rd		12,893	2,429 *22,080 x .11*	10,464 *12,893 – 2,429*
After 3rd payment	11,616 *22,080 - 10,464*	4th		12,894* *11,616+1,278*	1,278 *11,616 x .11*	11,616*
After 4th payment	0					

* The final loan payment has been adjusted to pay off the principal balance completely, plus interest for the fourth year.

2. a. $4,400   IS
    b. $4,400   SOCF
    c. $31,507   BS
    d. $8,493   SOCF
    e. $9,427   SOCF
    f. $22,080   BS
    g. $3,466   IS
    h. $3,466   SOCF

3. **Assets**	**Liabilities**	**Shareholders' Equity**	
		CC	**Retained earnings**
(5,788) Cash	1,600 FIT payable 496 FICA payable 116 Medicare taxes payable		(8,000) Salary expense

4. **Assets**	**Liabilities**	**Shareholders' Equity**	
		CC	**Retained earnings**
(2,824) Cash	(1,600) FIT payable (496) FICA payable (116) Medicare taxes payable		(612) Payroll tax expense

5. (Appendix) Annual interest payments: $10,000,000 x .055 x 1 year = $550,000

Present value of annual interest payments: $550,000 x 12.46221 = $ 6,854,215.50
Present value of maturity amount: $10,000,000 x 0.37689 =   3,768,900.00
Bond issue price (total present value): $10,623,115.50

CHAPTER 8
Accounting for Shareholders' Equity

Chapter Overview

When a business begins or wants to expand, it needs to obtain financing. The two sources of financing are debt financing (money from creditors) and equity financing (money from owners). Chapter 7 helps you to understand debt financing. Chapter 8 will help you to understand equity financing. You will see how the money a corporation receives from its owners, called shareholders or stockholders, is obtained and shown on the financial statements. You will also see how the corporation reports its earnings and its distributions of these earnings to shareholders on the financial statements.

Chapter Highlights

1. All companies, whether they are sole proprietorships, partnerships, or corporations, receive contributions from owners. Corporation owners are called stockholders or shareholders. Shareholders' equity represents these owners' claims to the assets after the liabilities have been paid. Shareholders' equity is made up of contributed capital (owners' contributions) and retained earnings (earnings kept by the business). Contributed capital (or paid-in capital) is divided into two parts, capital stock and additional paid-in capital, which together represent the amount received from owners in cash (or sometimes other assets, like property).

2. To begin, a corporation must receive a corporate charter from the state where the firm is located. The charter authorizes the maximum number of shares a corporation is allowed to issue (sell). The number of **issued shares** cannot exceed the number of **authorized shares**. All corporations have **common stock** which has specific rights: 1) to vote for members of the board of directors; 2) to share in the corporation's profits; 3) to share in any assets left if the corporation is to dissolve; and 4) to buy more shares when the corporation issues new stock.

- The dollar amount of common stock equals the number of shares issued times the par value of the common stock. The **par value** is an arbitrary fixed per-share amount stated on the stock certificate. Many states do not require a par value because it has little meaning today. The state and/or the corporate charter define the minimum amount of capital the company must maintain in order to protect creditors. If shareholders' equity falls below this minimum amount, the company is restricted from paying dividends.

- The par value is not to be confused with the market price the stock sells for when issued. The par value is typically much lower than the market price. The difference between the market price (the value received from the shareholder) and the par value, when the stock is issued, is called **additional paid-in capital** or **paid-in capital in excess of par**.

3. Shareholders take risks in hope of receiving cash **dividends** and an increase in the stock's market value. The board of directors determines how much and when a dividend will be paid and are not legally obligated to do so until the dividend is declared.

- The declaration date is the date the board of directors decides a dividend will be paid. A legal liability is created and recorded as:

Assets	Liabilities	Shareholders' equity	
		CC	Retained earnings
	+ Dividends payable		- Dividends

- The record date determines who will receive the dividends. Stocks are frequently traded on the stock market, so whoever owns the stock on the record date will receive the full dividend (even if the new shareholder held the stock for only one day). After this date the stock is said to trade ex-dividend.

- The payment date is when the cash is actually paid to the shareholders. The effect on the accounting equation is to reduce assets (Cash) and reduce liabilities (Dividends payable).

4. Some corporations issue **preferred stock** that has preference over common stock for dividends and claims on assets if the corporation were to dissolve. Common shareholders, however, typically have other rights that preferred shareholders do not, such as voting rights.

- The amount of dividends a preferred shareholder receives equals the dividend rate times the par value stated on the preferred stock. The dividends remaining, after the preferred stock dividends have been met, go to the common shareholders.

- There are two types of preferred stock. Cumulative preferred stock means the dividend accumulates so that no common shareholder can receive dividends until all past, unpaid dividends (called dividends in arrears) have been paid to the cumulative preferred shareholders. Noncumulative preferred stock means dividends do not accumulate so that no past, unpaid dividends will be paid, unless the board of directors decides otherwise.

5. A corporation will sometimes buy back its own stock in the stock market. These shares held by the corporation are called **treasury stock**. Treasury stock is a **contra-equity** account that reduces total shareholders' equity. The number of **outstanding shares** is the number of shares issued minus the number of shares in treasury.

- A corporation may buy back its own stock for several reasons. 1) to give employees stocks for bonuses or stock option plans; 2) to return excess cash to shareholders by buying back their shares or to use the excess cash to decrease the amount of equity compared to its debt; 3) to increase the company's earnings per share; 4) to reduce

the cash needed to pay future dividends by decreasing the number of shares outstanding; or 5) to reduce chances of a hostile takeover.

- The recording of a repurchase of treasury stock requires both assets (Cash) and shareholders' equity (Treasury stock) to be decreased by the cost to repurchase the stock (cost method). No gains or losses are recorded when a company purchases treasury stock or later resells it. If the stock is later reissued at a price that is more than this cost, the entry would be:

Assets	Liab.	Shareholders' equity	
		Contributed capital	**Retained earnings**
+ Cash		+ Treasury stock *(cost)* + Paid-in capital from treasury stock transactions *(price − cost)*	

If the price is less than cost, then additional paid-in capital would be reduced (instead of increased) by the difference between the cost and the price. If insufficient paid-in capital is available, then retained earnings would be reduced for the remaining amount.

6. A corporation may issue a **stock dividend** instead of a cash dividend. The stock dividend gives the shareholders more direct claim to equity by converting retained earnings to common stock (sometimes called capitalizing retained earnings). The effect of a stock dividend is:

Assets	Liab.	Shareholders' equity	
		Contributed capital	**Retained earnings**
		+ Common stock + Additional paid-in capital	- Retained earnings

A small stock dividend is a distribution of fewer than 25% of outstanding shares and is recorded at market value. Larger stock dividends are recorded at par value. A common shareholder's percentage ownership does not increase with a stock dividend because all the other common shareholders receive the same proportion.

7. A **stock split** is when a company increases the number of shares and proportionately decreases the par value. A 2-for-1 stock split means that the number of shares authorized, issued, and outstanding becomes two times the number before the split and the par value of a single share becomes one-half of the par value before the split. The market price of the stock should halve. There is no effect from a stock split on the accounting equation or the corporation's financial position. The only change is the par value and the number of shares reported parenthetically in the shareholders' equity sections of the financial statements.

8. **Retained earnings**, known as earned capital (not contributed capital), is the net income minus dividends declared since the company began. It can be expressed as beginning retained earnings plus net income minus dividends and is typically shown in the statement of changes in shareholders' equity. Some corporations may show changes in retained earnings in a separate statement.

9. Initial public offering (IPO) is the issuance of a corporation's stock to the public for the first time. In protecting investors, the Securities and Exchange Commission (SEC) requires the corporation to provide it with many reports, such as a prospectus that includes financial statements before "going public." Companies will go public to obtain significant contributed capital. The increase in shareholders' equity helps improve the capital structure (the amount of equity versus debt).

10. There are two ratios to help users analyze the shareholders' equity of a corporation. In general, the higher these ratios, the better.

- The **return on equity (ROE)** measures how profitable the company was in using the common shareholders' investment. ROE is calculated as net income (minus preferred stock dividends) divided by the average common shareholders' equity.

- **Earnings per share (EPS)** is shown on the income statement and is a popular measure used to evaluate a company's performance and predict future stock prices. Basic or primary EPS is calculated as net income (minus preferred stock dividends) divided by the weighted average number of common shares outstanding. The denominator should be a weighted average since shares may be issued or repurchased during the period. Another type of EPS is called diluted EPS and is calculated as if all convertible securities were converted into common stock. The effect is to dilute or reduce EPS because the larger number of shares in the denominator would make EPS smaller.

11. The risks associated with equity from an owner's point of view are that the owner may lose money and the management of the company may not act in the best interest of the owner. To minimize the risk of loss, you should diversify your investments by buying stock in many different companies. If a company or industry fails, the hope is that the resulting loss would be offset by other stock doing well. Many of the risks of damage from unethical management have been addressed by the Sarbanes-Oxley Act of 2002. Controls that monitor the behavior and decisions of management – such as boards of directors and independent audits – will help minimize these risks.

Featured Exercise

Part A: Fill in the accounting equation below for the events of Team Shorts, Inc. that occurred during 2011.

Team Shorts, Inc.		Assets =	Liab. +	Shareholders' equity	
				Contributed capital	**Retained earnings**
	Cash	All other assets			
Beginning balances, January 1, 2011	$500	Receivables (net) $ 6,000 Inventory 10,500 Prepaid insurance 600 Truck (net) 16,000	Accounts payable $5,000 Interest payable 700 Notes payable 7,000	Common stock, $1 par value $10,000 Additional paid-in capital 5,000	Retained earnings $5,900
a	Received $6,000 by issuing 4,000 shares of its $1 par value common stock.				
b	Purchased $20,000 of inventory on account.				
c	Made sales of $40,000 on account. The cost of the sales was $30,000.				
d	Collected $44,000 of its receivables.				
e	Repurchased 200 shares of treasury stock for $400.				
f	Paid $4,000 for payroll costs.				
g	Sold 50 shares of treasury stock for $100.				
h	Declared a $3,000 dividend payable in 2012.				
i	Adjusting entries are $200 for bad debts expense, $600 for insurance, $4,000 for depreciation, and $700 for interest owed.				

Part B: Using Parts A and B, prepare the shareholders' equity section of the balance sheet at December 31, 2011. The number of shares authorized is 100,000 shares.

Part C: Answer the following questions using the information from Parts A and B and assuming the average number of shares outstanding during 2011 is 13,900 shares.

1. How many shares of common stock are issued as of December 31, 2011?

2. How many shares of common stock are outstanding as of December 31, 2011?

3. What was the average price at which a share of common stock was issued?

4. Calculate the return on equity.

5. Calculate the earnings per share given the weighted average shares outstanding is 11,925 shares.

6. If Team Shorts, Inc., did a 2-for-1 stock split, what would be the number of shares issued and what would be the par value of its common stock?

Solution

Part A:

Team Shorts, Inc.		Assets =		Liab. +	Shareholders' equity	
		Cash	All other assets		Contributed capital	Retained earnings
Beginning balances, January 1, 2011		$500	Receivables (net) $ 6,000 Inventory 10,500 Prepaid insurance 600 Truck (net) 16,000	Accounts payable $5,000 Interest payable 700 Notes payable 7,000	Common stock, $1 par value $10,000 Additional paid-in capital 5,000	Retained earnings $5,900
a	Received $6,000 by issuing 4,000 shares of its $1 par value common stock.	6,000			4,000 Common stock 2,000 Additional paid-in capital	
b	Purchased $20,000 of inventory on account.		20,000 Inventory	20,000 Accounts payable		
c	Made sales of $40,000 on account. The cost of the sales was $30,000.		40,000 Receivables (30,000) Inventory			40,000 Sales (30,000) Cost of goods sold
d	Collected $44,000 of its receivables.	44,000	(44,000) Receivables			
e	Repurchased 200 shares of treasury stock for $400.	(400)			(400) Treasury stock	
f	Paid $4,000 for payroll costs.	(4,000)				(4,000) Payroll expense
g	Sold 50 shares of treasury stock for $100.	100			100 Treasury stock	
h	Declared a $3,000 dividend payable in 2012.			3,000 Dividends payable		(3,000) Dividends
i	Adjusting entries are $200 for bad debts expense, $600 for insurance, $4,000 for depreciation, and $700 for interest owed.		(200) Allowance for uncollectible accounts (600) Prepaid insurance (4,000) Accum. deprec.	700 Interest payable		(200) Bad debts expense (600) Insurance expense (4,000) Deprec. expense. (700) Interest expense

Part B:

December 31, 2011

Shareholders' equity

Common stock, par value $1 per share,	
authorized 100,000 shares, issued 14,000 shares	$14,000
Additional paid-in capital	7,000
Retained earnings	3,400
Treasury stock: 150 shares	(300)
Total shareholders' equity	$24,100

Part C:

1. Shares issued equals 14,000 shares.
2. Shares outstanding equals 13,850 (or 14,000 issued minus 150 treasury stock)
3. The average issue price equals $1.50 (or the sum of $14,000 common stock plus $7,000 additional paid-in capital divided by 14,000 shares of common stock issued).

4. $$\text{Return on equity} = \frac{\text{net income} - \text{preferred dividends}}{\text{average shareholders' equity}} = \frac{\$500\text{-}0}{(\$24,100 + \$20,900)/2} = 2.2\%$$

5. $$\text{Earnings per share} = \frac{\text{net income} - \text{preferred dividends}}{\text{average shares outstanding}} = \frac{\$500\text{-}0}{11,925 \text{ shares}} = \$0.04$$

6. The number of shares issued would be 28,000, or double the number of shares issued prior to the split. The par value of its common stock would be $0.50, or one half of the par value prior to the split.

Review Questions and Exercises

Completion Statements

Fill in the blank(s) to complete each statement.

1. The two sources of financing are debt financing (money from creditors), and _____ (money from owners).

2. Shareholders' equity is made up of _____ (owners' contributions) and _____ (earnings kept by the business).

3. When a corporation repurchases its own common stock, the shares are called _____. Since these shares reduce shareholders' equity, the account is called a _____-equity account.

4. The number of shares _____ always equals the number of shares _____ minus the number of shares in the _____.

5. Contributed capital (or paid-in capital) is divided into two parts: _____ and _____.

6. The difference between the market price (the value received from the shareholder) and the par value is called _____ or _____.

7. The _____ date is the date the board of directors decides a dividend will be paid and a legal liability is created. Whoever owns the stock on the _____ date will receive the full dividend. The _____ date is when the cash is actually paid to the shareholders.

8. There are two types of preferred stock: _____ preferred stock, which means that dividends accumulate, and _____ preferred stock, which means dividends do not accumulate.

9. A _____ is the division of the current shares of stock by some factor to increase the number of shares and decrease the par value by the same factor.

10. The _____ measures how profitable the company was in using the common shareholders' investment and is calculated as net income (minus preferred stock dividends) divided by the average common shareholders' equity.

True/False

Indicate whether each statement is true (T) or false (F).

_____1. The number of shares outstanding will always equal the number of shares issued minus the number of shares held as treasury stock.

_____2. The earnings per share is the amount of dividends the shareholder will receive.

_____3. The par value per share is the price the shareholders will pay when the shares are issued.

_____4. A company might repurchase its own stock as treasury stock to have shares it can later give to employees as part of a stock option plan.

_____5. Preferred shareholders do not have voting rights, but do have preference to dividends.

_____6. A stock dividend has the effect of reducing retained earnings and reducing cash.

_____7. Both stock dividends and stock splits increase the actual number of shares a shareholder will own, as well as increase the percentage of the shareholder's ownership.

_____8. The average issue price of common stock can be determined by dividing the sum of the balances in Common Stock and Additional Paid-in Capital by the number of shares issued.

Multiple Choice

Select the best answer for each question.

_____1. The preferred stock dividend amount is calculated by:
A. dividing the total dividend by the number of shares of preferred stock plus common stock outstanding.
B. multiplying the dividend rate times the market price per share times the number of preferred stock shares outstanding.
C. multiplying the dividend rate times the par value per share times the number of preferred stock shares outstanding.
D. multiplying the total dividend times the percentage of preferred stock to common stock.

_____2. Diluted earnings per share (EPS) is reported on the income statement so that users can see what effect:
A. cumulative preferred stock dividends have on EPS.
B. contingent liabilities will have on EPS.
C. treasury stock has on EPS.
D. the convertible securities would have on EPS if they were converted into common stock.

_____3. Retained earnings is:
A. net income divided by the weighted average number of shares outstanding.
B. the amount received in excess of par value.
C. the net income minus dividends since the inception of the company.
D. the minimum legal amount of earnings required to be kept by the company.

_____4. Stockup, Inc., issued 1,000 shares of $1 par value common stock for $3,000. The common stock account will be increased by:
A. $3,000.
B. $2,000.
C. $1,000.
D. none of these.

_____5. Stock that has dividends in arrears is called:
A. cumulative preferred stock.
B. convertible preferred stock.
C. cumulative common stock.
D. noncumulative preferred stock.

_____ 6. Aria's, Inc., has 1,000 shares of 5%, $100 par value cumulative preferred stock and 10,000 shares of $1 par value common stock outstanding. The company has not paid dividends in two years. In its third year, it paid the common shareholders a $2 per-share dividend. How much did the preferred shareholders receive per share?
A. $100 per share
B. $15 per share
C. $6 per share
D. $5 per share

_____ 7. Aria's, Inc., has 1,000 shares of 5%, $100 par value cumulative preferred stock, and 10,000 shares of $1 par value common stock. The company has not paid a dividend in two years. In its third year, it paid the common shareholders a $2 per-share dividend. What was the total amount of dividends paid?
A. $35,000
B. $30,000
C. $20,000
D. $20,150

_____ 8. At the beginning of the year, the balance in retained earnings was $400,000. During the year sales were $1,000,000, of which $800,000 was collected and expenses were $750,000, of which $400,000 was paid. The company has outstanding 10,000 shares of 6%, $100 par value preferred stock, and 100,000 shares of $0.10 par value common stock. The dividend paid to the common shareholders was $1 per share. Calculate the ending retained earnings.
A. $490,000
B. $410,000
C. $240,000
D. $ 90,000

_____ 9. Mr. Cello bought 4,000 shares of Ventures, Inc., $1 par value common stock directly from Ventures, Inc. for $80,000. When Mr. Cello sold 1,000 of his shares to Mr. Bilo for $30,000, the result for Ventures, Inc. will be:
A. shareholders' equity will decrease by $80,000.
B. net income will increase by $10,000 from the gain on the sale of common stock.
C. Shareholders' equity will be unaffected by the sale.
D. Both A and B above are correct.

_____ 10. A company has treasury stock which cost $50,000. If it resells this stock for $40,000, then:
A. additional paid-in capital is reduced by $10,000.
B. additional paid-in capital is reduced by $50,000.
C. treasury stock is increased by $40,000.
D. shareholders' equity is increased by $50,000.

Exercises

1. For each of the transactions below, show the effect on the accounting equation by circling one item in each column.

a. On January 1, 2011, Ventures, Inc., declared a $50,000 dividend. The date of record is January 31, 2011 and the date of payment is February 15, 2011.

Total assets	Total liabilities	Total shareholders' equity	
		Contributed capital	Retained earnings
Increase	Increase	Increase	Increase
Decrease	Decrease	Decrease	Decrease
No effect	No effect	No effect	No effect

b. On January 31, 2011, Ventures, Inc., updated its stock records.

Total assets	Total liabilities	Total shareholders' equity	
		Contributed capital	Retained earnings
Increase	Increase	Increase	Increase
Decrease	Decrease	Decrease	Decrease
No effect	No effect	No effect	No effect

c. On February 15, 2011, Ventures, Inc., paid the $50,000 dividend in a above.

Total assets	Total liabilities	Total shareholders' equity	
		Contributed capital	Retained earnings
Increase	Increase	Increase	Increase
Decrease	Decrease	Decrease	Decrease
No effect	No effect	No effect	No effect

d. On February 28, 2011, Ventures, Inc., repurchased $5,000 of its own stock.

Total assets	Total liabilities	Total shareholders' equity
		Contributed capital + Retained earnings
Increase	Increase	Increase
Decrease	Decrease	Decrease
No effect	No effect	No effect

e. On March 31, 2011, Ventures, Inc., issued a $10,000 stock dividend.

Total assets	Total liabilities	Total shareholders' equity	
		Contributed capital	Retained earnings
Increase	Increase	Increase	Increase
Decrease	Decrease	Decrease	Decrease
No effect	No effect	No effect	No effect

f. On May 31, 2011, Ventures, Inc., split its stock 2 for 1.

Total assets	Total liabilities	Total shareholders' equity	
		Contributed capital	Retained earnings
Increase	Increase	Increase	Increase
Decrease	Decrease	Decrease	Decrease
No effect	No effect	No effect	No effect

2. Capital Venture, Inc., began operations in January 2011 by issuing common stock for $10 per share. Net income for 2011 was $500,000 and dividends of $100,000 were declared. Fill in the missing amounts in the spaces provided.

	December 31, 2011
6% preferred stock, $50 par value, 500 shares authorized and issued	(a)
Common stock, $1 par value, 8,000,000 shares authorized, (b) _____ shares issued	$900,000
Additional paid-in capital in excess of par	(c)
Retained earnings	(d)
Treasury stock (1,000 shares at cost)	(25,000)
Total shareholders' equity	(e)

(f) How many shares are outstanding as of December 31, 2011?

3. Team Shorts had an initial public offering and sold 200,000 shares of $2 par value common stock for a total of $3,000,000.

a	What was the average selling price for each share of stock?	
b	What amount should be reported for Common stock?	
c	What amount should be reported for Additional paid-in capital?	

Solutions

Completion Statements

1. equity financing
2. contributed capital, retained earnings
3. treasury stock, contra
4. outstanding, issued, treasury
5. capital stock (or common stock), additional paid-in capital
6. paid-in capital in excess of par, additional paid-in capital
7. declaration, record, payment
8. cumulative, noncumulative
9. stock split
10. return on equity

True/False

1. True
2. False   EPS is a company's net income (not dividends), minus preferred stock dividends if any, on a per-share basis.
3. False   The par value represents the maximum responsibility of a shareholder and does not have any relationship to the market price of that share.
4. True
5. True
6. False   A stock dividend's effect on the accounting equation is to reduce retained earnings and increase common stock. A cash (not stock) dividend reduces cash when it is paid.
7. False   Both stock dividends and splits increase the number of shares a shareholder will own. However, since all shareholders receive the same proportion of stock, their ownership percentage remains the same.
8. True

Multiple Choice

1. C   Preferred stock typically has a dividend rate and par value stated on the certificate. The preferred stock dividend is the dividend rate times the par value. Common stock does not have a dividend rate and will receive the dividends that remain only after the preferred shareholders' dividends have been met.
2. D   The diluted EPS assumes that all of the company's convertible securities have been converted into common stock. This makes the denominator larger, causing the EPS to be smaller or diluted.
3. C   Retained earnings equals beginning retained earnings plus net income minus dividends.
4. C   The common stock account will be increased by the par value times the number of shares issued or $1 times 1,000 shares.
5. A   Only cumulative preferred shareholders have the right to receive past, unpaid dividends before other shareholders receive any dividends.
6. B   The preferred dividend per share is $5, which equals the dividend rate, 5%, times the par value of $100. Since the stock is cumulative, the dividend will equal $15 per share (3 years x $5).
7. A   The cumulative preferred shareholders receive $15 per share. The total dividends paid is $35,000, which equals $15,000 to preferred shareholders (or $15 per share times 1,000 shares) plus $20,000 to common shareholders (or $2 per common share times 10,000 shares).

8. A   Beginning retained earnings of $400,000 plus net income of $250,000 (or $1,000,000 minus $750,000) minus dividends of $160,000 (6% times $100 par value times 10,000 preferred shares plus $1 times 100,000 common shares) equals ending retained earnings of $490,000.

9. C   When the company issued 4,000 shares to Mr. Cello, its contributed capital increased by $80,000. When Mr. Cello sells his shares to another party, there is no effect on Ventures' shareholders' equity.

10. A   The reissuance of treasury stock at an amount below cost causes cash to increase by $40,000 and treasury stock to increase by $50,000. Additional paid-in capital is decreased by $10,000 to balance the accounting equation.

Exercises

1.	Total assets	Total liabilities	Total shareholders' equity	
			Contributed capital	Retained earnings
a	No effect	Increase	No effect	Decrease
b	No effect	No effect	No effect	No effect
c	Decrease	Decrease	No effect	No effect
d	Decrease	No effect	Decrease	
e	No effect	No effect	Increase	Decrease
f	No effect	No effect	No effect	No effect

2.	December 31, 2009
6% preferred stock, $50 par value, 500 shares authorized and issued	(a) $25,000 *$50 par value x 500 shares*
Common stock, $1 par value, 8,000,000 shares authorized, (b) 900,000 shares issued *($900,000/$1 par value)*	$900,000
Additional paid-in capital in excess of par	(c) $8,100,000 *($10 - 1) x 900,000 shares*
Retained earnings	(d) $400,000 *$500,000 – 100,000*
Treasury stock (1,000 shares at cost)	(25,000)
Total shareholders' equity	(e) $9,400,000

(f)   900,000 shares issued minus 1,000 treasury shares equals 899,000 shares outstanding.

3.		
a	What was the average selling price for each share of stock?	$15 *$3,000,000/200,000 shares*
b	What amount should be reported for the common stock?	$400,000 *$2 x 200,000 shares*
c	What amount should be reported for the additional paid-in capital?	$2,600,000 *($15 - $2) x 200,000 shares*

CHAPTER 9
PREPARING AND ANALYZING THE STATEMENT OF CASH FLOWS

Chapter Overview

The statement of cash flows, which describes in detail all of a company's cash receipts and cash payments, is one of the financial statements required by GAAP. In this chapter you will learn to prepare the three sections of the statement of cash flows: 1) cash from operating activities, which may be prepared using either the direct or the indirect method; 2) cash from investing activities; and 3) cash from financing activities. In learning to prepare the statement of cash flows, you should gain a clearer understanding of the difference between accrual accounting and cash-basis accounting. You will also learn to analyze the statement of cash flows.

Chapter Highlights

1. Cash is a very important asset. Many companies go bankrupt each year because they do not have enough cash at the right time to pay their bills. A cash budget is useful for estimating in advance the cash inflows and outflows that a company expects. If a company expects a shortfall, it can plan ahead and secure a line of credit, borrow the money needed, or change the timing of expected cash receipts and payments. At the end of the accounting period, managers can use this same budget to evaluate performance by comparing it with actual events. This year's cash budget is also useful for planning next year's cash activity.

2. GAAP and IFRS allow two ways of preparing the cash from operating activities section of the statement of cash flows: the **direct method** and the **indirect method**. With the direct method, cash inflows and outflows are shown directly. With the indirect method, the statement begins with net income, an accrual-based number, and adjusts it to cash from operating activities. Regardless of the method used, net cash from operating activities should be the same dollar amount. The other two sections, cash from investing activities and cash from financing activities, are prepared in the

same way for both the direct and indirect methods.

3. The first section of the statement of cash flows shows cash from operating activities, where the cash inflows and outflows from the normal, day-to-day activities are reported. Typical operating cash inflows are:
- Cash collected from customers
- Cash collected for interest

Typical operating cash outflows are:
- Cash paid to employees
- Cash paid to vendors for inventory
- Cash paid for operating expenses
- Cash paid for interest
- Cash paid for taxes

4. The second section of the statement of cash flows is the investing section, also known as **cash from investing activities**, where the cash inflows and outflows for long-term business assets and for investments are reported. Typical investing cash inflows are:
- Cash received from the sale of property, plant, and equipment
- Cash from the sale of marketable securities
- Cash received when amounts loaned to others are repaid

Typical investing cash outflows are:
- Cash paid to buy property, plant, and equipment
- Cash paid for investments
- Cash loaned to others

5. The third section of the statement of cash flows is the financing section, also known as **cash from financing activities**, where the cash inflows and outflows for the principal on loans, contributions from shareholders, and payments to shareholders are reported. Typical financing cash inflows are:
- Cash received from the sale of stock
- Cash received from borrowing

Typical financing cash outflows are:
- Cash paid for treasury stock
- Cash paid to retire debt principal
- Cash paid for dividends

6. Most companies keep their accounting records on an accrual basis so that they can easily prepare financial statements in accordance with GAAP. If a company sells goods on account, it will recognize sales revenue for goods that have been sold even if cash has not yet been received. Uncollected accounts receivable represent revenue that has been earned but has not been collected in cash. Moreover, the company may have collected cash during the accounting period from sales on account recorded in a previous accounting period. For both of these reasons, the amount of cash received during an accounting period will not necessarily be the same as the revenue earned during that period.

To convert the accrual-basis sales revenue found on the income statement to cash collected from customers for the statement of cash flows, you must analyze the change in accounts receivable during the accounting period by looking at balance sheets for both the beginning and end of the period. If accounts receivable increased during the period, then some of the current period's sales have not yet been collected from customers. This increase in accounts receivable should be subtracted from sales revenue to determine the amount of cash collected.

Every revenue or expense reported on the accrual-basis income statement may be different from the amount of cash actually received or paid. Each income statement line item must be examined along with changes in the related current asset or current liability accounts to determine the amount of cash actually received or paid. For example, a company might show salary expense of $30,000 on its income statement. This represents the cost of services provided by employees during the accounting period, regardless of whether these employees have been paid in cash or not. If the related current liability account, salaries payable, also decreased $400 during the period, then the company must have paid cash for more than just the $30,000 current period's expense. The

decrease in salaries payable should be added to the $30,000 salary expense to determine the amount of cash paid to employees.

7. There are two possible ways to prepare the cash from operating activities section of the statement of cash flows. The direct method begins with the income statement. Each revenue and expense must be analyzed to determine the amount of cash received or paid. In your textbook, look at Team Shirts' third month of business – March – to see how to convert revenues to cash collected and expenses to cash paid.

- Team Shirts' income statement shows sales revenue of $2,000 for the month ended March 31. During the month, accounts receivable grew from $150 at the beginning of the month to $2,000 at the end of the month, an increase of $1,850. This means that none of March's $2,000 in sales revenue has been received in cash yet. Cash collected from customers must be $2,000 in sales revenue minus the $1,850 increase in accounts receivable, or $150.

- Team Shirts' income statement shows cost of goods sold of $800 for the same month. The first step in calculating cash paid for inventory is to determine how much inventory was purchased during March. Inventory grew from $100 at the beginning of the month to $300 at the end of the month, an increase of $200. Team Shirts must have purchased enough inventory to cover the $800 in cost of goods sold and to increase its inventory by $200 as well, a total of $1,000 in inventory purchased. However, this does not tell us how much cash the company actually paid for inventory, since often inventory is purchased on account, not for cash. We must also look at changes in accounts payable for the period. Accounts payable went from $800 at the beginning of the month to $0 at the end of the month, a decrease of $800. The company must have paid the full $1,000 for March's purchases plus another $800 for inventory purchased in a previous period, a total of $1,800 cash paid for inventory in March.

- The March income statement for Team Shirts shows depreciation expense of $100. This represents part of the historical cost of equipment allocated to expense for the current accounting period. No cash is ever paid for depreciation expense.

- The company's income statement shows insurance expense of $50 for the month. During the month, the balance in Prepaid insurance went from $125 at the beginning of the month to $75 at the end of the month, a decrease of $50. Clearly, the $50 in March insurance expense came from a policy purchased in a previous month, not from a current cash payment. No cash was paid for insurance in March.

- Finally, Team Shirts' income statement shows interest expense of $30. During March, the balance in Interest payable increased from $0 at the beginning of the month to $30 at the end of the month. The company owes the entire $30 in interest. No cash was paid for interest during the month.

- Although we have covered all of the line items on the income statement, we must look at the balance sheet to make sure that all changes in current assets and current liabilities have been included. Property, plant, and equipment, represented by the $3,900 in the Computer account, is not a current asset, so it does not affect cash from operating activities. Among the current liabilities, Other Payables decreased from $50 at the beginning of the month to $0 at the end of the month. Although no other operating expenses appear on the income statement, the company must have paid $50 for other expenses reported during a previous accounting period. Notes payable is a long-term liability, not a current liability, so it does not affect cash from operating activities.

The cash from operating activities section for Team Shirts' statement of cash flows, prepared using the direct method, looks like this:

Cash from operating activities:

Cash collected from customers	$ 150
Cash paid to vendors	(1,800)
Cash paid for other expenses	(50)
Net cash from operating activities	$(1,700)

8. The Financial Accounting Standards Board (FASB) and the International Accounting Standards Board (IASB) encourage companies to use the direct method to prepare the operating activities section of the statement of cash flows. However, since companies using the direct method must also provide a reconciliation of net income and cash from operating activities, which is essentially the same as using the indirect method, most companies use the indirect method to report cash flows from operating activities.

Using the indirect method, the operating activities section begins with net income. Any amounts that affect net income but do not affect cash are removed. These items include depreciation, amortization, and gains/losses from the sale of long-term assets. Then changes in each current asset and current liability account are analyzed to determine the effect on cash. Team Shirts' income statement shows net income of $1,020. To this amount, add $100 in depreciation expense because this expense decreases income but does not decrease cash.

- Accounts receivable grew from $150 at the beginning of the month to $2,000 at the end of the month, an increase of $1,850. If accounts receivable increases, it means that sales revenue has not been collected in cash. This $1,850 increase in accounts receivable should be subtracted from net income for the calculation of cash from operating activities.

- Inventory increased from $100 at the beginning of March to $300 at the end of March. This $200 increase in a current asset represents an inventory purchase that might have been paid for in cash, and should be subtracted from net income because it potentially decreases the cash provided by operating activities.

- Prepaid insurance went from $125 at the beginning of the month to $75 at the end of the month, a decrease of $50. This decrease in a current asset represents an expense on the income statement that decreased income without requiring a decrease in cash as well. The $50 should be added to net income in calculating cash from operating activities.

- Prepaid rent was $0 at the beginning of March and $0 at the end of March, too. Since it did not change, it did not affect either income or cash for the month, and it can be ignored.

- The change in the Computer account, a long-term asset, does not affect cash from operating activities because buying and selling property, plant, and equipment is an investing activity, not an operating activity.

- Accounts payable went from $800 at the beginning of March to $0 at the end of March. This decrease in a current liability represents cash paid out by Team Shirts, and a decrease in cash provided by operating activities. Similarly, the $50 decrease in other payables decreases the cash provided by operating activities.

- Interest payable increased from $0 at the beginning of the period to $30 at the end of the period. This means that the $30 expense, which decreased net income on the income statement, did not decrease cash because the company did not pay anything for interest in March. This increase in a current liability should be added to net income in calculating cash from operating activities.

- Notes payable is a long-term liability, not a current liability. Increases and decreases in long-term debt are financing, not operating, activities.

The cash from operating activities section for Team Shirts' statement of cash flows, prepared using the indirect method, looks like this:

Net income	$ 1,020
+ Depreciation expense	100
- Increase in accounts receivable	(1,850)
- Increase in inventory	(200)
+ Decrease in prepaid insurance	50
- Decreases in payables (- 800 – 50 + 30)	(820)
Net cash from operating activities	$(1,700)

Notice that cash from operating activities is the same $(1,700) under both the direct and indirect methods.

9. The format of the cash from investing activities section is exactly the same, whether operating activities are presented under the direct method or indirect method. Analyze changes in noncurrent assets to determine cash received or paid for investing activities.

- In the month of March, the balance in Team Shirts' Computer account increased from $0 to $3,900, net of $100 accumulated depreciation. The original cost of the computer must have been $4,000. Since long-term assets are often expensive, it is possible that this entire amount was not paid in cash, thus we must look further in the company's records. Team Shirts paid $1,000 in cash and signed a note for the $3,000 remainder. Only the cash paid will appear in the investing activities section of the statement, but the $3,000 note will be shown in a footnote so that the statement includes all major investing activities, even those that did not involve cash.

10. Similarly, the format of the cash from financing activities section is exactly the same, whether operating activities are presented under the direct method or indirect method. Analyze changes in noncurrent liabilities and shareholders' equity accounts for evidence of financing activities.

- Notes payable increased from $0 at the beginning of March to $3,000 at the end of March. However, Team Shirts did not receive cash for the note payable, but instead used it to finance the purchase of equipment. Since no cash was received, the note will not be reported in the financing activities section of the statement, but will be described in a note to the financial statements.

- There was no change in Team Shirts' Common stock account during March. Apparently no cash was received from the sale of stock. Retained earnings went from $1,220 to $2,240 during the month, an increase of $1,020. Since this increase is exactly equal to net income, no dividends were declared or paid.

The investing and financing activities sections of Team Shirts' statement of cash flows will look like this:

Cash from investing activities:

Purchase of computer*	(1,000)
Net cash from investing activities	(1,000)

Cash from financing activities: 0

* A $4,000 computer was purchased for $1,000 cash and a $3,000 note payable.

11. GAAP require that companies that use the indirect method disclose cash paid for interest and taxes somewhere in the financial statements.

12. Investors hope to see a positive cash flow from operating activities. In the long run, a company must generate positive operating cash flow or it will not survive. The investing activities section of the statement of cash flows shows the company's future plans. Negative investing cash flow means the company has invested in long-term assets, which may indicate expansion, or at least replacement of aging productive assets. Failure to invest in property, plant, and equipment may mean the company has a problem. The financing activities section shows changes in how the company is financed, with debt or with equity.

Financial analysts sometimes calculate **free cash flow**, which is net cash from operating activities minus cash paid for dividends and capital expenditures. This is used as a measure of a company's ability to make future investments.

13. Investors' risks associated with the statement of cash flows include management's misclassification of cash inflows and outflows. Analysts interpret positive net cash from operating activities as a signal for positive future growth. Thus, management may be pressured into acting unethically and misclassifying cash inflows from investing or financing activities as cash inflows from operating activities. Management could also create positive cash from operating activities by misclassifying operating cash outflows as investing or financing activities.

Featured Exercise

Megabucks, Inc.
Income Statement
For the Year Ended December 31, 2012

Sales revenue		$2,000,000
Expenses		
Cost of goods sold	$1,080,000	
Salary expense	572,000	
Depreciation expense	24,000	
Other operating expenses	138,000	
Interest expense	38,800	1,852,800
Net income		$ 147,200

Megabucks, Inc.
Comparative Balance Sheets
At December 31, 2012 and 2011

	2012	2011	Increase (Decrease)
Cash	$ 120,800	$ 40,800	$ 80,000
Accounts receivable	84,000	132,000	(48,000)
Inventory	408,000	384,000	24,000
Equipment (net of depreciation)	480,000	504,000	(24,000)
Total	$1,092,800	$1,060,800	
Accounts payable	$ 98,400	$ 63,200	$ 35,200
Salaries payable	7,600	16,000	(8,400)
Interest payable	9,600	21,600	(12,000)
Bonds payable	400,000	400,000	0
Common stock	104,000	104,000	0
Retained earnings*	473,200	456,000	17,200
Total	$1,092,800	$1,060,800	

*During 2012, Megabucks declared and paid a cash dividend of $130,000.

Part A: Prepare a statement of cash flows for the year ended December 31, 2012, using the direct method.

Megabucks, Inc.
Statement of Cash Flows
For the Year Ended December 31, 2012

Part B: Prepare a statement of cash flows for the year ended December 31, 2012, using the indirect method.

Megabucks, Inc.
Statement of Cash Flows
For the Year Ended December 31, 2012

Solution

Part A

Megabucks, Inc.
Statement of Cash Flows
For the Year Ended December 31, 2012

Cash from operating activities

Cash collected from customers	$ 2,048,000	
Cash paid to vendors	(1,068,800)	
Cash paid for salaries	(580,400)	
Cash paid for other operating expenses	(138,000)	
Cash paid for interest	(50,800)	
Net cash from operating activities		$ 210,000

Cash from investing activities   0

Cash from financing activities

Cash paid for dividends	(130,000)	
Net cash from financing activities		(130,000)

Net increase (decrease) in cash	$ 80,000
Beginning cash balance	40,000
Ending cash balance	$ 120,000

Part B

Megabucks, Inc.
Statement of Cash Flows
For the Year Ended December 31, 2012

Cash from operating activities

Net income	$147,200	
+ Depreciation expense	24,000	
+ Decrease in Accounts receivable	48,000	
- Increase in Inventory	(24,000)	
+ Increase in Accounts payable	35,200	
- Decrease in Salaries payable	(8,400)	
- Decrease in Interest payable	(12,000)	
Net cash from operating activities		$210,000

Cash from investing activities   0

Cash from financing activities

Cash paid for dividends	(130,000)	
Net cash from financing activities		(130,000)

Net increase (decrease) in cash	$ 80,000
Beginning cash balance	40,000
Ending cash balance	$ 120,000

Review Questions and Exercises

Completion Statements

Fill in the blank(s) to complete each statement.

1. The first section of the statement of cash flows is _____.

2. The second section of the statement of cash flows is _____.

3. The third section of the statement of cash flows is _____.

4. There are two ways to present cash flows from operating activities: the _____ method and the _____ method.

5. Companies that use the direct method of calculating cash from operating activities must also provide a _____.

6. Companies that use the indirect method of calculating cash from operating activities must also report cash paid for _____ and cash paid for _____ somewhere in their financial statements.

7. Investors hope to see _____ cash flow from operating activities.

8. Investors look at cash used by _____ for evidence of expansion.

9. The cash from _____ section shows how a company finances its assets.

10. A _____ is a detailed plan of a company's estimated cash receipts and disbursements.

True/False

Indicate whether each statement is true (T) or false (F).

_____ 1. Both the Financial Accounting Standards Board and the International Accounting Standards Board encourage companies to use the direct method of reporting cash from operating activities.

_____ 2. Most companies use the direct method of reporting cash from operating activities.

_____ 3. Depreciation expense decreases a company's cash.

_____ 4. A company that uses the direct method will show more cash from operating activities than a company that uses the indirect method.

_____ 5. There are two acceptable ways to report cash from investing activities: the direct method and the indirect method.

_____ 6. Only new companies need to prepare a cash budget to obtain financing.

_____ 7.   Negative cash flow from investing activities is usually good.

_____ 8.   If a company issues a five-year note payable to buy equipment, the note will not appear on the statement of cash flows because it does not involve receipt or payment of cash.

_____ 9.   Only the largest companies are required to prepare a statement of cash flows.

_____ 10. If a company uses the indirect method of calculating cash from operating activities, its statement of cash flows begins with net income.

Multiple Choice

_____ 1.   In the long run, a company must generate positive cash flow from _____ or it will not survive.
- A. operating activities
- B. investing activities
- C. financing activities
- D. operating, investing, or financing activities

_____ 2.   Which of the following financial statements explains why a company's cash balance changed over a period of time?
- A. Income statement
- B. Balance sheet
- C. Statement of cash flows
- D. Both B and C

Use the following information to answer the next three questions:
Our Feathered Friends, Inc., reported credit sales of $1,500,000 for 2012. Cost of goods sold was $700,000. The following additional information is available from the company's records:

	December 31, 2012	December 31, 2011
Accounts receivable	$50,000	$40,000
Inventory	75,000	80,000
Accounts payable	30,000	25,000

_____ 3.   How much cash did the company collect from customers in 2012?
- A. $1,500,000
- B. $1,510,000
- C. $1,490,000
- D. $10,000

_____ 4.   How much inventory did the company buy from vendors in 2012?
- A. $700,000
- B. $5,000
- C. $705,000
- D. $695,000

_____ 5. How much cash was paid to vendors in 2012?
   A. $690,000
   B. $695,000
   C. $700,000
   D. $705,000

Use the following information to answer the next two questions. Both of these companies are merchandisers that began operations this year.

	X Company	Y Company
Cash from operating activities	$ 20,000	$ 60,000
Cash from investing activities	(200,000)	(100,000)
Cash from financing activities	230,000	90,000
Net increase in cash	$ 50,000	$ 50,000

_____ 6. Which of these two companies appears to have made the larger purchases of property, plant, and equipment during the year?
   A. X Company
   B. Y Company
   C. Both companies have made the same purchases.
   D. Neither company has made any purchases.

_____ 7. Which of these two companies is likely to pay the larger cash dividend per share of stock next month?
   A. X Company
   B. Y Company

_____ 8. Oblique, Inc., prepares its statement of cash flows using the indirect method. In calculating cash from operating activities, increases in current assets other than Cash should be:
   A. added to net income.
   B. subtracted from net income.
   C. ignored.

_____ 9. Oblique, Inc., prepares its statement of cash flows using the indirect method. In calculating cash from operating activities, increases in current liabilities should be:
   A. added to net income.
   B. subtracted from net income.
   C. ignored.

_____ 10. Cash flows from investing activities can be discovered by analyzing changes in a company's:
   A. current asset accounts.
   B. current liability accounts.
   C. long-term asset accounts.
   D. long-term liabilities and shareholders' equity accounts.

Exercises

1. Put an X in the appropriate box to identify each of these activities as operating, investing, or financing.

	Activity	Operating	Investing	Financing
a	Cash paid to purchase treasury stock			
b	Cash received for interest			
c	Cash paid to buy machinery			
d	Cash paid to employees			
e	Cash paid for stock of other companies			
f	Cash received from the sale of the company's own stock			
g	Cash paid for interest			
h	Cash paid for dividends			
i	Cash paid for taxes			
j	Cash received from customers			
k	Cash received on loans previously made to other companies			
l	Cash received from selling equipment			
m	Cash paid for rent on warehouse			
n	Cash paid to retire the principal on debt			
o	Cash collected on accounts receivable			
p	Cash received from selling investments in stock of other companies			
q	Cash paid to buy land that will be used for the company's new store			
r	Cash paid for utilities used in one of the company's stores			
s	Cash paid for inventory			
t	Cash received from borrowing			
u	Cash loaned to other companies			

2. The column below on the left lists line items from the income statement. The column on the right lists current assets and current liabilities. Match each income statement item with the related balance sheet account(s) used for preparing the statement of cash flows.

_____ 1. Sales   A. Interest payable

_____ 2. Salary expense   B. Other payables

_____ 3. Cost of goods sold   C. Inventory and Accounts payable

_____ 4. Interest expense   D. Interest receivable

_____ 5 Interest revenue   E. Salaries payable

_____ 6. Insurance expense   F. Accounts receivable

_____ 7. Operating expenses   G. Prepaid rent

_____ 8. Rent expense   H. Prepaid insurance

3. Use the information below to prepare the cash flows from investing activities and cash flows from financing activities sections of the statement of cash flows. Some of the items listed are not investing or financing activities.

a. Sold equipment for $6,000 cash that had a book value of $8,000.

b. Paid $50,000 cash to retire bonds payable.

c. Bought an $80,000 building by making an $8,000 cash down payment and signing a 20-year mortgage note for the remainder.

d. Made a $4,000 payment on an installment note. $600 of this payment was interest and the rest was principal.

e. Issued 5,000 shares of $1 par value common stock for $20 per share.

f. The company had 500 shares of treasury stock that cost $8,000. It sold these shares for $10,000.

g. Declared and paid a cash dividend of $40,000.

h. Paid $12,000 for the bonds of another company to be held as a long-term investment.

i. Received $1,000 interest from the investment in bonds of another company.

4. Describe two unethical ways management could misclassify cash inflows and outflows to appear more favorable to analysts.

Solutions

Completion Statements
1. cash from operating activities
2. cash from investing activities
3. cash from financing activities
4. direct; indirect
5. reconciliation of net income and cash from operating activities
6. interest; income taxes
7. positive
8. investing activities
9. financing activities
10. cash budget

True/False
1. True
2. False   Around 90% of companies use the indirect method.
3. False   The entry to record depreciation expense decreases the book value of the asset and decreases shareholders' equity. Cash is never paid for depreciation expense.
4. False   Cash from operating activities should be the same regardless of the method used.
5. False   There is only one acceptable way to report cash from investing activities. There are two acceptable ways to report cash from operating activities.
6. False   Lenders expect to see a cash budget from all borrowers.
7. True
8. False   Noncash investing and financing activities are described in the notes to the statement of cash flows, so that the statement summarizes all important investing and financing activities.
9. False   The statement of cash flows is one of the financial statements required by GAAP.
10. True

Multiple Choice
1. A   In the long run, a business must be able to generate enough cash from normal, day-to-day activities to pay for its operations, investments in long-term assets, loans from creditors, and dividends to shareholders. In the short run, a company can raise cash by borrowing or by selling stock. However, if it cannot generate a positive cash flow from operating activities to pay back the loans, eventually creditors will be unwilling to lend the company any more money. Similarly, it will become very difficult to raise additional cash by issuing more shares of stock, since investors will be unwilling to buy more shares.
2. C   A is wrong because the income statement shows revenues earned and expenses incurred, not cash received and cash paid. B is wrong because the balance sheet shows the cash balance at a single point in time, not the detailed changes in cash during the accounting period. Only the statement of cash flows shows the inflows and outflows of cash during an accounting period.
3. C   The $10,000 increase in Accounts receivable ($50,000 – 40,000) means that some customers who purchased merchandise on account in 2012 have not yet paid the company. Credit sales of $1,500,000 minus the $10,000 increase in Accounts receivable equal $1,490,000. Or, $40,000 beginning accounts receivable, plus $1,500,000 in additional accounts receivable from sales during the year, minus $50,000 ending accounts receivable equals $1,490,000.
4. D   The $5,000 decrease in Inventory ($75,000 – 80,000) means that some of the merchandise sold came from beginning inventory. Cost of goods sold of $700,000, minus the $5,000 decrease in inventory, equals $695,000. Or $700,000 in cost of goods sold, plus $75,000 in ending inventory, means that the company had $775,000 of merchandise available for sale during the year. If

$80,000 of this merchandise came from beginning inventory, the remaining $695,000 must have been purchased during the year. ($700,000 +75,000 – 80,000 = $695,000)

5. A The $5,000 increase in Accounts payable ($30,000 – 25,000) means that the company did not pay for all of the inventory it purchased in 2012. Purchases of $695,000, minus the $5,000 increase in Accounts payable, equals $690,000. Or, beginning accounts payable of $25,000, plus $695,000 in additional accounts payable during the year, minus $30,000 in ending accounts payable, equals $690,000 paid in cash.

6. A Company X has paid more cash for investing activities. Purchases of property, plant, and equipment are investing activities.

7. B Y Company has generated more cash from operating activities than X Company and is in a better position for paying dividends. Also, Y Company, with less cash coming in from financing activities, probably has less debt, so it doesn't need to worry as much about cash for future interest payments. Furthermore, less cash from financing activities probably means that Y Company issued fewer shares of stock than X Company. Each share of Y Company stock can receive a larger cash dividend without requiring as much total cash as X Company would need for the same dividend per share.

8. B Increases in current assets such as inventory or prepaid rent represent purchases of goods or services that might have required a payment of cash. An increase in the current asset Accounts receivable means that some of the current period's sales have not been collected in cash yet.

9. A Increases in current liabilities such as Accounts payable or Salaries payable represent purchases of goods or services that were not paid for in cash. They are associated with expenses that decreased net income, but did not decrease cash.

10. C Typical investing activities are purchases or sales of stock in another company or property, plant, and equipment. These are long-term assets. A and B are wrong because changes in current assets and current liabilities are used to analyze cash from operating activities. D is wrong because changes in long-term liabilities and shareholders' equity accounts are indicators of financing activities.

Exercises

1.	Activity	Operating	Investing	Financing
a	Cash paid to purchase treasury stock			X
b	Cash received for interest	X		
c	Cash paid to buy machinery		X	
d	Cash paid to employees	X		
e	Cash paid for stock of other companies		X	
f	Cash received from the sale of the company's own stock			X
g	Cash paid for interest	X		
h	Cash paid for dividends			X
i	Cash paid for taxes	X		
j	Cash received from customers	X		
k	Cash received on loans previously made to other companies		X	
l	Cash received from selling equipment		X	
m	Cash paid for rent on warehouse	X		
n	Cash paid to retire the principal on debt			X
o	Cash collected on accounts receivable	X		
p	Cash received from selling investments in stock		X	
q	Cash paid to buy land		X	
r	Cash paid for utilities used in one of the company's stores	X		
s	Cash paid for inventory	X		
t	Cash received from borrowing			X
u	Cash loaned to other companies		X	

2.

F	1.	Sales/ Accounts receivable
E	2.	Salary expense/ Salaries payable
C	3.	Cost of goods sold/ Inventory and Accounts payable
A	4.	Interest expense/ Interest payable
D	5	Interest revenue/ Interest receivable
H	6.	Insurance expense/ Prepaid insurance
B	7.	Operating expenses/ Other payables
G	8.	Rent expense/ Prepaid rent

3.

Cash from investing activities

Sale of equipment	$ 6,000	
Purchase of building*	(8,000)	
Purchased bonds of another company	(12,000)	
Net cash from investing activities		$(14,000)

Cash from financing activities

Retired bonds payable	$(50,000)	
Repayment on loan	(3,400)	
Issued common stock	100,000	
Sold treasury stock	10,000	
Paid dividends	(40,000)	
Net cash from financing activities		$ 16,600

* An $80,000 building was purchased by making an $8,000 down payment and signing a 20-year mortgage note for the remainder.

4. Analysts interpret positive net cash from operating activities as a signal for positive future growth. Thus, management may be pressured into acting unethically and misclassifying cash inflows from investing or financing activities as cash inflows from operating activities. Management could also create positive cash from operating activities by misclassifying operating cash outflows as investing or financing activities.

CHAPTER 10
USING FINANCIAL STATEMENT ANALYSIS TO EVALUATE FIRM PERFORMANCE

Chapter Overview

This chapter introduces accounting for two new items that are sometimes found on the income statement, discontinued operations and extraordinary items. Techniques for analyzing financial statements are illustrated and discussed as well. Vertical and horizontal analyses are introduced, and ratios are presented as well.

Chapter Highlights

1. Because the earnings a company reports are so important, the Financial Accounting Standards Board (FASB) requires that two particular items be presented separately on the income statement and not be included with income from continuing operations. They are 1) discontinued operations, and 2) extraordinary items. Each of these is shown net of tax, that is, the tax expense or tax benefit is combined with the dollar amount of the gain or loss to show the after-tax effect of the item on earnings. You can remember the order in which they are presented by the letters **C-D-E**: income from **C**ontinuing operations, **D**iscontinued operations, and **E**xtraordinary items. If a company had both of these items, its income statement would look something like this:

   Revenues
   - Expenses
   Income before taxes
   - Income tax expense
   Income from continuing operations
   Discontinued operations:
   +/- Income or loss from discontinued operations, net of tax
   +/- Gain or loss on disposal, net of tax
   Income before extraordinary item
   +/- Extraordinary item, net of tax
   Net income

2. **Discontinued operations** are a part of a company's past activities that will not be continued in the future. They represent a major portion of the business, usually a segment or an entire division, that will no longer earn profits (or incur losses) for the company. The actual disposal of the segment will happen only once and thus will not affect future earnings, so the impact on income must be shown separately in the financial statements. Then analysts can better predict the company's future earnings. IFRS also requires a separate presentation of discontinued operations.

If a company has discontinued operations, the first part of its income statement will show revenue, expenses, and income taxes for continuing operations. Then, under a heading called "Discontinued operations," it will show the after-tax income or loss from operating the discontinued segment during the accounting period. A second line item, still under "Discontinued operations," shows the after-tax gain or loss from the actual sale or disposal of the segment.

3. **Extraordinary items** are events that are both unusual in nature and infrequent in occurrence. Accountants must use professional judgment to decide if an item should be reported as extraordinary. Natural disasters, for example, will sometimes be considered extraordinary and sometimes not, depending upon how frequently they occur in a particular area. Other possible extraordinary items are the one-time cost of complying with new laws or the loss of assets in a foreign country seized by that country's government. IFRS do not allow extraordinary items.

If any event qualifies as an extraordinary item, it will be shown on the income statement, net of tax, after income from continuing operations and any discontinued operations.

4. **Horizontal analysis** is a technique used to evaluate an individual financial statement line item over a period of time. Often a specific past year is chosen as a base year. The increase or decrease in the same line item for other years is

then expressed as a percentage of the base year. For example:

Property, plant and equipment		
2012	2011	2010
$130,000	$120,000	$100,000
30%	20%	100%

In this example, 2010 is the base year. In 2011, PP&E has increased $20,000 ($120,000 minus $100,000). This $20,000 increase divided by the $100,000 base year equals 20%. During 2011, PP&E increased 20%. In 2012, PP&E was $30,000, or 30%, more than the base year of 2010.

This is just one way to do horizontal analysis. Sometimes the analyst simply compares each year with the previous year, rather than with a common base year:

Property, plant and equipment		
2012	2011	2010
$130,000	$120,000	$100,000
8%	20%	100%

In this example, PP&E in 2011 is still $20,000 (or 20%) more than it was in 2010. However, PP&E in 2012 is $10,000 more than in 2011, an 8% increase over the $120,000 of PP&E in 2011 ($10,000 divided by $120,000).

5. **Vertical analysis**, also called **common-sizing**, expresses each line item on a particular year's financial statement as a percentage of a single item on that financial statement. The most common vertical analysis is performed on the income statement, where each line item on the statement is expressed as a percentage of sales for the period. Managers and analysts can then see if a particular item of expense is growing disproportionately. This technique is more useful if two or more periods are available for comparison.

6. Ratio analysis uses information on the financial statements to calculate specific values, which can then be used to determine a company's financial condition. Ratios for a particular accounting period are more useful when compared with: 1) ratios from other periods, 2) industry averages, or 3) other companies in the same industry.

Some analysts will use variations of the formulas presented in this book. It is important that you understand the company you are analyzing and apply the formulas consistently from one accounting period to the next. You should also read the notes to the financial statements carefully so that you know which accounting choices management has made.

7. **Liquidity ratios** measure a firm's ability to meet its short-term debt obligations and operating costs when they come due.

- The **current ratio** measures a company's ability to cover its current liabilities (due within the next year) with its current assets, which are cash and items that will be converted into cash or used in the business during the next year. The current ratio is calculated as:

$$\frac{\text{Total current assets}}{\text{Total current liabilities}}$$

- **Cash from operations to current liabilities** measures a company's ability to pay its current liabilities. It is similar to the current ratio, but it considers only cash from operating activities, not all current assets. It is calculated as:

$$\frac{\text{Net cash from operating activities}}{\text{Average current liabilities}}$$

- The **inventory turnover ratio** measures how quickly a company turns over (or sells) its inventory. It is calculated as:

$$\frac{\text{Cost of goods sold}}{\text{Average inventory}}$$

- The **accounts receivable turnover ratio** measures how quickly a company turns over (or collects) its accounts receivable. It is calculated as:

$$\frac{\text{Net credit sales}}{\text{Average net accounts receivable}}$$

8. **Solvency ratios** are a measure of a company's ability to pay its long-term obligations and to survive over time.

- The **debt-to-equity ratio** shows how much of a company's financing is provided by creditors and how much is provided by owners. The formula is:

$$\frac{\text{Total liabilities}}{\text{Total shareholders' equity}}$$

9. **Profitability ratios** evaluate a company's earnings for a period of time.

- **Return on assets** compares a company's earnings with the assets invested to generate those earnings:

$$\frac{\text{Net income}}{\text{Average total assets}}$$

- The **asset turnover ratio** measures how efficiently a company uses its assets:

$$\frac{\text{Net sales}}{\text{Average total assets}}$$

- **Return on equity** compares a company's earnings with the investment made by the common shareholders:

$$\frac{\text{Net income} - \text{preferred dividends}}{\text{Average common shareholders' equity}}$$

- The **profit margin ratio** measures the percentage of each sales dollar that becomes net income:

$$\frac{\text{Net income}}{\text{Net sales}}$$

- The **gross profit ratio** measures the percentage of each dollar of sales that is left over after covering the cost of the merchandise:

$$\frac{\text{Gross profit}}{\text{Net sales}}$$

A small decrease in the gross profit percentage can make a big difference in a company's profitability.

- **Earnings per share** expresses the company's income on a per-share basis:

$$\frac{\text{Net income} - \text{preferred dividends}}{\substack{\text{Weighted average number of shares of} \\ \text{common stock outstanding}}}$$

Companies are required to show earnings per share on the income statement.

10. Two **market indicators** are of interest to shareholders because they analyze the current market price of the stock, which is the amount a new investor would pay for a share.

- The **price-earnings ratio** compares the market price of a share of stock with the earnings that each share generates:

$$\frac{\text{Market price per common share}}{\text{Earnings per share}}$$

A high price-earnings ratio shows that investors believe the company has potential for future growth. However, it can also be an indicator of an over-valued stock.

- The **dividend yield** ratio compares the dividend paid on a single share of stock with the market price of that share:

$$\frac{\text{Dividend per share}}{\text{Market price per share}}$$

Dividend yields may be quite low, since many investors expect to profit from increases in the market price of the stock rather than dividends. However, some investors are dependent on dividend income and prefer stocks with a high dividend yield.

11. EBITDA, earnings before interest, taxes, depreciation and amortization, has become a popular measure of a firm's performance. These items are eliminated because they involve management discretion and estimation or because they arise from financing choices of debt rather than equity. Some analysts feel that looking at EBITDA makes it easier to compare different companies.

12. To minimize the risk of investing in stock, you should either find a financial advisor or become an expert from your own study and analysis of stocks. You also need to understand financial accounting and financial statement analysis. Investors should diversify, or invest in a variety of stocks, so that losses in one stock are offset by gains in another. A diversified portfolio, or group of investments, allows shareholders to minimize (but not eliminate) risk.

13. (Appendix 10A) There are several events that have a direct effect on shareholders' equity that are not reported on the income statement. Two of them are owner contributions (which increase contributed capital) and dividends to corporate owners (which decrease retained earnings). However, there are two other items that are part of **other comprehensive income.** The first item is unrealized gains and losses from foreign currency translations and the second is unrealized gains and losses on certain types of investments. Neither of these items appears on the income statement because they do not really reflect a firm's performance. The gains and losses from these items are included in **accumulated other comprehensive income** in the shareholders' equity section of the balance sheet.

13. (Appendix 10B) Companies will often invest surplus cash in the stocks and bonds of other companies. Management's plans to sell or hold these securities determine how they should be treated.

- **Held-to-maturity securities** are debt securities that the company plans to keep until they mature. Equity securities (stocks) cannot be held-to-maturity securities because they do not have maturity dates. These debt securities are recorded at cost and shown as assets on the balance sheet at historical cost, (plus any unamortized premium or minus any unamortized discount). Changes in market value do not affect the recorded value of held-to-maturity securities.

- **Trading securities** are either debt or equity securities that the company has purchased in hope of making a short-term profit. These securities are first recorded at cost. However, before the company issues financial statements, it must revalue these securities and show them as current assets on the balance sheet at their market values, known as marking-to-market. If the market value is higher than cost, the company has an **unrealized gain,** (holding gain) and if the market value is lower than cost, the company has an **unrealized loss** (holding loss). Unrealized gains and losses on trading securities appear on the company's income statement.

- **Available-for-sale securities** are either debt or equity securities that the company does not plan to sell in the short run, but does not intend to hold to maturity, either. These securities are initially recorded at cost and revalued to market value at the balance sheet date. Any unrealized gain or loss does not appear on the income statement, however. Instead it is included in accumulated other comprehensive income in the shareholders' equity section of the balance sheet.

Featured Exercise

Virtual Company
Consolidated Balance Sheet
At December 31

millions, except share data	2012	2011	2010
Current assets			
Cash and cash equivalents	$ 5.6	$ 16.2	$ 14.9
Accounts receivable, less allowances	18.9	17.5	20.4
Inventories	32.4	39.4	38.6
Other current assets	3.8	1.2	2.3
Total current assets	60.7	74.3	76.2
Property, plant & equipment, net	145.7	135.8	122.4
Other assets	1.4	2.1	1.1
Total assets	207.8	212.2	199.7
Current liabilities			
Accounts payable	2.5	13.4	15.2
Current portion of long-term debt	24.3	22.9	21.5
Other current liabilities	1.9	2.1	0.7
Total current liabilities	28.7	38.4	37.4
Long-term debt	126.0	118.6	115.8
Other liabilities	1.6	1.4	1.2
Shareholders' equity			
Common stock, $0.10 par, 20,000,000 shares authorized.			
Issued 14,000,000 shares in 2012, 13,700,000 in 2011			
and 13,650,000 in 2010	1.4	1.4	1.4
Capital in excess of par value	36.3	35.2	34.7
Retained earnings	25.9	22.1	18.7
Treasury stock at cost	(9.7)	(8.2)	(7.8)
Accumulated other comprehensive income	(2.4)	3.3	(1.7)
Total shareholders' equity	51.5	53.8	45.3
Total liabilities and shareholders' equity	$ 207.8	$ 212.2	$ 199.7

Virtual Company
Consolidated Statement of Earnings
For the Year Ended December 31

millions, except share data	2012	2011	2010
Net sales	$ 120.8	$ 140.4	$ 109.5
Cost of goods sold	65.7	82.5	58.3
Selling and administrative expense	39.7	37.3	32.8
Operating income	15.4	20.6	18.4
Interest expense	1.1	0.7	1.0
Earnings before income taxes	14.3	19.9	17.4
Income taxes	5.0	7.0	6.1
Net earnings	$ 9.3	$ 12.9	$ 11.3

Part A: Use the financial statements for Virtual Company to complete the ratios in the chart below. If you cannot calculate a ratio, explain why. The following additional information may be helpful:

	2012	2011	2010
Market price per share	$9.00	$13.00	$12.80
Dividend per common share	$0.60	$0.60	$0.58
Weighted average number of common shares outstanding during the year	13,800,000	13,680,000	13,600,000

Partial information from the Statement of Cash Flows for the year ended December 31	2012	2011	2010
Cash from operations in millions	$25.2	$40.6	$30.9

		2012	2011	2010
1	Current ratio			
2	Cash from operations to current liabilities			
3	Inventory turnover ratio			
4	Accounts receivable turnover ratio			
5	Debt-to-equity ratio			
6	Return on assets			
7	Asset turnover ratio			
8	Return on equity			
9	Profit margin ratio			
10	Gross profit ratio			
11	Earnings per share			
12	Price-earnings ratio			
13	Dividend yield			

Part B: Prepare a vertical analysis of Virtual Company's income statements for all three years.

	2012		2011		2010	
Net sales	$ 120.8		$ 140.4		$ 109.5	
Cost of goods sold	65.7		82.5		58.3	
Selling and administrative expense	39.7		37.3		32.8	
Operating income	15.4		20.6		18.4	
Interest expense	1.1		0.7		1.0	
Earnings before income taxes	14.3		19.9		17.4	
Income taxes	5.0		7.0		6.1	
Net earnings	$ 9.3		$ 12.9		$ 11.3	

Part C: Prepare a horizontal analysis of the following selected items for Virtual Company. Use 2010 as the base year.

1		2012	2011	2010
	Accounts receivable	$18.9	$17.5	$20.4

2		2012	2011	2010
	Property, plant & equipment, net	$145.7	$135.8	$122.4

3		2012	2011	2010
	Net sales	$120.8	$140.4	$109.5

4		2012	2011	2010
	Net earnings	$9.3	$12.9	$11.3

Part D: (Appendix A) What two items might be part of Virtual Company's Accumulated other comprehensive income on its balance sheet?

1. _____

2. _____

Solution

Part A:		2012	2011	2010
1	Current ratio	$\dfrac{\$60.7}{\$28.7} = 2.11$	$\dfrac{\$74.3}{\$38.4} = 1.93$	$\dfrac{\$76.2}{\$37.4} = 2.04$
2	Cash from operations to current liabilities	$\dfrac{\$25.2}{(\$28.7 + 38.4)/2} = 0.75$	$\dfrac{\$40.6}{(\$38.4 + 37.4)/2} = 1.07$	*Can't calculate average current liabilities for 2010*
3	Inventory turnover ratio	$\dfrac{\$65.7}{(\$32.4+39.4)/2} = 1.8$	$\dfrac{\$82.5}{(\$39.4+38.6)/2} = 2.1$	*Can't calculate average inventory for 2010*
4	Accounts receivable turnover ratio	$\dfrac{\$120.8}{(\$18.9+17.5)/2} = 6.6$	$\dfrac{\$140.4}{(\$17.5+20.4)/2} = 7.4$	*Can't calculate average A/R for 2010*
5	Debt-to-equity ratio	$\dfrac{\$28.7+126.0+1.6}{\$51.5} = 3.0$	$\dfrac{\$38.4+118.6+1.4}{\$53.8} = 2.9$	$\dfrac{\$37.4+115.8+1.2}{\$45.3} = 3.4$
6	Return on assets	$\dfrac{\$9.3}{(\$207.8 + 212.2)/2} =$ $0.044 = 4.4\%$	$\dfrac{\$12.9}{(\$212.2 + 199.7)/2} =$ $0.063 = 6.3\%$	*Can't calculate average assets for 2010*
7	Asset turnover ratio	$\dfrac{\$120.8}{(\$207.8 + 212.2)/2} =$ 0.575 times	$\dfrac{\$140.4}{(\$212.2 + 199.7)/2} =$ 0.682 times	*Can't calculate average assets for 2010*
8	Return on equity	$\dfrac{\$9.3 - 0}{(\$51.5 + 53.8)/2} =$ $0.177 = 17.7\%$	$\dfrac{\$12.9 - 0}{(\$53.8 + 45.3)/2} =$ $0.260 = 26.0\%$	*Can't calculate average shareholders' equity for 2010*
9	Profit margin ratio	$\dfrac{\$9.3}{\$120.8} = 7.7\%$	$\dfrac{\$12.9}{\$140.4} = 9.2\%$	$\dfrac{\$11.3}{\$109.5} = 10.3\%$
10	Gross profit ratio	$\dfrac{\$120.8-65.7}{\$120.8} = 45.6\%$	$\dfrac{\$140.4-82.5}{\$140.4} = 41.2\%$	$\dfrac{\$109.5-58.3}{\$109.5} = 46.8\%$
11	Earnings per share	$\dfrac{\$9,300,000}{13,800,000} = \$0.67$	$\dfrac{\$12,900,000}{13,680,000} = \$0.94$	$\dfrac{\$11,300,000}{13,600,000} = \$0.83$
12	Price-earnings ratio	$\dfrac{\$9.00}{\$0.67} = 13.4$	$\dfrac{\$13.00}{\$0.94} = 13.8$	$\dfrac{\$12.80}{\$0.83} = 15.4$
13	Dividend yield	$\dfrac{\$0.60}{\$9.00} = 0.067 = 6.7\%$	$\dfrac{\$0.60}{\$13.00} = 0.046 = 4.6\%$	$\dfrac{\$0.58}{\$12.80} = 0.045 = 4.5\%$

Part B:	2012		2011		2010	
Net sales	$ 120.8	100.0%	$ 140.4	100.0%	$ 109.5	100.0%
Cost of goods sold	65.7	54.4%	82.5	58.8%	58.3	53.2%
Selling and admin. expense	39.7	32.9%	37.3	26.6%	32.8	30.0%
Operating income	15.4	12.7%	20.6	14.7%	18.4	16.8%
Interest expense	1.1	0.9%	0.7	0.5%	1.0	0.9%
Earnings before income taxes	14.3	11.8%	19.9	14.2%	17.4	15.9%
Income taxes	5.0	4.1%	7.0	5.0%	6.1	5.6%
Net earnings	$ 9.3	7.7%	$ 12.9	9.2%	$ 11.3	10.3%

Part C:		2012	2011	2010
1	Accounts receivable	$18.9	$17.5	$20.4
		$\dfrac{\$18.9 - 20.4}{\$20.4} = (7.4)\%$	$\dfrac{\$17.5 - 20.4}{\$20.4} = (14.2)\%$	100%

2	Property, plant & equipment, net	$145.7	$135.8	$122.4
		$\dfrac{\$145.7 - 122.4}{\$122.4} = 19.0\%$	$\dfrac{\$135.8 - 122.4}{\$122.4} = 10.9\%$	100%

3	Net sales	$120.8	$140.4	$109.5
		$\dfrac{\$120.8 - 109.5}{\$109.5} = 10.3\%$	$\dfrac{\$140.4 - 109.5}{\$109.5} = 28.2\%$	100%

4	Net earnings	$9.3	$12.9	$11.3
		$\dfrac{\$9.3 - 11.3}{\$11.3} = -17.7\%$	$\dfrac{\$12.9 - 11.3}{\$11.3} = 14.2\%$	100%

Part D (Appendix A)
1. Unrealized gains and losses from foreign currency translations.
2. Unrealized gains and losses on certain investments (available-for-sale securities).

Review Questions and Exercises

Completion Statements

Fill in the blank(s) to complete each statement.

1. _____ are events that are both unusual in nature and infrequent in occurrence.

2. _____ measures the percentage of each dollar of sales that is left over after covering the cost of the merchandise.

3. The _____ ratio shows how much of a company's financing is provided by creditors and how much is provided by owners.

4. _____ are a part of a company's past activities that will not be continued in the future.

5. _____ expresses each item on a particular year's financial statement as a percentage of a single item on that financial statement.

6. _____ is a technique used to evaluate an individual financial statement line item over a period of time. Often a specific past year is chosen as a base year.

7. _____ is the only ratio that companies are required to include with their financial statements. It appears on the _____.

8. To calculate the return on assets, you need two financial statements, the _____ and the _____.

9. (Appendix B) _____ are debt securities that the company plans to keep until they mature.

10. (Appendix B) _____ are either debt or equity securities that the company has purchased in hope of making a short-term profit.

11. (Appendix B) _____ are either debt or equity securities that the company does not plan to sell in the short-run, but does not intend to hold to maturity, either.

12. (Appendix A) _____ is the total of all items that affect shareholders' equity except for transactions with shareholders.

True/False

Indicate whether each statement is true (T) or false (F).

_____ 1. The current ratio will always be greater than 1.0.

_____ 2. The current ratio measures a company's solvency.

_____ 3. To prepare a vertical analysis of a company's income statement, you should divide each line item on the statement by total assets.

_____ 4. The asset turnover ratio is a measure of a company's profitability.

_____ 5. The accounts receivable turnover ratio is a measure of a company's profitability.

_____ 6. Ratios are more meaningful when they are compared with other companies in the same industry or with industry averages.

_____ 7. Investors should buy stocks with the highest possible price-earnings ratio.

_____ 8. Stock with a high dividend yield is a good investment.

_____ 9. To be classified as an extraordinary item, an event must be both unusual in nature and infrequent in occurrence.

_____ 10. Gains and losses from discontinued operations are shown separately on a company's income statement.

_____ 11. (Appendix A) Comprehensive income will always be greater than net income.

_____ 12. (Appendix B) Trading securities are shown on the balance sheet at historical cost.

_____ 13. (Appendix B) Held-to-maturity securities are shown on the balance sheet at historical cost, plus any unamortized premium minus any unamortized discount.

_____ 14. (Appendix B) Available-for-sale securities are shown on the balance sheet at historical cost.

Multiple Choice

Select the best answer for each question.

_____ 1. Beta Business has total current assets of $1,000,000 and total current liabilities of $400,000. Its current ratio is:
   A. 2.00.
   B. 2.25.
   C. 2.50.
   D. 0.40.

2. Beta Business has total current assets of $1,000,000 and total current liabilities of $400,000. If the company collects $100,000 of its accounts receivable, its current ratio will:
   A. increase.
   B. decrease.
   C. stay the same.
   D. The answer cannot be determined from the information given.

3. Beta Business has total current assets of $1,000,000 and total current liabilities of $400,000. If the company purchases $100,000 of inventory for cash on the last day of the accounting year, its inventory turnover ratio will:
   A. increase.
   B. decrease.
   C. stay the same.
   D. The answer cannot be determined from the information given.

4. Beta Business has total current assets of $1,000,000 and total current liabilities of $400,000. If the company purchases $100,000 of inventory and promises to pay for it in the next two weeks, its current ratio will:
   A. increase.
   B. decrease.
   C. stay the same.
   D. The answer cannot be determined from the information given.

5. Last year Iota, Inc., had earnings per share of $1.95. In December this year, Iota repurchased some of its own common stock. Assume that net income this year is exactly the same as it was last year. This purchase of treasury stock will _____ the number of shares of common stock outstanding and _____ earnings per share.
   A. increase   increase
   B. increase   decrease
   C. decrease   decrease
   D. decrease   increase

6. Last year Madd Hatter, Inc., bought baseball caps for $3 each and sold them for $9. This year the company's supplier is charging $4 for each cap, but Madd Hatter can not raise its prices because competition is too tough. If Madd Hatter continues to sell caps for $9, its gross profit per cap will _____ and its gross profit ratio will _____.
   A. increase   increase
   B. increase   decrease
   C. decrease   decrease
   D. decrease   increase

7. Nu News, Inc., has total current assets of $1,000,000 and total current liabilities of $500,000. If the company pays $100,000 of accounts payable, its current ratio will:
   A. increase.
   B. decrease.
   C. stay the same.
   D. The answer cannot be determined from the information given.

_____ 8. If a company increases its collection effort, it hopes to see its accounts receivable turnover ratio _____, because the average amount of accounts receivable will _____.
   A. increase   increase
   B. increase   decrease
   C. decrease   decrease
   D. decrease   increase

_____ 9. One of Caribbean Cruises' ships hit an iceberg just off Miami and sank. Icebergs in the Caribbean are both unusual and infrequent, so the company plans to treat the $10,000,000 uninsured loss as an extraordinary item. The company's tax rate is 35%. What effect will this event have on net income for the year?
   A. Net income will decrease $3,500,000.
   B. Net income will decrease $6,500,000.
   C. No effect. Extraordinary items appear on the balance sheet as a direct increase or decrease to retained earnings.
   D. No effect. Companies are not required to report extraordinary items because they will have no effect on future earnings.

_____ 10. Which of the following ratios would most interest a banker who is thinking about making a long-term loan to a company?
   A. Return on equity
   B. Return on assets
   C. Dividend yield
   D. Debt-to-equity

Exercises

1. Classify each of the ratios listed in the table below by putting an X in the appropriate box.

		Liquidity	Solvency	Profitability	Market indicator
a	Return on assets				
b	Profit margin ratio				
c	Current ratio				
d	Return on equity				
e	Debt-to-equity ratio				
f	Gross profit ratio				
g	Accounts receivable turnover ratio				
h	Dividend yield				
i	Inventory turnover ratio				
j	Cash from operations to current liabilities				
k	Earnings per share				
l	Price-earnings ratio				
m	Asset turnover ratio				

2. 2012 was a very eventful year for Buck's Better Bacon.
- Buck's decided to discontinue its manure processing division, which wasn't very profitable even in good years. On October 31, Buck's sold the division for a small gain of $10,000. Up to the date of sale, the division earned revenues of $50,000 and had expenses of $45,000.
- In August, Buck's Iowa research farm was leveled by an earthquake. Uninsured damages amounted to $300,000. Buck's will treat this disaster as an extraordinary loss, since earthquakes in Iowa are both unusual and infrequent.
- Normal continuing operations earned revenues of $900,000. Expenses were $600,000. Buck's has a 30% tax rate that applies to all income.

Prepare an income statement for the year ended December 31, 2012, in good form.

Buck's Better Bacon, Inc.
Income Statement
For the Year Ended December 31, 2012

Solutions

Completion Statements

1. Extraordinary items
2. Gross profit ratio
3. debt-to-equity
4. Discontinued operations
5. Vertical analysis
6. Horizontal analysis
7. Earnings per share; income statement
8. income statement; balance sheet
9. (Appendix B) Held-to-maturity securities
10. (Appendix B) Trading securities
11. (Appendix B) Available-for-sale securities
12. (Appendix A) Comprehensive income

True/False

1. False   A company's current ratio will be greater than 1.0 only when its current assets are greater than its current liabilities.
2. False   The current ratio measures a company's liquidity.
3. False   Divide each line item on the income statement by net sales, not total assets.
4. True
5. False   The accounts receivable turnover ratio measures a company's liquidity.
6. True
7. False   Although a high price-earnings ratio may indicate that investors expect future growth, a high price-earnings ratio may also be the sign of an over-valued stock.
8. False   Some investors are dependent on dividend income and prefer stocks with a high dividend yield. However, many investors expect to profit from increases in the market price of the stock rather than dividends. For them, a low dividend yield is fine.
9. True
10. True
11. False   (Appendix A) Comprehensive income is net income plus other comprehensive income. The elements of other comprehensive income include losses as well as gains, so it's possible that comprehensive income will be smaller than net income.
12. False   (Appendix B) Trading securities are shown at their market value as of the balance sheet date.
13. True   (Appendix B)
14. False   (Appendix B) Available-for-sale securities are shown at their market value as of the balance sheet date.

Multiple Choice

1. C $1,000,000/$400,000 = 2.5
2. C   If Beta collects $100,000 of accounts receivable, its cash will increase $100,000 while its accounts receivable decrease $100,000. Total current assets will still be $1,000,000.
3. B   Buying additional inventory on the last day of the year will increase the amount in Inventory and increase the company's average inventory. Since the denominator (average inventory) is larger, the ratio will decrease.
4. B   Both current assets and current liabilities increase by $100,000. $1,100,000/$500,000 = 2.2

5. D Treasury stock is subtracted from shareholders' equity and reduces the number of shares held by those outside the company. With fewer shares outstanding, the denominator of the EPS calculation will be smaller, and earnings for each outstanding common share will be larger.

6. C Last year the company's gross profit was $6 per cap, which is 67% of sales. This year, gross profit will be only $5 per cap, or 56%.

7. A Right now the company's current ratio is $1,000,000/$500,000, or 2.0. If it pays $100,000 of accounts payable, both current assets and current liabilities will decrease by $100,000. $900,000/$400,000 = 2.25

8. B If a company collects its receivables more quickly, fewer dollars will remain uncollected in accounts receivable at any given point in time. The denominator of the accounts receivable turnover ratio will decrease, which increases the ratio itself.

9. B. Extraordinary items appear on the income statement after discontinued operations. They are shown net of tax. The $10,000,000 loss will result in a tax savings of 35% times $10,000,000, or $3,500,000. The overall impact of the extraordinary loss is to reduce income by $10,000,000 – 3,500,000 = $6,500,000.

10. D The debt-to-equity ratio compares the amount of debt financing the company already has to the amount of financing provided by its shareholders. A banker would look at this ratio to determine if a company could take on additional debt. The other ratios listed in this question are of more interest to shareholders than creditors.

Exercises

1.		Liquidity	Solvency	Profitability	Market indicator
a	Return on assets			X	
b	Profit margin ratio			X	
c	Current ratio	X			
d	Return on equity			X	
e	Debt-to-equity ratio		X		
f	Gross profit ratio			X	
g	Accounts receivable turnover ratio	X			
h	Dividend yield ratio				X
i	Inventory turnover ratio	X			
j	Cash from operations to current liabilities	X			
k	Earnings per share			X	
l	Price-earnings ratio				X
m	Asset turnover ratio			X	

2.

Buck's Better Bacon, Inc.
Income Statement
For the Year Ended December 31, 2012

Revenues		$900,000
Expenses		600,000
Income before taxes		300,000
Income tax expense		90,000
Income from continuing operations		210,000
Discontinued operations		
Income from discontinued operations, net of $1,500 tax	$3,500 [1]	
Gain or loss on disposal, net of $3,000 tax	7,000 [2]	10,500
Income before extraordinary item		220,500
Extraordinary loss from earthquake, net of $90,000 tax savings [3]		(210,000)
Net income		$ 10,500

---

[1] Revenue	$50,000
Expenses	45,000
Income before tax	5,000
Taxes (30%)	1,500
Net income	$ 3,500

[2] $10,000 gain x 30% = $3,000 tax

[3] The loss is tax deductible, so Buck's will save 30% x $300,000, or $90,000 in taxes. The $300,000 loss decreases income, but the $90,000 saved in taxes increases income, so the overall effect on profits is a decrease of $210,000.

CHAPTER 11
QUALITY OF EARNINGS, CORPORATE GOVERNANCE, AND IFRS

Chapter Overview

In this chapter, you will learn about the significance of earnings per share and the common ways management may manipulate earnings. You will also learn about the importance of effective corporate governance and how the Sarbanes-Oxley Act of 2002 is designed to help prevent future corporate misconduct. In addition, the differences between U.S. GAAP and IFRS are summarized at the end of the chapter.

Chapter Highlights

1. When evaluating a firm's performance, investors focus heavily on earnings per share. If a company's earnings do not meet Wall Street's and financial analysts' expectations, the company's stock price will most likely fall. This creates pressure for management to manipulate earnings in order to meet expectations. Manipulation compromises the quality of earnings and raises concerns that earnings reported to the public may not truly reflect a company's performance.

2. Two accounting authors, Leopold Bernstein and John Wild (*Analysis of Financial Statements),* say the quality of earnings is affected in three ways:

- Management's choice of accounting methods has an impact on the quality of earnings. Conservative choices, which report lower net income and lower assets or higher liabilities, tend to result in higher quality earnings. A conservative method of depreciating long-term assets would be choosing shorter estimated useful lives or lower salvage values, because this results in higher depreciation expense for the year and lower earnings. A conservative choice of inventory method, such as using LIFO rather than FIFO, leads to reporting higher cost of goods sold and lower net income and total assets. It also matches more current costs

with revenue, which many analysts believe gives higher quality earnings.

- The quality of earnings is also affected by the degree of risk a company faces. A company that faces fewer risks will tend to have higher quality earnings. The more risks a company faces, the more likely management will feel pressure to manipulate earnings.

- The quality of earnings will be lower for companies that record revenues early and/or expenses late.

3. Many of the accounts on the financial statements are estimates which require judgment. Although most managers and accountants do their best to make sound ethical judgments, the opportunity exists for making choices that inflate company earnings. There are three accounting procedures used to "**cook the books,**" which means to manipulate or falsify financial statements to make the company's performance look better or worse than it truly is.

- **Big bath** charges occur in an accounting period when a company's earnings per share will fail to meet investors' expectations. The theory is that management should maximize its loss in this period by recording expenses that belong in future accounting periods and by writing off assets that may need to be written off in future periods. Management's goal is to make the already bad year worse so that future earnings will look better without the expenses and write-offs that have already been reported. To identify this type of manipulation, you should look for unusual amounts of expenses and write-offs compared with previous years. You should also read the notes to the financial statements and management's discussion and analysis of the company in periodicals.

- **Cookie jar reserves** involve the estimated reserve accounts, such as allowance for uncollectible accounts and estimated warranty liability. Management may increase or decrease these reserves in order to manipulate earnings. If this year's earnings are going to be higher than investors' expectations, there is an incentive to smooth earnings by increasing current period expenses, which in turn increases the allowance accounts. This provides a larger reserve, or cookie jar, to dip into in future periods when earnings may not be meeting investors' expectations. Ratio analyses of the company's reserve accounts and reading the notes to the financial statements may help to identify this type of manipulation.

- Management may also manipulate earnings by recognizing revenues either too early or too late. GAAP requires that revenues be recorded when the earnings process is complete and collection is reasonably assured. This rule is open to interpretation and sometimes abused. Management abuses can range from recording revenues in the wrong accounting period to recording fictitious revenues. Reading the company's revenue recognition policy in the first note to the financial statements may help to identify these abuses. Ratio analysis such as accounts receivable to sales should also help to identify manipulation when the current year is compared with prior years.

4. Understanding the causes of the business failures of the past decade may help to prevent similar problems from occurring in the future. Over-reliance on earnings per share is part of the problem. Some executives manipulate earnings to bolster stock prices so they may benefit personally when selling their shares of the company's stock. Management's use of estimates and interpretations of accounting rules must be better disclosed in the financial statements. Top management must establish ethical behavior and demand it from others in the company, since the tone at the top has a large impact on the behavior of other employees in the company. Auditors have to be independent of their clients so they can be objective in performing audits. Steps to address these problems and issues should help reduce fraud,

although there is no way for accounting rules to completely stop fraud.

5. The Sarbanes-Oxley Act of 2002 (SOX) was enacted in response to the scandals and financial debacles of the early 2000's. The aim of the new regulation is to improve corporate governance. **Corporate governance** is the way a company governs itself and interacts with its board of directors, management, shareholders, auditors, and any others with a stake in the company. The following groups are directly impacted by SOX:

- Management is now required to include in the annual report a report on the effectiveness of the company's internal controls. The external auditors must attest to the accuracy of this report. The CEO and the CFO now must certify that they have reviewed the annual financial statements and swear that they are aware of no false statements or significant omissions. Management must provide a way, including a hotline, for anonymously reporting any fraudulent activity in the company. Management is not allowed to punish an employee for disclosing suspected fraud (whistle-blowing).

- The board of directors (BOD), elected by the shareholders to represent their interests, has an audit committee that oversees the company's financial matters. SOX requires that this audit committee be independent and have no members who are company managers. The audit committee is responsible for hiring, compensating, and overseeing the work of the company's external auditors (public accounting firm).

- External auditors are hired by the audit committee of the company's BOD and provide an opinion on whether the firm's financial statements fairly present the company's financial position and the results of operations in accordance with GAAP. SOX requires that the external auditors be independent of their clients and prohibits the auditors from also performing consulting services. The auditors are now required to report directly to the audit committee and not to the company's management team.

- The Public Company Accounting Oversight Board (PCAOB) was newly formed to regulate the auditing profession. The SEC appoints the members and approves all its rules. All publicly-traded companies are required to follow PCAOB rules.

A major criticism of SOX is that it is expensive to implement, particularly the requirement for establishing and reporting on the company's internal controls. However, this cost seems to be declining for many firms after the year of initial adoption. Some people argue that the real problem is a lack of managers' ethical values, which will not be solved by legislation. All business managers must be familiar with the accounting rules for their area and identify risks so that adequate internal controls may be adopted.

6. It is difficult to measure the quality of corporate governance. Many experts believe that the most important factor in good corporate governance is an ethical climate. Other attributes include:
- Highly qualified, experienced directors on the board who are independent of management

- Review of major management and financial decisions by the board of directors

- Transparent, easy-to-understand financial information for shareholders

- Independent, ethical auditors

To assess the quality of corporate governance, more investors are using rating systems provided by such companies as Moody's and others. Investors can also check companies' Web sites and annual reports or 10-Ks filed with the SEC for corporate governance policies. Another indication of a company's quality of corporate governance is the report on a company's internal control system and the results of the external auditors' review of the system.

7. The overall difference between U.S. GAAP and IFRS is that U.S. GAAP is generally described as rule based, while IFRS is generally described as principle based. Accounting choices improve the usefulness of financial information for users. Since no two businesses are exactly the same, management can choose the accounting treatment which best reflects the company's activities. IFRS, which should be fully implemented in the U.S. by 2014, provides less detailed guidance for financial reporting, so auditors will need to use more judgment in expressing their opinion on financial statements.

Both sets of standards have similar goals of providing useful information. Both require an accrual-based income statement, balance sheet, and statement of cash flows, although the format of the statements may be different. For example, a balance sheet prepared under IFRS, shown in Exhibit 11.2 of your textbook, reflects a different version of the basic accounting equation: Assets − Liabilities = Equity. The balance sheet shows long-term assets followed by current assets. However, current liabilities are still shown before long-term liabilities, and shareholders' equity is at the end.

Major differences between U.S. GAAP and IFRS include:
- IFRS does not allow LIFO inventory costing.

- U.S. GAAP generally define the lower-of-cost-or-market (LCM) for inventory as replacement cost. IFRS define LCM as net selling price, which is generally higher than replacement cost, so there will probably be fewer LCM write-downs under IFRS, which also allow reversals of previous LCM write-downs.

- IFRS allow property, plant, and equipment to be written up or down based on appraisals, and allow write-downs to be reversed in later years if the assets' values recover. U.S. GAAP require a write-down only in the case of an asset's impairment, and do not allow any reversal. U.S. GAAP never allow property, plant, and equipment's value to be increased to current appraisal value.

- U.S. GAAP require that research and development costs (R&D) be expensed when incurred, except for computer software development costs. IFRS still require that research be expensed, but allow development costs to be treated as assets and amortized over future periods.

- U.S. GAAP allow recognition of intangible assets only if they have been purchased from others outside the business. Internally-developed intangible assets such as patents or brand names are not recognized as assets under U.S. GAAP. IFRS, on the other hand, allow recognition of internally-developed intangible assets if their future benefit is probable and can be measured reliably.

- IFRS require more reporting of contingent liabilities. Both probable and reasonably possible contingent liabilities must be reported in the body of the financial statements under IFRS. On the other hand, U.S. GAAP require financial statement presentation only for probable contingent liabilities, but allow reasonably possible contingent liabilities to be reported only in the notes to the financial statements.

- U.S. GAAP allow special separate treatment at the bottom of the income statement for extraordinary items that are both unusual and infrequent. IFRS do not allow special treatment, but require that extraordinary items be reported as part of income from continuing operations.

- On the statement of cash flows, U.S. GAAP include interest received and interest paid as part of cash from operating activities. IFRS allow interest received to be either an operating activity or an investing activity. Interest paid may be either an operating activity or a financing activity.

Featured Exercise

Part A: Identify whether each of the following will make earnings per share higher, lower, or not affected by putting an X in the correct column.

	Krupt, Inc.	Higher	Lower	Not affected
1.	included in its sales for the year the goods that were delivered FOB destination at year end but had not yet arrived at the buyer's place of business.			
2.	included goods in inventory that were purchased FOB shipping point at year end but had not yet arrived.			
3.	recorded the repair of its trucks as a capital expenditure.			
4.	estimated the useful lives of the majority of its long-term assets to be five years when the industry average is more like ten years.			
5.	repurchased 40% of its shares outstanding at year end in order to inflate the price of its stock.			

Part B: For each of the following, identify whether Krupt, Inc.'s manipulations are considered "Big Bath Charges," "Cookie Jar Reserve," and/or "Revenue Recognition" manipulations. There can be more than one correct answer for each.

	Krupt, Inc.	Big Bath Charges	Cookie Jar Reserve	Revenue Recognition
1.	included in its sales for the year the goods that were delivered FOB destination at year end but had not yet arrived at the buyer's place of business.			
2.	overstated its bad debts expense.			
3.	recorded many capital expenditures as revenue expenditures.			
4.	underestimated its warranty expense.			
5.	wrote off 30% of its intangible assets which were still considered to have future economic benefit.			

Part C: Describe the new responsibilities or changes required by SOX for each of the following groups:

1. Management:

2. Board of directors:

3. External auditors:

4. Public Company Accounting Oversight Board:

Part D: Put an X in the appropriate box to identify each accounting treatment as U.S. GAAP or IFRS. Some items may be both U.S. GAAP and IFRS.

	Accounting treatment	U.S. GAAP	IFRS
1.	Require a statement of cash flows		
2.	Allow recognition of internally-developed intangible assets if their future benefit is probable and can be measured reliably		
3.	Require that development costs be expensed when incurred, except for computer software development costs		
4.	Require accrual accounting		
5.	Allow LIFO for inventory valuation		
6.	Allow special separate treatment at the bottom of the income statement for extraordinary items		
7.	Allow development costs for all projects to be treated as assets and amortized over future periods		
8.	Never allow property, plant, and equipment's value to be increased to current appraisal value		
9.	Allow choices among acceptable accounting treatments		
10.	Often described as principle based		

Solution

Part A:

	Krupt, Inc.	Higher	Lower	Not affected
1.	included in its sales for the year the goods that were delivered FOB destination at year end but had not yet arrived at the buyer's place of business.	X		
2.	included in inventory the goods that were purchased FOB shipping point at year end but had not yet arrived.			X
3.	recorded the repair of its trucks as capital expenditures.	X		
4.	estimated the useful lives of the majority of its long-term assets to be five years when the industry average is more like ten years.		X	
5.	repurchased 40% of its shares outstanding at year end in order to inflate the price of its stock.	X		

Part B:

	Krupt, Inc.	Big Bath Charges	Cookie Jar Reserve	Revenue Recognition
1.	included in its sales for the year the goods that were delivered FOB destination at year end but had not yet arrived at the buyer's place of business.			X
2.	overstated its bad debts expense.	X	X	
3.	recorded many capital expenditures as revenue expenditures.	X		
4.	underestimated its warranty expense.		X	
5.	wrote off 30% of its intangible assets which were still considered to have future economic benefit.	X		

Part C:
1. Management must report on the internal controls. The CEO and CFO must certify that they are unaware of any false statements in or omissions from the annual financial statements. They must provide means for anonymous reporting of fraudulent activity.
2. The board of directors is required to have an audit committee of independent directors which cannot include company management.
3. The external auditors must be independent of and not perform consulting services for their clients. They must report directly to the audit committee and not to the company's managers.
4. The PCAOB was newly formed to regulate the auditing profession.

Part D:

	Accounting treatment	U.S. GAAP	IFRS
1.	Require a statement of cash flows	X	X
2.	Allow recognition of internally-developed intangible assets if their future benefit is probable and can be measured reliably		X
3.	Require that development costs be expensed when incurred, except for computer software development costs	X	
4.	Require accrual accounting	X	X
5.	Allow LIFO for inventory valuation	X	
6.	Allow special separate treatment at the bottom of the income statement for extraordinary items	X	
7.	Allow development costs for all projects to be treated as an asset and amortized over future periods		X
8.	Never allow property, plant, and equipment's value to be increased to current appraisal value	X	
9.	Allow choices among acceptable accounting treatments	X	X
10.	Often described as principle based		X

Review Questions and Exercises

Completion Statements

Fill in the blank(s) to complete each statement.

1. _____ is net income divided by the weighted average number of outstanding shares of (common) stock.

2. _____ the _____ is a slang term that means to manipulate or falsify the firm's accounting records to make the firm's financial performance or position look better than it actually is.

3. The _____ theory is the type of manipulation where management maximizes a current loss to get rid of expenses that belong on future years' income statements.

4. The term for manipulating earnings by misstating reserves such as the allowance for uncollectible accounts is called _____ reserves.

5. _____ describes how a firm governs itself and is executed by the board of directors.

True/False

Indicate whether each statement is true (T) or false (F).

_____ 1. External auditors are required to audit all publicly-traded companies' internal control systems and write an opinion which is to be included with each company's annual report.

_____ 2. The cookie jar reserve is a term used to describe the manipulation of earnings by misstating allowance and/or reserve accounts.

_____ 3. The quality of earnings per share is improved when a company chooses an inventory method that results in a lower cost of goods sold.

_____ 4. The SOX Act requires external auditors to report directly to management to avoid any miscommunication.

_____ 5. The purpose of the PCAOB is to regulate the auditing profession.

_____ 6. IFRS is another term for U.S. GAAP.

_____ 7. Both U.S. GAAP and IFRS allow recognition of internally-developed intangible assets.

_____ 8. IFRS allow long-term assets to be written up or down based on appraisals.

_____ 9. U.S. GAAP provide more detailed rules for accountants to follow than IFRS.

_____ 10. U.S. GAAP require accrual accounting while IFRS allows cash-basis accounting.

Multiple Choice

_____ 1. Which of the following may indicate a company is manipulating earnings using big bath charges?
A. Higher than usual revenues for the year
B. Higher than usual expenses for the year
C. Lower than usual allowance for uncollectible accounts at year-end
D. Lower than usual payables at year-end

_____ 2. Which of the following is a new requirement imposed by the SOX Act?
A. The CFO must be part of the audit committee.
B. The external auditors must oversee the PCAOB.
C. Management is required to have external auditors assess and give an opinion as to the effectiveness of the company's internal control system.
D. All of the above are new requirements.

_____ 3. The quality of earnings is considered to be higher if:
A. management chooses the conservative methods of accounting.
B. the level of internal and external risks of the company is higher.
C. the revenues are recognized early or expenses are postponed to a later period.
D. All of the above will lead to higher quality of earnings.

_____ 4. Which of the following is an indication of good corporate governance?
   A. Boards of directors are independent of management.
   B. Boards of directors are involved in major managerial and financial decisions.
   C. Financial statements are transparent.
   D. All of the above indicate good corporate governance.

_____ 5. The SOX Act now requires external auditors to:
   A. no longer provide information processing consulting services to their audit clients.
   B. assess and give an opinion on the effectiveness of the board of directors.
   C. be paid by the PCAOB instead of their audit clients in order to strengthen independence.
   D. be on the client's board of directors.

USE THE FOLLOWING INFORMATION TO ANSWER THE NEXT TWO QUESTIONS:
This month Tom's Wear tried calculating its bad debts expense two different ways. Using a percentage of credit sales, bad debts expense would be $1,500. Based on an aging of accounts receivable, however, bad debts expense would be $1,750.

_____ 6. If Tom's Wear decides to report $1,750 of bad debts expense, this accounting choice would be considered:
   A. conservative.   C. basic.
   B. fundamental.   D. aggressive.

_____ 7. If Tom's Wear decides to report $1,500 of bad debts expense, this accounting choice would be considered:
   A. conservative.   C. basic.
   B. fundamental.   D. aggressive.

_____ 8. Who is ultimately responsible for the accuracy of a company's financial statements?
   A. management
   B. the board of directors
   C. the external auditors
   D. the PCAOB

_____ 9. Who is responsible for giving an opinion on whether or not a company's financial statements fairly present the company's financial position and results of operations?
   A. management
   B. the board of directors
   C. the external auditors
   D. the PCAOB

_____ 10. PharmX spent $5,000,000 this year on research and $2,000,000 on development of a new product. Under IFRS, the company's earnings will be _____ under U.S. GAAP.
   A. higher than
   B. lower than
   C. the same as

Exercises

1. Put an X in the appropriate box to identify each of the following as overstating, understating, or not affecting earnings per share.

		Overstating	Understating	Not affecting
a.	Recorded capital expenditures as revenue expenditures			
b.	Depreciated land			
c.	Overstated the allowance for uncollectible accounts			
d.	Reported a current liability as a long-term liability			
e.	Paid a cash dividend to all shares outstanding			

2. Match each group with its new responsibilities required by the SOX Act.

_____ Management   A. Reports directly to the audit committee, not the executives

_____ Board of directors   B. Members are appointed by the SEC

_____ External auditors   C. Includes an audit committee independent of company executives

_____ PCAOB   D. Must provide a mechanism for anonymous reporting of fraudulent activities.

3. Ace Electronics just spent $200,000 to buy forty new electronic cash registers for its chain of stores. Due to rapid changes in technology, Ace expects to use these cash registers for four or five years, after which they will be worthless because they are obsolete.

a. How much depreciation expense will Ace record each year using the straight-line method and an estimated useful life of four years?

b. How much depreciation expense will Ace record each year using the straight-line method and an estimated useful life of five years?

c. If Ace has 1,000,000 weighted-average shares of common stock outstanding, how much difference will the choice of useful life make in the company's earnings per share?

d. Which useful life would be considered aggressive? _____

e. Which useful life would improve the quality of Acme's earnings? _____

4. American Enterprises, Inc., has been preparing its financial statements using U.S. GAAP. For each of the following items, show the financial statement effect of reporting the event under IFRS instead of U.S. GAAP.

a. American Enterprises has been valuing its inventory using LIFO, which is not allowed under IFRS. Prices have been rising slowly but steadily. If the company switches to FIFO, so that it can issue financial statements under IFRS, then:

Inventory on the balance sheet will be (circle one)   higher   lower   the same

Total assets will be (circle one)   higher   lower   the same

Cost of goods sold will be (circle one)   higher   lower   the same

Net income will be (circle one)   higher   lower   the same

b. American Enterprises has a factory which cost $10,000,000 and has accumulated depreciation of $4,000,000. A recent independent appraisal found that the market value of the factory is $13,000,000. Under IFRS:

PP&E on the balance sheet could be (circle one)   higher   lower

c. American Enterprises spent $1,000,000 this year to develop its AmFam trademark internally. Under IFRS:

Total assets will be (circle one)   higher   lower   the same

Total operating expenses will be (circle one)   higher   lower   the same

Net income will be (circle one)   higher   lower   the same

Solutions

Completion Statements
1. Earnings per share
2. Cooking (the) books
3. big bath
4. cookie jar
5. Corporate governance

True/False
1. True
2. True
3. False   The quality of earnings improves when a company chooses the more conservative method which yields lower net income and total assets. The inventory method that results in a lower cost of goods sold and higher reported net income is not conservative.
4. False   The external auditors must report directly to the audit committee and board of directors, not management.
5. True
6. False   There are many differences between U.S. GAAP (generally accepted accounting principles) and IFRS (international financial reporting standards).
7. False   U.S. GAAP allow recognition of purchased intangible assets, but not of internally-developed intangible assets.
8. True
9. True
10. False   Both U.S. GAAP and IFRS require accrual accounting.

Multiple Choice
1. B   Big bath charges maximize an already losing company's losses in that period by recording expenses that belong in future accounting periods and writing off assets that may need to be written off in future periods. A is incorrect because big bath charges relate to overstating expenses, not revenues. C is wrong because manipulating allowances (or reserves) downward results in expenses being understated, not overstated. D is incorrect because payables would be overstated, not understated.
2. C   A is wrong because the audit committee must be independent of management in order to ensure objectivity. B is incorrect because the PCAOB oversees the external auditors.
3. A   B is incorrect because the higher the risks, the higher the potential for manipulated earnings. C is incorrect because quality is diminished if revenues are overstated and expenses are understated.
4. D
5. A   B is incorrect because the auditors report to, not on, the board of directors. C is incorrect because the auditors are paid by their clients, not the PCAOB. D is incorrect because the auditors must be independent of their clients.
6. A   If Tom's Wear reports higher bad debts expense, then reported net income and total assets will be lower, which is a conservative choice.
7. D   If Tom's Wear reports lower bad debts expense, then reported net income and total assets will be higher, which is an aggressive choice.
8. A
9. C
10. A   Under U.S. GAAP, PharmX must report both research and development costs as expenses. Under IFRS, PharmX could report the $2,000,000 of development costs as an asset, which would be amortized over the life of the new product. Less expense would appear on the IFRS income statement this year, so earnings would be higher under IFRS.

Exercises

1.		Overstating	Understating	Not affecting
a.	Recorded capital expenditures as revenue expenditures		X	
b.	Depreciated land		X	
c.	Overstated the allowance for uncollectible accounts		X	
d.	Reported a current liability as a long-term liability			X
e.	Paid a cash dividend to all shares outstanding			X

2. Management: D   Board of directors: C   External auditors: A   PCAOB: B

3.
    a. ($200,000 − 0) / 4 years = $50,000
    b. ($200,000 − 0) / 5 years = $40,000
    c. (50,000 − 40,000) / 1,000,000 shares = $0.01 per share
    d. five years, because it leads to reporting lower expenses and higher income
    e. four years, because it leads to reporting higher expenses and lower income, so net income and total assets are less likely to be overstated

4.
    a. FIFO uses older, lower prices for cost of goods sold and newer, higher prices for inventory
      Inventory on the balance sheet will be **higher**
      Total assets will be **higher**
      Cost of goods sold will be **lower**
      Net income will be **higher**
    b. IFRS allows assets to be written up to appraisal values.
      PP&E on the balance sheet could be **higher**
    c. IFRS allows companies to capitalize the costs of internally-developed intangible assets such as trademarks. These costs must be expensed under U.S. GAAP.
      Total assets will be **higher**
      Total operating expenses will be **lower**
      Net income will be **higher**

APPENDIX B
THE MECHANICS OF AN ACCOUNTING SYSTEM

Chapter Overview

This chapter covers the mechanics of the accounting information system. The accounting information system is referred to as the **general ledger system** and is where financial events are recorded, summarized, and reported. The general ledger system is often a small part of many large companies' integrated information systems called **enterprise-wide resource planning systems (ERP)**. ERP's include accounting information along with data for other parts of the business like marketing, production, and human resources. This chapter will focus on a manual general ledger system so that you can better understand how information is recorded, classified, and summarized for the financial statements in a computerized system.

Chapter Highlights

1. The accounting equation worksheet that we have been using to record business events is too awkward to use for a real-world company that has a large number of transactions. Accountants use a **general ledger system** to keep track of a company's financial transactions. Information from this system can be used to prepare the four basic financial statements.

2. As transactions occur, they are recorded by a bookkeeper in a **journal**. Some companies have separate journals for frequently recurring events like sales, cash receipts, and cash payments. Each journal entry shows the date of the transaction, the specific accounts and dollar amounts involved, and a brief explanation of the event. Since the journal lists events in chronological order, it is difficult to use in preparing financial statements when there are many transactions.

3. To make statement preparation easier, all events in the journal are copied, or **posted**, to another book, called the **general ledger**, which has a separate page for each account. The general ledger page for a particular account shows all the increases and decreases to that account and calculates a running balance. Every company must decide how many accounts it wants to use to keep track of financial events. Some companies that want to have detailed information will have many hundreds of accounts, while smaller companies may have only a few dozen. Most companies combine similar accounts when they prepare financial statements, so the statements do not show all the underlying detail that is in the general ledger.

4. Before a company prepares financial statements, it will prepare a **trial balance**, a list of all the accounts in the general ledger with their balances. The trial balance is reviewed to decide which accounts need adjustments so that the income statement will reflect all revenue earned and all expenses incurred during the accounting period.

5. Accountants use a system of debits and credits to record financial events in the journal and ledger. **Debit (DR)** means the left side of an account and **credit (CR)** means the right side. Look at the accounting equation:

$$\text{Assets} = \text{Liabilities} + \text{Shareholders' equity}$$

- Assets are on the left-hand side of the accounting equation, and are increased with left-handed, debit entries. If debits make assets go up, then credits make them go down.

- Liabilities are on the right-hand side of the accounting equation, and are increased with right-handed, credit entries. If credits make liabilities go up, then debits make them go down.

- Shareholders' equity, on the right-hand side of the accounting equation, is increased with right-handed, credit entries. Shareholders' equity is decreased by debit entries. Revenue, which increases shareholders' equity, is increased with a credit entry. Expenses decrease shareholders' equity. An increase in an expense is a decrease in shareholders' equity, a debit entry. Dividends also decrease shareholders' equity, a debit entry.

- Recording a debit entry is called **debiting** an account. Recording a credit entry is called **crediting** an account.

6. The general ledger, which has a separate page for each account, usually has separate columns for debits, credits, and each account's running balance. Accountants often use **T-accounts** to represent pages in the general ledger.

- The **normal balance** of an account is the type of entry (either debit or credit) that increases the account. For example, the normal balance of an asset account is a debit balance, because debits increase assets.

Asset	
increases with a debit entry (normal balance)	

Liability	
	increases with a credit entry (normal balance)

Shareholders' equity	
	increases with a credit entry (normal balance)

Revenue	
	increases with a credit entry (normal balance)

Expense	
increases with a debit entry (normal balance)	

- For any journal entry, the dollars of debits must always equal the dollars of credits, just as the accounting equation must always balance.

7. The **accounting cycle** is a system for recording and summarizing financial information to produce financial statements.

- The first step in the accounting cycle is recording journal entries as business events take place. For example, if a business collects $500 in cash for services performed for a client, the business needs to record a $500 increase in the asset Cash and $500 of Revenue, which increases shareholders' equity.

Date	Transaction	Debit	Credit
1/1/01	Cash	500	
	Revenue		500
	To record revenue earned	1-1	

The debit entry is always shown first. Some entries may have more than one debit. The credit entry follows all of the debit(s) and is always indented. Each journal entry also includes the date and a brief explanation of the business event that is being recorded. The "1-1" is a reference number so that the journal entries can be traced to the general ledger or vice versa.

- The next step in the accounting cycle is posting from the journal to the general ledger. This is usually done on a daily or weekly basis. Using T-accounts to represent pages in the general ledger, the revenue transaction shown above would be posted as follows:

Cash		Revenue	
1-1 500			500 1-1

- At the end of every accounting period, the accountant prepares an **unadjusted trial balance**, a three-column list of all accounts in the general ledger with their debit or credit ending balances.

Account	DR	CR

The debits and credits are shown in separate columns so that the accountant can see that total debits equal total credits. The accountant uses this unadjusted trial balance to review all of the account balances and identify those accounts that require adjusting entries. These are needed so that the income statement will properly reflect all revenue earned and all expenses incurred during the accounting period. Adjustments always affect balance sheet accounts as well.

- Step four is to prepare and post adjusting journal entries. Adjusting entries include the following: 1) Accrued revenues must be recorded for revenue earned, even if cash has not yet been collected. 2) Accrued expenses must be recorded, so that the income statement will show all expenses incurred to earn revenue, even if payment has not yet been made. 3) Deferred revenues which were originally recorded as Unearned revenue, a liability because cash was received from customers before goods or services were delivered, may need to be adjusted. The accountant examines all deferred revenue accounts to determine how much revenue has been earned and decreases the liability accounts and increases Sales or Service revenue accounts. 4) Finally, deferred expenses, where the company paid in advance for items before they were used in the business, may need to be adjusted for the amounts used. For instance, the assets Prepaids and Supplies used up to generate revenue must be decreased and the related expense accounts increased.

- The next step in the accounting cycle is to prepare an **adjusted trial balance**. Like all trial balances, this is simply a three-column list of all the accounts in the general ledger with their debit or credit balances. If the total debits equal the total credits, and all accounts that need adjustment have been properly adjusted, this adjusted trial balance can be used to prepare the financial statements.

- Preparation of the four basic financial statements is the next step. The accountant prepares the income statement, statement of changes in shareholders' equity, balance sheet, and statement of cash flows.

- After the financial statements have been prepared, the accountant must get the general ledger ready to record events for the next fiscal year. Revenue accounts, expense accounts, and Dividends are **temporary accounts**. All amounts in these accounts are transferred to Retained earnings through a process called **closing the accounts**. Their balances are reduced to zero so that they can be used to accumulate revenues, expenses, and dividends for the next year. The current year's revenue, expenses, and dividends will not be combined with prior years' revenue, expenses, and dividends.

Revenue accounts are closed by debiting the separate revenue accounts for the amount of their ending, credit balances, and making a single, offsetting credit to Retained earnings. For example, suppose the Sales account has a credit balance of $400,000, representing all of the sales revenue the company has earned for the fiscal year. This account would be closed by debiting Sales for $400,000 and crediting Retained earnings for $400,000. Now the balance in Sales is zero and Retained earnings has increased by $400,000. The Sales account can now be used to record sales for the next fiscal year.

All expense accounts are closed in a similar way. However, expense accounts normally have debit balances. They usually are closed by making a single debit entry to Retained earnings for the total of all expenses, and making separate credit entries to each individual expense account. After this journal entry is posted, all of the expense accounts have zero balances and Retained earnings has decreased by the amount of all the fiscal year's expenses. The expense accounts are now ready to be used for the next year.

Corporations often use an account called Dividends that is debited when dividends are declared by the board of directors. Although dividends are not expenses, this account is also closed to Retained earnings by debiting Retained earnings and crediting Dividends.

After **closing entries** have been made, the balance in Retained earnings, a shareholders' equity account, has been increased by revenues and decreased by expenses and dividends. Now the balance sheet should balance because total assets equal total liabilities plus total shareholders' equity.

Asset accounts, liability accounts, and shareholders' equity accounts are **permanent accounts** or **real accounts**. Their balances are not reduced to zero at the end of the fiscal year. Instead, the ending balances in these accounts become the beginning balances for the following year.

- The final step in the accounting cycle is preparing a **post-closing trial balance**. Like any other trial balance, this is a three-column list of accounts with their debit or credit balances. However, only balance sheet accounts appear on the post-closing trial balance because the revenue, expense, and dividends accounts have zero balances. The accountant uses this trial balance to check that debits equal credits and to make sure that all the temporary accounts have been properly closed.

Featured Exercise

Part A: Tom's Wares, Inc. is in its second month of business. Complete Tom's Wares' general journal by recording the transactions based on the descriptions given below (for account titles, see the general ledger on the following page):

GENERAL JOURNAL

Date	Transaction	Debit	Credit
3/1			
	1) Collected $5,000 from a customer for goods to be delivered next month		
3/1			
	2) Delivered $4,000 of goods that cost $2,500 to a customer who had paid in the prior month		
3/1			
	3) Borrowed $16,000 on a 10-month, 6% note payable		
3/3			
	4) Paid $800 of its accounts payable		
3/21			
	5) Paid $900 to its employee for work performed during the month		
3/31			
	6) Declared and paid a $500 cash dividend to its shareholder		

Part B: Post the journal entries above to the general ledger below (BB equals beginning balance):

GENERAL LEDGER

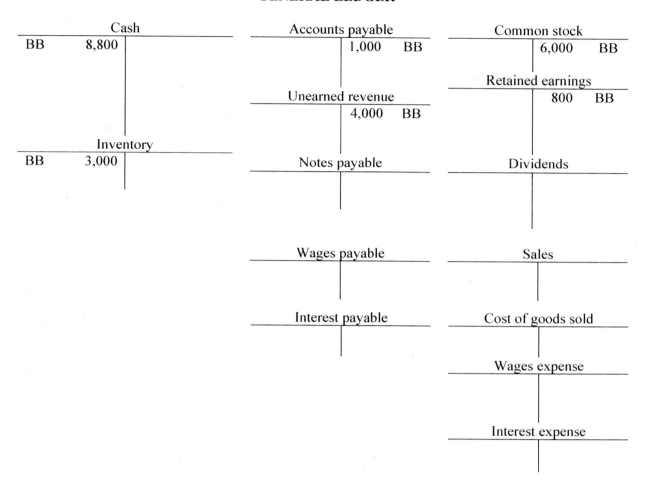

Part C: Prepare the Unadjusted Trial Balance at March 31, 2012 below:

Tom's Wares, Inc. Unadjusted Trial Balance March 31, 2012		
	Debit	**Credit**
Cash		
Inventory		
Accounts payable		
Unearned revenue		
Notes payable		
Common stock		
Retained earnings		
Dividends		
Sales		
Cost of goods sold		
Wages expense		
Totals		

Part D: Record the necessary adjusting entries below:

GENERAL JOURNAL (continued)

Date	Transaction	Debit	Credit
3/31			
	A1) Recorded interest on the $16,000, 10-month, 6% note payable		
3/31			
	A2) Recorded the $300 owed to its employee for work performed in the last week of March. Payday is on April 3.		

Part E: Post the adjusting entries from Part D to the general ledger (T-accounts) on the previous page and then prepare the Adjusted Trial Balance at March 31, 2012 below:

Tom's Wares, Inc. Adjusted Trial Balance March 31, 2012		
	Debit	**Credit**
Cash		
Inventory		
Accounts payable		
Unearned revenue		
Notes payable		
Interest payable		
Wages payable		
Common stock		
Retained earnings		
Dividends		
Sales		
Cost of goods sold		
Wages expense		
Interest expense		
Totals		

Part F: After the financial statements are prepared, the closing entries are recorded in the general journal. Record the closing entries below:

GENERAL JOURNAL (continued)

Date	Transaction	Debit	Credit
3/31			
	C1) Closed the revenue account to retained earnings		
3/31			
	C 2) Closed the expense accounts to retained earnings		
3/31			
	C3) Closed dividends to retained earnings		

Part G: Post the closing entries from Part F to the general ledger (T-accounts) in Part B and prepare the Post-Closing Trial Balance at March 31, 2012 below:

Tom's Wares, Inc. Post-Closing Trial Balance March 31, 2012		
	Debit	**Credit**
Cash		
Inventory		
Accounts payable		
Unearned revenue		
Notes payable		
Interest payable		
Wages payable		
Common stock		
Retained earnings		
Totals		

Solution

Part A:

GENERAL JOURNAL

Date	Transaction	Debit	Credit
3/1	Cash	5,000	
	Unearned revenue		5,000
	1) Collected $5,000 from a customer for goods to be delivered next month		
3/1	Unearned revenue	4,000	
	Cost of goods sold	2,500	
	Sales		4,000
	Inventory		2,500
	2) Delivered $4,000 of goods that cost $2,500 to a customer who had paid in the prior month		
3/1	Cash	16,000	
	Notes payable		16,000
	3) Borrowed $16,000 on a 10-month, 6% note payable		
3/3	Accounts payable	800	
	Cash		800
	4) Paid $800 of its accounts payable		
3/21	Wages expense	900	
	Cash		900
	5) Paid $900 to its employee for work performed during the month		
3/31	Dividends	500	
	Cash		500
	6) Declared and paid a $500 cash dividend to its shareholder		

Part B:

GENERAL LEDGER

Cash

BB	8,800		
3/1	5,000		
3/1	16,000		
		800	3/3
		900	3/21
		500	3/31

Inventory

BB	3,000		
		2,500	3/1

Accounts payable

		1,000	BB
3/3	800		

Unearned revenue

		4,000	BB
		5,000	3/1
3/1	4,000		

Notes payable

	16,000	3/1

Wages payable

	300	A2

Interest payable

	80	A1

Common stock

	6,000	BB

Retained earnings

		800	BB
		4,000	C1
C2	3,780		
C3	500		

Dividends

3/31	500		
		500	C3

Sales

		4,000	3/1
C1	4,000		

Cost of goods sold

3/1	2,500		
		2,500	C2

Wages expense

3/21	900		
A2	300		
		1,200	C2

Interest expense

A1	80		
		80	C2

Part C:

Tom's Wares, Inc. Unadjusted Trial Balance March 31, 2012	Debit	Credit
Cash	27,600	
Inventory	500	
Accounts payable		200
Unearned revenue		5,000
Notes payable		16,000
Common stock		6,000
Retained earnings		800
Dividends	500	
Sales		4,000
Cost of goods sold	2,500	
Wages expense	900	
Totals	32,000	32,000

Part D:

GENERAL JOURNAL (continued)

Date	Transaction	Debit	Credit
3/31	Interest expense	80	
	Interest payable		80
	A1) Recorded interest on the $16,000, 10-month, 6% note payable		
3/31	Wages expense	300	
	Wages payable		300
	A2) Recorded the $300 owed to its employee for work performed in the last week of March. Payday is on April 3.		

Part E:

Tom's Wares, Inc. Adjusted Trial Balance March 31, 2012	Debit	Credit
Cash	27,600	
Inventory	500	
Accounts payable		200
Unearned revenue		5,000
Notes payable		16,000
Interest payable		80
Wages payable		300
Common stock		6,000
Retained earnings		800
Dividends	500	
Sales		4,000
Cost of goods sold	2,500	
Wages expense	1,200	
Interest expense	80	
Totals	32,380	32,380

Part F: **GENERAL JOURNAL** (continued)

Date	Transaction	Debit	Credit
3/31	Sales	4,000	
	Retained earnings		4,000
	C1) Closed the revenue account to retained earnings		
3/31	Retained earnings	3,780	
	Cost of goods sold		2,500
	Wages expense		1,200
	Interest expense		80
	C 2) Closed the expense accounts to retained earnings		
3/31	Retained earnings	500	
	Dividends		500
	C3) Closed dividends to retained earnings		

Part G:

Tom's Wares, Inc. Post-Closing Trial Balance March 31, 2012		
	Debit	**Credit**
Cash	27,600	
Inventory	500	
Accounts payable		200
Unearned revenue		5,000
Notes payable		16,000
Interest payable		80
Wages payable		300
Common stock		6,000
Retained earnings		520
Totals	28,100	28,100

Review Questions and Exercises

Completion Statements

Fill in the blank(s) to complete each statement.

1. As transactions occur, they are recorded in a _____.

2. The transactions listed in the journal are copied to another book called the _____.

3. The process of entering data in the general ledger is called _____.

4. Expenses are increased with _____ entries.

5. A(n) _____ is a list of all accounts and their debit or credit balances.

6. Distributions to corporate shareholders are called _____.

7. Revenues are increased with _____ entries.

8. Asset accounts, liability accounts, and shareholders' equity accounts are _____ accounts because their balances are not reduced to zero at the end of the fiscal year.

9. Revenue, expense, and dividend accounts are _____ accounts because their balances are reduced to zero at the end of a fiscal year by transferring amounts to Retained earnings.

10. ERP stands for _____system.

True/False

Indicate whether each statement is true (T) or false (F).

_____1. ERP stands for electronic reporting principles.

_____2. The journal groups together transactions that affect a particular account.

_____3. Assets are decreased with debit entries.

_____4. Revenue accounts are closed by debiting them and crediting Retained earnings.

_____5. Preparing a post-closing trial balance is an unnecessary extra step because it just repeats the information found on the balance sheet.

_____6. Revenue, expense, and dividend accounts must be closed before financial statements can be prepared.

_____7. Accounting information is only one part of an enterprise-wide resource planning system.

_____8. For every journal entry, the dollar amount of debits must equal the dollar amount of credits.

_____9. All accounts begin each fiscal year with zero balances.

_____10. Adjusting entries must be prepared before financial statements are prepared.

Multiple Choice

Select the best answer for each question.

_____1. The adjusting entry to accrue interest on a note payable will include:
A. a debit to Interest revenue.
B. a debit to Interest receivable.
C. a debit to Interest expense.
D. a debit to Interest payable.

_____ 2. The adjusting entry to record depreciation on equipment will include:
   A. a credit to Equipment.
   B. a credit to Depreciation expense.
   C. a credit to Accumulated depreciation.
   D. a credit to Cash.

_____ 3. Which of the following events will cause the adjusted trial balance to be out of balance?
   A. An adjusting entry to record the cost of supplies used was recorded as a $200 debit to Supplies expense and a $200 debit to Supplies.
   B. An adjusting entry to record the amount of prepaid insurance that had expired was recorded as a $100 debit to Insurance expense and a $100 credit to Prepaid insurance. However, the $100 amount of the adjusting entry was wrong because $300 of insurance had actually expired.
   C. Both A and B will cause the adjusted trial balance to be out of balance.
   D. Neither A nor B will cause the adjusted trial balance to be out of balance.

_____ 4. On October 1, Team Shirts, Inc., accepted a $500 advance payment from a customer. This event was recorded as a debit to Cash and a credit to Unearned revenue. On October 10, Team Shirts delivered the merchandise to the customer, but made no additional journal entry. Before Team Shirts prepares financial statements, the company must:
   A. do nothing. The cash receipt was properly recorded when the advance payment was received from the customer.
   B. prepare a closing entry to reduce the balance in Unearned revenue to zero.
   C. record another journal entry that debits Cash and credits Sales.
   D. prepare an adjusting entry that debits Unearned revenue and credits Sales.

_____ 5. Which of the following events will cause the adjusted trial balance to be out of balance?
   A. An entire day's worth of transactions were not posted from the journal to the general ledger.
   B. An adjusting entry to record the $400 of prepaid rent that had expired was recorded as a debit to Prepaid rent and a credit to Rent expense.
   C. Both A and B will cause the adjusted trial balance to be out of balance.
   D. Neither A nor B will cause the adjusted trial balance to be out of balance.

_____ 6. Which of the following items are increased with debit entries?
   A. Assets and liabilities
   B. Assets and revenues
   C. Assets and expenses
   D. Assets and shareholders' equity

_____ 7. For each journal entry, the total debits _____ equal the total credits.
   A. sometimes
   B. usually
   C. always
   D. never

_____ 8. Closing entries:
   A. are prepared to prove that debits equal credits.
   B. are prepared before financial statements.
   C. get the temporary accounts ready for the next accounting period.
   D. always increase a corporation's retained earnings.

_____ 9. An ERP includes:
   A. accounting information for financial statements.
   B. human resources information.
   C. information about production and distribution of products.
   D. all of these.

Exercises

1. First put an X in the appropriate box to identify each of these accounts as an asset, liability, shareholders' equity, revenue, or expense account. Then indicate the normal balance of the account with a DR or CR. Finally, identify each account as permanent (P) or temporary (T).

	Account	Asset	Liability	Share-holders' equity	Revenue	Expense	Normal balance	Permanent or temporary
a	Cash							
b	Accounts receivable							
c	Sales							
d	Unearned revenue							
e	Inventory							
f	Cost of goods sold							
g	Accounts payable							
h	Prepaid insurance							
i	Insurance expense							
j	Notes receivable							
k	Interest revenue							
l	Interest receivable							
m	Notes payable							
n	Interest expense							
o	Interest payable							
p	Equipment							
q	Depreciation expense							
r	Accumulated depreciation							
s	Salary expense							
t	Salaries payable							
u	Common stock							
v	Retained earnings							
w	Dividends							
x	Prepaid rent							
y	Rent expense							
z	Other payables							

2. Prepare the journal entries needed for each of the following situations.

a. On April 1, 2012, Tim's Ware sold merchandise for $800. Twenty percent of the customers paid cash and the rest promised to pay next month. The merchandise originally cost Tim's Ware $500.

Record the sale.

Date	Transaction	Debit	Credit

Record the cost of goods sold.

Date	Transaction	Debit	Credit

b. On December 31, 2012, the unadjusted trial balance shows Supplies of $300. However, only $50 of supplies remain. Prepare the adjusting journal entry at December 31, 2012.

Date	Transaction	Debit	Credit

c. In March of 2010, Able Bakery bought a delivery van that cost $25,000, expecting to use the van for five years. Able Bakery does not prepare monthly financial statements, so it makes adjusting entries only once a year. Prepare the adjusting journal entry at December 31, 2012 using straight-line depreciation.

Date	Transaction	Debit	Credit

d. On December 31, 2012, the unadjusted trial balance for Tim's Ware shows Prepaid insurance of $2,400. This represents the amount the company paid in August for a two-year policy effective September 1, 2012. Tim's Ware does not prepare monthly financial statements, so it makes adjusting entries only once a year. Prepare the adjusting journal entry at December 31, 2012.

Date	Transaction	Debit	Credit

e. On October 5, 2012, *Tanks a Lot*, the monthly magazine for tropical fish fanciers, received payment for one-year subscriptions from twenty new subscribers. A subscription to *Tanks a Lot* costs $24 for twelve monthly issues. All twenty new subscriptions will begin November 1, 2012.

Record the cash received October 5, 2012.

Date	Transaction	Debit	Credit

Tanks a Lot does not prepare monthly financial statements, so it makes adjusting entries only once a year. Prepare the adjusting journal entry at December 31, 2012.

Date	Transaction	Debit	Credit

f. On December 31, 2012, the adjusted trial balance for Tim's Ware shows Sales of $50,000 and Dividends of $10,000.

Record the closing entry for Sales at December 31, 2012.

Date	Transaction	Debit	Credit

Record the closing entry for Dividends at December 31, 2012

Date	Transaction	Debit	Credit

Solutions

Completion Statements

1. journal
2. ledger or general ledger
3. posting
4. debit
5. trial balance (can be unadjusted, adjusted, or post-closing)
6. dividends
7. credit
8. permanent (or real)
9. temporary
10. enterprise-wide resource planning

True/False

1. False ERP stands for enterprise-wide resource planning system, which is an integrated software program used by large companies to manage all of their information.

2. False The journal shows financial events in chronological order, the same order in which they take place. The general ledger groups together transactions that affect a particular account.

3. False Assets are on the left-hand side of the accounting equation. They are increased with left-handed, debit entries. Assets are decreased with credit entries.

4. True

5. False The post-closing trial balance is used to verify that debits still equal credits after closing entries have been made in the journal and posted to the general ledger. The accountant also reviews the post-closing trial balance to make sure that all of the temporary accounts have zero balances. Furthermore, since many companies group accounts together and show them as a single financial statement line item, the post-closing trial balance might show more detail than the balance sheet.

6. False Financial statements are prepared after adjusting entries but before closing entries. Since closing reduces the balances in temporary accounts to zero, it would be impossible to prepare an income statement after closing, because it would show $0 revenue and $0 expenses.

7. True

8. True

9. False Only in the first year of a company's operations is it true that all accounts begin with zero balances. In subsequent years, only the temporary accounts (revenues, expenses, and Dividends) begin the fiscal year with zero balances. Permanent accounts (asset, liability, and shareholders' equity accounts) have balances carried forward from the end of the previous fiscal year.

10. True

Multiple Choice

1. **C**   The adjustment for accrued interest on a note payable includes a debit to Interest expense and a credit (not a debit) to Interest payable. The adjusting entry to accrue interest on a note receivable (not payable) would include a debit to Interest receivable and a credit (not a debit) to Interest revenue.

2. **C**   The adjusting entry for depreciation on equipment includes a debit (not a credit) to Depreciation expense and a credit to Accumulated depreciation. Although the entry decreases the carrying value of the equipment, it is not made directly to the Equipment account. Depreciation does not require a payment of cash, so the entry will not decrease (credit) the Cash account.

3. **A**   For every journal entry, the dollars of debits must equal the dollars of credits. A journal entry that involves two debit entries with no offsetting credit(s) will cause the general ledger and the adjusted trial balance to be out of balance. Since debits equal credits, the error described in B will not cause the adjusted trial balance to be out of balance. Even though the dollar amounts are wrong for two of the accounts, total debits will still equal total credits.

4. **D**   It is true that the cash receipt was recorded properly on October 1. No additional debit to Cash should be recorded. However, the company also recorded Unearned revenue, a liability to deliver goods in the future. Now that the merchandise has been delivered, an adjusting entry is needed to remove the liability and record the sale that has finally taken place. A closing entry would reduce the balances in revenue, expense, and Dividends accounts to zero, but it would not affect the Unearned revenue account, which is a liability.

5. **D**   Although the dollar amounts for many of the accounts may be incorrect, the debits will still equal the credits. Even a backwards entry like B will not make the trial balance out of balance, since the entry has both a debit and a credit for the same amount.

6. **C**   Assets are on the left-hand side of the accounting equation and are increased with left-handed, debit entries. Liabilities and shareholders' equity are on the right-hand side of the accounting equation and are increased with right-handed, credit entries. It follows that liabilities and shareholders' equity are decreased with debit entries. Since expenses decrease shareholders' equity, an increase in an expense account is recorded with a debit.

7. **C**   Total debits must always equal total credits for each journal entry in order for the accounting system to remain in balance.

8. **C**   Closing entries reduce the balances in the temporary accounts (revenues, expenses, and Dividends) to zero. Closing entries also increase Retained earnings for revenues. However, closing entries decrease Retained earnings for expenses and dividends. If expenses and dividends are greater than revenues for an accounting period, closing entries will decrease (not increase) Retained earnings.

9. **D**   An enterprise resource planning system stores data that is shared by many departments company-wide.

Exercises

l	Account	Asset	Liability	Share. equity	Revenue	Expense	Normal balance	Permanent or temporary
a	Cash	X					DR	P
b	Accounts receivable	X					DR	P
c	Sales				X		CR	T
d	Unearned revenue		X				CR	P
e	Inventory	X					DR	P
f	Cost of goods sold					X	DR	T
g	Accounts payable		X				CR	P
h	Prepaid insurance	X					DR	P
i	Insurance expense					X	DR	T
j	Notes receivable	X					DR	P
k	Interest revenue				X		CR	T
l	Interest receivable	X					DR	P
m	Notes payable		X				CR	P
n	Interest expense					X	DR	T
o	Interest payable		X				CR	P
p	Equipment	X					DR	P
q	Depreciation exp.					X	DR	T
r	Accum. depreciation	X					CR	P
s	Salary expense					X	DR	T
t	Salaries payable		X				CR	P
u	Common stock			X			CR	P
v	Retained earnings			X			CR	P
w	Dividends			X			DR	T
x	Prepaid rent	X					DR	P
y	Rent expense					X	DR	T
z	Other payables		X				CR	P

2.

a.

	Transaction	Debit	Credit
4/01/12	Cash	160	
	Accounts receivable	640	
	Sales		800
	To record sales		

	Transaction	Debit	Credit
4/01/12	Cost of goods sold	500	
	Inventory		500
	To record cost of goods sold		

b.

	Transaction	Debit	Credit
12/31/12	Supplies expense	250	
	Supplies		250
	To record supplies used		
	$300 – 50 = $250		

c.

	Transaction	Debit	Credit
12/31/12	Depreciation expense	5,000	
	Accumulated depreciation		5,000
	To record depreciation expense		
	$25,000 / 5 years = $5,000		

d.

	Transaction	Debit	Credit
12/31/12	Insurance expense	400	
	Prepaid insurance		400
	To record insurance expense		
	($2,400 / 24 months) times 4 months = $400		

e.

	Transaction	Debit	Credit
10/05/12	Cash	480	
	Unearned revenue		480
	To record cash received for subscriptions		

	Transaction	Debit	Credit
12/31/12	Unearned revenue	80	
	Subscription revenue		80
	To record revenue earned		
	($24 / 12 months) times 2 months times 20 subscribers = $80		

f.

	Transaction	Debit	Credit
12/31/12	Sales	50,000	
	Retained earnings		50,000
	To close the Sales account		

	Transaction	Debit	Credit
12/31/12	Retained earnings	10,000	
	Dividends		10,000
	To close the Dividends account		